Power into Art

Power into Art

KARL SABBAGH

ALLEN LANE
THE PENGUIN PRESS

ALLEN LANE
THE PENGUIN PRESS

Published by the Penguin Group
Penguin Books Ltd, 27 Wrights Lane, London W8 5TZ, England
Penguin Putnam Inc., 375 Hudson Street, New York, New York 10014, USA
Penguin Books Australia Ltd, Ringwood, Victoria, Australia
Penguin Books Canada Ltd, 10 Alcorn Avenue, Toronto, Ontario, Canada M4V 3B2
Penguin Books (NZ) Ltd, Private Bag 102902, NSMC, Auckland, New Zealand

Penguin Books Ltd, Registered Offices: Harmondsworth, Middlesex, England

First published 2000
10 9 8 7 6 5 4 3 2 1

Rusting machinery in the power station © Tom Miller; Rooflights being removed,
Wall mock-up, External shot of the gallery with cranes, Overview of the Light Beam,
The Grand Staircase, The inside of the building, Level 1 visitor area, The ramp outside,
The ramp inside © Schal/Keyfoto; The steel structure, Turbine Hall nearing completion,
External shot of Bankside nearing completion © Martin Leith for the Tate; All other
illustrations © Karl Sabbagh.

The moral right of the author has been asserted

Set in Monotype Sabon and Linotype ITC Officina
Typeset by Rowland Phototypesetting Ltd, Bury St Edmunds, Suffolk
Printed and bound in Great Britain by Clays Ltd, St Ives plc

A CIP catalogue record for this book is available from the British Library

ISBN 0-713-99280-0

Contents

Part Three: 1997–8
Structures and Symbols

Part Four: 1998–9
Art and Artifice

Part Five: 1999–2000
Tate Accompli

Acknowledgements

First, of course, I wish to thank the Trustees of the Tate and Sir Nicholas Serota for agreeing unreservedly to let me observe the processes of designing and building a new modern art gallery from the earliest stages of the competition to find an architect. Nick Serota could not have been more supportive during the entire process, and his support set the tone for the participation of others who, while wondering what they were letting themselves in for, nevertheless took seriously the task of explaining, describing and showing their own roles in the project. Second, Peter Wilson at the Tate also understood exactly what I saw as my task and helped me to carry it out in the way I wanted, providing backing where needed and persuading others to help where they were reluctant. Lars Nittve, who joined the Tate halfway through my project and had little choice about assisting me, nevertheless entered into the spirit of my inquiries and was always helpful. Adrian Hardwicke, charged with facilitating my arrangements for contacting people, visiting the Tate sites and attending meetings, accepted the doubling of his workload with grace and charm.

The architects, Jacques Herzog and Harry Gugger, along with their English colleague Michael Casey, were very helpful at every stage of the project. Harry Gugger in particular bore the burden of my demands, giving me interviews and allowing me into working situations even on those few occasions when he was obviously uncomfortable about doing so.

Among the other participants in the project, Ian Blake of Schal was particularly helpful in the early stages of construction and Andy Butler of Stanhope revealed much about the complexities of turning a core and shell into a functioning building.

Needless to say, I am grateful to everyone who spoke to me and my colleague, Belinda Aird, during the six years of the Tate project, many of them up to a dozen times or more, and I am only sorry that for those in the know, there will be obvious gaps, and areas where the coverage of a topic seems thin. Unfortunately, to pursue every interesting story that I came across would have required a book four times as long as this one.

Channel 4 deserve my gratitude for commissioning the project as a television series way back in 1994, and committing the funds to cover the project for the whole period. I am particularly grateful to Waldemar Januszczak, the then commissioning editor for arts programmes, who spotted the potential of the topic on the day the Tate announced that it had acquired Bankside Power Station.

At Skyscraper Productions, I have been particularly helped by Belinda Aird, who in helping to gather material for the television series also provided much that was useful for the book. The detailed knowledge of the Tate project that she acquired over the years has often helped me to understand knotty problems to do with the steel, the glazing or the walls, and to understand why X left when he did, or why Y and Z didn't get on with each other. Lorayne Crawford has also been an invaluable colleague, in particular through her management of the hundreds of thousands of words of transcribed interviews.

Two sets of friends were invaluable at the stage when I needed to gather my thoughts and write large portions of the book. Patrick and Judy Wright gave me hospitality in their holiday house in France, and Josh Simpson and Cady Coleman made available the guest house on their beautiful estate and glass workshop in Massachusetts. Both couples provided the mixture of daytime seclusion and evening hospitality that I find so helpful to the writing process.

I have shown the manuscript to several key individuals and I have usually – but not always – taken their advice. This is very much a personal view of the process, rather than a handbook for architects and construction managers, and so I have concentrated on the stories that interested me as a writer and observer rather than attempting to cover the whole field. But my understanding of the process and the starting point for my choice of stories has been the hundred or more participants in the process who gave me their time and helped me to understand this complex and fascinating building. Even if I have not quoted from them directly, each one of the following people has made an important contribution to the writing of this book, and I thank them for that:

Will Alsop, Tadao Ando, Bernard Angus, Dawn Austwick, Reto Barblan, Peter Barnicoat, Graham Bennett, Colin Berry, Christine Binswanger, Iwona Blazwick, Louise Bourgeois, Andy Bramwell, David Burnsall, David Chipperfield, George Cochrane, Michael Craig-Martin, Janet de Botton, Oierre de Meuron, Judy Dixey, Peter Emerson, Jeremy Fraser, Peter Gannon, Ron German, Steve Gibson, Gerry Gorovoy, Catherine Graham-Harrison, Nicholas Grimshaw, Jim Grundy, Don Hands, Adrian Hardwicke, Gary Hatton, John Hendry, Paul Hewlett, John Hirst, Hans Hollein, Michael and Patty Hopkins, Caro Howell, Jan Kaplicky, Cynthia King, Rem Koolhaas, Richard Koshalek, Rob Lamarre, Amanda Levete, Jeremy Lewison, Stuart Lipton, Joe Lock, Ivor Lovesey, Rick Mather, Phil Monk, Frances Morris, Sandy Nairne, Mike O'Rorke, Jennie Page, Tim Parsons, Renzo Piano, Jonathan Raynes, Peter Rogers, Dale Sager, Claudio Silvestrin, Colin Slee, Bob Spring, Geoffrey Taylor, Faith Wainwright, Adrian Waters, Hilary Wines, Bill Woodrow, Nick Woolcott, Mohsen Zhikri.

List of Illustrations

Dramatis personae

People

Dawn Austwick – *project director, Tate Modern*

Peter Barnicoat – *site manager, Schal*

Colin Berry – *senior construction manager, Schal*

Christine Binswanger – *partner, Herzog and de Meuron*

Iwona Blazwick – *head of exhibitions and displays, Tate Modern*

Ian Blake – *project director, Schal*

Andy Bramwell – *TGMA project coordinator, Tate*

Andy Butler – *project manager, Stanhope Properties*

Michael Casey – *architect, Herzog and de Meuron*

George Cochrane – *development officer (community liaison), Tate Modern*

Pierre de Meuron – *partner, Herzog and de Meuron*

Ian Fraser – *partner, Davis Langdon Everest*

Ron German – *project director, Stanhope Properties*

Harry Gugger – *partner, Herzog and de Meuron*

Jacques Herzog – *partner, Herzog and de Meuron*

John Hirst – *engineer, Ove Arup*

Caro Howell – *education officer, Tate Modern*

Stuart Lipton – *chief executive, Stanhope Properties*

Sandy Nairne – *director of regional and public services, Tate*

Lars Nittve – *director, Tate Modern*

Paul Morrell – *senior partner, Davis Langdon Everest*

Frances Morris – *curator, displays, Tate Modern*

Mike O'Rorke – *project director, Schal*

Jonathan Raynes – *project manager, Schal*

Peter Rogers – *director, Stanhope Properties*
Dale Sager – *project director, Schal*
Nicholas Serota – *director, Tate*
Faith Wainwright – *engineer, Ove Arup*
Peter Wilson – *director of buildings and gallery services, Tate*
Nick Woolcott – *project director, Schal*

Companies

Schal – *construction managers*
Stanhope Properties – *project advisers to the Tate*
Ove Arup – *engineers*
Herzog and de Meuron – *architects*
Davis Langdon Everest – *cost consultants*

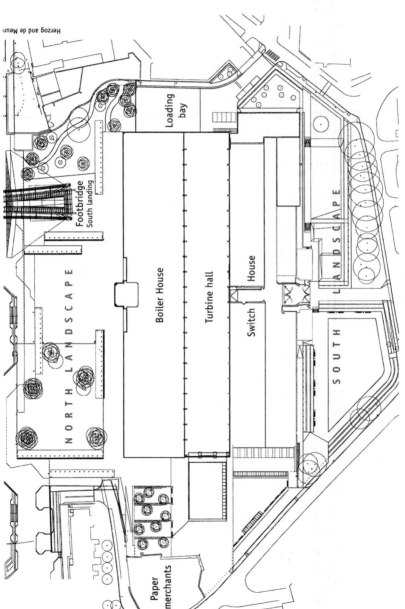

Herzog and de Meur...

Footbridge
South landing

NORTH LANDSCAPE

Paper merchants

Loading bay

Boiler House

Turbine hall

Switch House

SOUTH LANDSCAPE

Site plan showing building and landscape

The site plan of Bankside, showing the building in its finished landscape layout, including the end of the footbridge across the Thames to St Paul's. Two of the divisions of the old power station into Boiler House and Turbine Hall have been adopted for the Tate Modern. When the museum was completed the Switch House was still owned by Nuclear Electric, but the Tate hoped to expand into that area in the future.

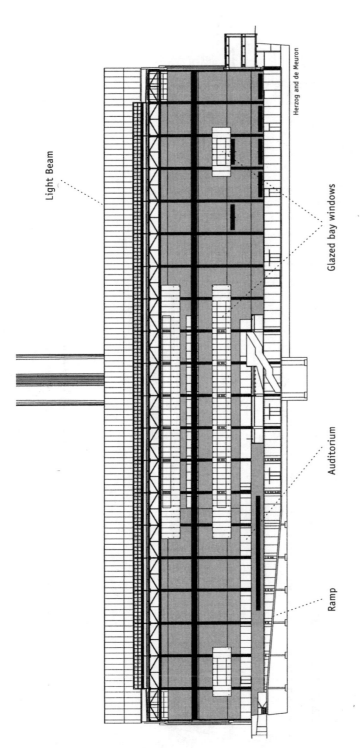

Light Beam

Glazed bay windows

Herzog and de Meuron

Auditorium

Ramp

Turbine Hall interior elevation

The wall of the Boiler House seen from the Turbine Hall. The wall is flat apart from bay windows at Levels 3 and 5 where the permanent collection is displayed. The auditorium windows also look out on to the Turbine hall.

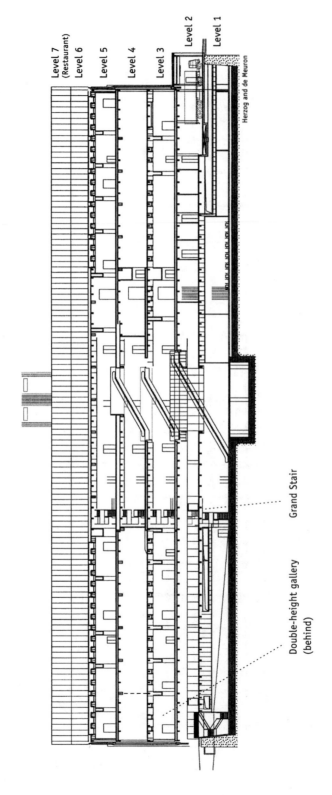

Level 7 (Restaurant)
Level 6
Level 5
Level 4
Level 3
Level 2
Level 1

Herzog and de Meuron

Double-height gallery (behind)

Grand Stair

Cross-section of floors

The ramp brings visitors down from the west entrance to Level 1 of the Turbine Hall. Level 2 has the cafeteria and auditorium, but visitors can take the escalator directly to Level 3 to visit the first two suites of galleries. At the west end is the entrance to the double-height gallery. Level 4 contains special exhibition spaces, and Level 5 has the other two suites for the permanent collection. The restaurant is in the top level of the Light Beam, Level 7.

Prologue

On Sunday 23 January 1995, Pierre de Meuron's mother was listening to the radio in her home in Switzerland. She was surprised to hear the news that her son's architecture firm, Herzog and de Meuron, had won the competition to design the new Tate Gallery of Modern Art on Bankside in London, since he hadn't told her the news himself. When she telephoned him, he too was surprised to hear it since he himself hadn't been told. Shortly afterwards, Nicholas Serota, Director of the Tate, rang to tell Jacques Herzog the news and the next day Herzog and two of his partners were on their way to London for a 'surprise' announcement that by then was anything but a surprise.

Serota had wanted there to be as short a time as possible between the Tate Trustees' decision and the announcement, to reduce the chance of leaks. This project was the biggest Tate event for decades and Serota, showman that he is, wanted it to received the maximum publicity rather than leak out in dribs and drabs. British architecture correspondents are starved of big news stories and the fact that Britain's leading modern art gallery was giving a £130 million project to a foreign architect was sure to tantalize them.

But all the precautions were in vain. After the decision was made on Wednesday – a decision known to Serota and the Trustees, the competition jury, several senior staff and an advisory committee – someone in the know passed it on.

Sunday morning's *Observer* newspaper printed the news as a strong rumour; Swiss Radio broadcast it as fact; and Herzog and de Meuron were off on a five-year roller-coaster ride on their most ambitious project yet.

The irony was, they nearly hadn't entered the competition. They were a small practice with several other large projects in Europe and their first inclination was to say 'no' when the competition was announced. Then Ricky Burdett, an advocate of contemporary architecture and one of the Tate's architectural advisers, rang and suggested that Herzog and de Meuron should enter. He knew of their work and clearly for him, even at that stage, they were one of the favourites to tackle the unusual task the Tate had set itself.

One reason it was unusual was that the Tate had decided to build its new art gallery in an existing building – the old Bankside Power Station designed by Giles Gilbert Scott. Scott's massive all-brick envelope, built to enclose turbines, boilers, gas scrubbers and transformers, was seen by many as a key statement in 1950s architecture, although in its grimy and secluded state in an unfashionable quarter of London it wasn't on anybody's 'must see' list. But as well as seeing its architectural merit, Serota and the Tate Trustees were enticed by its central location, on the south bank of the Thames opposite St Paul's Cathedral.

On Tuesday 25 January 1995, twenty or so journalists assembled in a single storey visitor centre that had already been commandeered by the Tate, next to the main gate of Bankside Power Station. As the journalists listened to the build-up by Serota and Dennis Stevenson, chairman of the Trustees, the Herzog and de Meuron architects were secreted just outside the visitor centre. In spite of the leaks, the secrecy plan had gone ahead. The night before, the architects had flown to London and dined with Serota and Stevenson at Wilton's, chosen as being quintessentially English and a 'safe' restaurant where they would not be recognized. With a dramatic flourish, their names were announced to the press and they walked through the door to polite applause from a less-than-startled audience.

Inside the power station, 35 metres tall and 152 metres long, safe areas had been cordoned off for journalists and visitors. Only the Turbine Hall, a vast echoing space with rusting turbines in a line from one end to the other, was visible. This area was divided from the river side of the building, called the Boiler House, by a framework of steel, beyond which were boilers, flue-gas washing equipment, and other large metal components of the process of power generation.

After the press conference the journalists wandered into the area, accompanied by the architects. Jacques Herzog and his colleagues had already been here half a dozen times, in order to devise ways of turning the structure into a large modern art gallery. Now for the first time they had to treat the task as a real project rather than a hypothetical exercise. As they looked up at the rooflights, they could imagine the Light Beam, an extra two storeys across the length of the roof, that was a key part of their design. Off to the west, where there was now steel decking, turbines and a large window, would be the gently sloping ramp they had suggested to the Tate jury to bring visitors in from the west. And where the boilers and scrubbing equipment were now firmly locked into the steel framework would be seven floors of galleries, restaurants and shops. At least, that was the intention. Now there were to be five years of design and construction that this small firm of architects in Basel had to complete by the opening date, already fixed for spring 2000.

Part One

1994–6

Winning and Designing

Why a New Tate?

The Tate Gallery in London has for some time been an expansionist organization. In the last two decades it has established outposts in Liverpool and St Ives, in a move to make modern and contemporary art accessible to people who don't live in London. But the moves that began seriously in the late 1980s to establish another Tate in London were clearly propelled by different motives. There were two factors. First, there was the fact that the Tate was really two galleries: a national gallery of British art of the last 400 years; and Britain's major gallery of modern and contemporary art. Some people found this rather a good arrangement. To be able to wander from Turner to Tanguy or Dadd to Duchamp under one roof presented new opportunities and the possibility of discoveries to visitors. Others, including the Trustees of the Tate, had come to feel that there should be two buildings, each dedicated to the two separate functions of the Tate.

Secondly, there was the fact that over the years the Tate had acquired far more art than it could put on display at any one time. Millbank was able to display about 1,000 works of art. The Tate actually owned over 4,000 paintings, 1,300 sculptures, 3,500 works of art on paper and 9,000 prints. Only 10 per cent of their total collection was on display, although they actually showed a higher proportion of their 5,300 paintings and sculptures. Nevertheless, in their stores and in other outlying places, the Tate had plenty of art which was well worth displaying if only they had the space.

There was one other factor that influenced the decision to plan a new gallery – the approaching millennium, and the fund that the British government had announced that it would set up, using money from the National Lottery, to enable the country to mark the millennium with various major sporting and cultural projects. A large new gallery could be expected to cost over £100 million, and this would present the Tate with a major fund-raising challenge. By proposing a new gallery that would open in the year 2000, part of this £100 million could perhaps be extracted from the Millennium Fund.

The key figure at the Tate through the 1990s was its director, Nicholas Serota. It was he who initiated the project, although all key decisions were made by the Trustees. One criterion everyone thought was important was that any new site should be accessible to Londoners and visitors to the city. The Tate at Millbank is not the sort of place – like the National Gallery in Trafalgar Square – where tourists who might be visiting some other major attraction could stumble on the gallery, and visit it on impulse. While Millbank doesn't appear to suffer too much from its location – there have been constant references by the chairman of the Trustees to the 'football crowds' who turn up at the weekends – the Trustees and Serota didn't want anywhere further away from the centre for their new gallery and hoped to find somewhere more easily reached by large numbers of people.

But the task was not easy. Sites with the square footage they would need to make a significant statement were not often available in the centre of London, and when they became available they were extremely expensive. In 1992 and 93 Serota and his colleagues looked at a whole range of sites that might fit the bill. But nothing really gelled. Either the available sites weren't appealing enough or they were too expensive.

Peter Wilson, the Tate's Head of Gallery Services at the time, described what happened next: 'We were looking at the former Billingsgate Fishmarket which had been converted into a dealing floor but had become unlettable because of the recession. This project floundered (forgive the pun) and was overtaken by events – the National Lottery and so on. But one thing I was looking at was the possibility of river transport between Millbank and Billingsgate, so I went on the river bus a number of times and couldn't help noticing Bankside Power Station.' Wilson himself used to work in power stations, so the huge, distinguished (and distinctive) bulk of Bankside would have had particular significance for him as would the fact that it was up for sale and possible demolition. He mentioned the idea of

Bankside as a possible site for the new Tate more than once to Francis Carnwath, deputy director of the Tate at the time, and Carnwath went to see for himself. 'When he was on the visit,' Wilson continued, 'someone from the Twentieth Century Society was making a short TV piece about saving Bankside, made the connection between Francis and the Tate and asked him whether the Tate was interested. We became interested!'

Nick Serota adds a gloss to the story: 'Francis looked up at the building and as far as I know said something along the lines of "Oh, it's far too big for the Tate and we couldn't possibly take on a building on this scale". But something in it pricked my interest, and a couple of days later I was going home late one evening and I decided I'd have a look at Bankside. And I got down to the river front and suddenly realized that this was an extraordinary building. And then I thought, "Well, how big is it?" – it's actually very difficult to judge the scale. So I started at one end and I walked two hundred feet and got to the end of one wing and then I walked another hundred feet, which is the central section, and so the whole thing was five hundred feet long. Then I began to think, "Well, what if we were to do it in two phases?" And then it occurred to me that if I was in Frankfurt or Cologne and saw this building and was told that it was being converted to be a Museum of Modern Art, I wouldn't be surprised. And so it really began at that moment.'

Serota's account of how he fell for Bankside contains several characteristic elements of his relationship with the project that were to run through the whole design and construction process. First, where someone else might delegate, he likes to experience things for himself, as he did when he decided one evening to go and look at Bankside on his own. ('I was going home late one evening' rather makes it sound as if the visit was on his way home when in fact Bankside is in the opposite direction from Serota's North London home.) Second, he likes to understand the detail of things, down to measuring the dimensions of Bankside by pacing along the Thames Embankment late in the evening, and comparing the size with Millbank. Third, there is his Europeanism, linked to an understanding that the strength of the new gallery would lie in its response to some of the movements in modern and contemporary art – and architecture – that had not really got a look in in Britain.

For the six years of the Bankside project, Serota was alternately to infuriate and impress those who worked with him by his interventions in matters as detailed as the placing of smoke detectors or the choice of fabric on the auditorium seats. Listening to him talk about the project in 1995 in his high-ceilinged office over the front entrance of Millbank, you could sense that Bankside had come just at the time when he was feeling the need to find ways of displaying more modern and contemporary art, and when he saw the possibilities presented by an effective doubling of the amount of display space the Tate had at its disposal in London. It was also a fact that Serota had had job offers from other world-class galleries and it may be that the Trustees felt that allowing him to run the Bankside project would have the bonus of keeping him at the Tate until 2000 at least.

As the preliminary idea gathered momentum and strength, it became clear that the announcement that they were planning to convert an existing building would enrage those who felt that this was an excellent opportunity to build a brand-new building and enrich London's stock of institutional architecture by major architects. Sandy Nairne, appointed the Tate's Director of Regional and Public Services in 1994, was nervous about possible reactions. 'Everybody's instincts originally were for building a new building. It seems to make sense – if you want to build a museum of modern art, you want a new building. And of course there was the worry that if you didn't build a new building everybody would say, "Oh come on, it's never going to be as good".'

But to acquire the site, demolish the power station and build a brand-new building would have cost far more money than the Tate could raise. Building from scratch would have to take place on a cheaper site further from the centre of London with a small fraction of the 11,000 square metres of space that Bankside could provide.

It happened that Serota felt that building conversions often had advantages over new buildings. But in the beginning there were many who disagreed, even among the Trustees of the Tate who would ultimately make the decisions. Michael Craig-Martin, a painter, was one of them, although he was soon converted. 'I love contemporary architecture and I'm fascinated by it. I much preferred originally the idea that it was going to be a wholly new building, and I fully expected that it was going to be, until we went to see Bankside. When we saw Bankside, it was hard to believe what we had stumbled on, because the most obvious thing about it was it was immensely big, it was vastly big, it was two or three times as big as anything we'd ever imagined. It was far bigger than anything we could ever have hoped to build. Even if we had thought we could tear this down and start again, we'd never have gotten the whole site, we would never have gotten agreement, permission, money, to build a building of this scale. The most important thing for art is to have plenty of space. And for an institution whose role is to expand, to be able to have a building which allows for future development is a fantastic thing for a museum. Every other museum director in the world must be jealous of this project, because very often that is the problem.'

In 1994, Ricky Burdett was director of the Architecture Foundation, an architecture think-tank with premises and exhibition space in St James's in London. He played a major part in the Tate's competition to find an architect, and as someone at the sharp end of architectural philosophy he was well aware of the current of feeling that was generated by the Tate's interest in converting an old building. 'The choice not to go with a new building was met with very mixed reactions. There is a strong body of opinion which feels that there must be in London a site which can actually take a modern building where the external shape communicates what's happening inside and is a statement about the last century of this millennium, and I have very strong support for that as someone who promotes good architecture. On the other hand there are absolutely compelling reasons why Bankside is actually an interesting idea. It's interesting because the scale of it is so great. We see this in film, in photographs, as you walk through it. It's not a question of an interior re-furb job, it's much more than that.'

For Serota – who was personally very enthusiastic about a new gallery in an old building – the unpopularity of the idea had one worrying negative effect: 'I think there are one or two people who might well have given us money, and now will not, had we built an entirely new building. And those are people who probably had their views about architecture formed in the nineteen-fifties and sixties and for whom the approach we have taken runs somewhat counter to their philosophy of the notion of building new for each generation.'

But how much was this likely to matter to the ordinary punter, the Saturday afternoon visitor in search of an hour of diverting and stimulating museum-going? Unmotivated by a desire to keep Britain's world-class architectural practices in work, he or she is unlikely to think too hard about the issue of old versus new. The only factor that might operate is the public image created by the new gallery and its PR advisers when it finally opens. Clearly a new gallery in a new building has a publicity angle that a new gallery in an old building might not. The Guggenheim in Bilbao and the Getty in Los Angeles are both galleries which opened during the period of design and construction of the new Tate and they both attracted crowds of visitors who were at least as interested in the building as they were in the contents. But that does not mean that an art gallery in a new building is better per se than one in an old building.

One unusual aspect of Serota's enthusiasm for Bankside was that it seemed to matter that the building wasn't just any old building – there was power in the idea that it was a twentieth-century building that was going to be used for the display of twentieth (and twenty-first) century art. 'It will be extremely interesting to bring together a mid twentieth-century vision and a late twentieth-century vision. That collision in itself, that juxtaposition, is actually very characteristic of the time in which we live. I think that old buildings of this sort can provide rather wonderful spaces in which to show twentieth-century art. This discontinuity, this collision between different visions or different moments, is a very powerful one. Secondly, a building that has a certain patina and a certain age is also one in which the immediate contemporary can often be seen in better relief than in an absolutely new building. It's very striking if you go to Italy, for instance, and you see contemporary art installed in a Renaissance palace: it's not only that a tension exists between the art and its setting but also that you are made very conscious of the sense of living at a particular moment, of the art being made at a particular moment, and necessarily the kind of relationships that exist between it and art in the past.'

In 1994, despite whatever potential Serota and his colleagues saw in Bankside Power Station, the building that the Tate had chosen struck many passers-by as forbidding. For all of Sir Giles Gilbert

Scott's talents as an architect of a range of building types, from cathedrals to telephone boxes, his power stations – including the better-known Battersea Power Station – could not help being vast, monumental, rectilinear, and – since they were made of brick – rather dark, particularly after a few decades of London pollution. Where the sombre qualities of Battersea were relieved by four light-coloured chimneys, Bankside had one wider chimney, made of the same brick as the rest of the building. Although Bankside also had tall, slender mullioned windows, from the outside these made the building seem even darker since, before work began, they gave spectators a view of dark, rusting boilers and the flue-gas washing plant.

In fact, even to see Bankside took a bit of navigating. It was not on any main road but tucked away and invisible behind the road that led from Waterloo to London Bridge. The only place the casual visitor might see it from is the north side of the river, from the steps that lead from the south side of St Paul's Cathedral down to the river embankment. This view, because the building is usually silhouetted against the southern sky, often made the building seem blacker than it really is. The visitor who really wanted a close view of the river side of the building, its best side in design terms, had to meander down several side streets and hope to stumble on the river walk. Even here, it was only at the last moment that the Bankside chimney loomed into view over a terrace of three elegant seventeenth-century houses that had somehow survived centuries of urban neglect in the Borough of Southwark.

Even for Ricky Burdett, the architectural qualities of the building did not rate very highly, although Scott himself is a major twentieth-century British architect. 'I think it's not the most elegant building. It's rather crude in some of its mass volumes. It's two big chunks with one sort of big thing sticking in the middle of it, which reflects exactly what it was all about. Some of its detailing and some of its brickwork is quite nice but that doesn't turn me on. What is exciting is you've got this volume which you can interact with, you can have a dialogue with, you can break through it if you want and probably have a wonderful building in the future.'

When the Tate announced its plans, Bankside Power Station had been out of use for thirteen years. The main building had a rectangular floor plan, divided along its length into two separate areas parallel to the river by a row of steel columns. Out of the north side of the building rose a 99-metre-tall square brick-clad chimney. The area on the river side was filled from floor to ceiling with the rusting accompaniments of the power generation process. In the middle, underneath the base of the chimney, was the plant used to 'scrub' the waste gases from the furnaces before they were evacuated through the chimney. On either side of this area were the boilers that heated the water to produce the steam to drive the turbines. The south side of the building, the long area away from the river, was open from floor level to roof and contained four large turbines. These were supplied with steam from the boilers, which drove the huge rotating coils that generated the electricity.

On three sides of the building, the west, north and east, Scott had designed tall, mullioned windows, three sets on east and west, and six along the river side on the north. During all the discussions of the Bankside conversion, the two major divisions of the building were known as the Turbine Hall, the south half of the building, and the Boiler House, the north section.

The building was built in two stages, with the first part being opened in 1953 and an extension completed in 1963. But the fickle economics of supply, demand and fuel prices meant that the power station was no longer needed by 1981 and it was closed down. By 1994, when the Tate made its decision, the building had been disused for longer than it had been an active power station, with one small but important exception. London Electricity, the current owners, still maintained an active presence in a building that took up the south side of the power station, containing a set of transformers and a control room. The transformers were there to convert high voltage electricity from the national grid to a lower voltage for use in the community. It was purely a convenience for this to be sited in the old power station, but London Electricity did not particularly want to move, so they retained that part of the building when the rest was sold to the Tate. Although it was only a small percentage of the main building, the Switch House, as it was called, was to irritate the Tate and its architects for the next six years or more, partly because it constrained them in their planning of the site and partly because the transformers produced a pervasive hum throughout the main building, a hum which the Tate was eventually able to reduce but not eliminate.

When the Tate acquired the building, the general air of rust and decrepitude created a rather Gothic impression inside the echoing building. This was an impression that had attracted the makers of the movies *Judge Dredd* and *Richard III*, who had used the building in its current state as a location. Rain dripped into puddles, creating ripples in the reflections of the square rooflights 26 metres above the ground. Birds flew high up in the interior, depositing their droppings on rusting beams and disused equipment. Occasionally, from a few vantage points, there was a sudden glimpse of the dome of St Paul's through a broken window pane. And the eastern windows, if you cleaned away the grime, revealed the Globe Theatre under construction a hundred metres away.

There was a surprising amount of the power station below ground level. An echoing basement housed the foundations of the turbines, and more pipes and boilers. Then, to the south, under the Switch House, was an area that made Serota's eyes light up. When the Tate had decided to commit themselves to Bankside, they had not really known much about the space at basement level to the south of the main building. But as Peter Wilson began to explore the building he made a discovery. 'I think the biggest surprise is the sheer extent of space at basement level. We've discovered that there is space stretching not only underneath the London Electricity sub-station but out under the road, and that space leads on directly to the huge oil tanks which are buried under the lawn to the south of the building, where there's an enormous volume of space which we could exploit in the future.'

Spreading out from the building itself were several layers of territory which were to play a part in the Tate's discussions. They could be characterized as landscape, community and borough. From the beginning the Tate said that it wanted to put effort and money into getting each of these areas and its associated human ramifications right.

First, the landscape. On the river side of the building was an area of grassy mounds, brick amphitheatres and walls, and the river walkway itself, with a number of semi-mature trees scattered around. This was the result of attempts in 1981 to hide the power station from passers-by. The grassy areas were a favourite dog-walking space for residents, and the river walkway had a regular but sparse flow of walkers, cyclists and joggers. The sparseness was because in 1994 there really was very little to bring outsiders to the area. Only those in the know would be likely to penetrate to the river and its magnificent view of St Paul's. Ideally, in the Tate's view, the landscaping between the north side of the gallery and the river should all be part of one scheme, although on the map there was a convoluted boundary that marked off the power station's land from the area next to the river that belonged to the Borough of Southwark.

Outside the immediate boundary of the Tate's own property was the community – those people living adjacent to the site, whom the Tate had pledged to consult in its application for planning permission. This was partly to get the Borough of Southwark on its side and partly because of a genuine belief on the part of some of the Tate team that the new gallery should be a community project in a way that Millbank wasn't. Over the period of design and construction the Tate was to spend a lot of time and effort in consulting their neighbours-to-be, in a process that astonished the eventual architects, who were used to the designers of large urban projects being allowed to get on with it. In this case, the process of consultation was complicated by the fact that there were really two groups of immediate neighbours – one group of a hundred or so people in council flats to the west of the site, and the other consisting of three families in the row of seventeenth-century houses to the east.

And then there was the Borough of Southwark, who had greatly encouraged the Tate in its choice of Bankside by pledging a sum of money for developing their ideas in the early days of the project. For Southwark, a deprived borough with high unemployment, stretching from the river to the dingier southern edges of London, a world-class modern art gallery would complement its world-class Shakespearean replica theatre and enhance the cultural life of the borough as well as sucking in many visitors from the outside.

Architecture is always about more than walls, ceilings and floors. In architects' parlance, buildings have programmes – carefully written briefs that set out the functions a building has to perform. Usually the programme has little to say about the design but it is an essential benchmark for testing the design as it evolves. In the case of Bankside, the programme was unusually broad. It embraced topics as general as the need to assist with the regeneration of Southwark and as specific as catering for groups of people with different disabilities. And underlying it all was the brief to provide one of the most stimulating, innovative and original experiences of modern and contemporary art in the world.

2

Eyes on Bankside

Architecture competitions are not universally loved by architects. They would much rather be asked directly to design a project by a client who trusted them to do a great job and interfered as little as possible. On the other hand, when there *is* a competition, particularly one as juicy as Bankside, anybody who's anybody in the architecture world has to be seen on the list of entrants, or to let it be known widely why they are not applying.

Competitions are a lot of work and involve spending your own money for no guaranteed return. But a museum of modern art is likely to provide a greater stimulus and more kudos than, say, a hospital, office block or hotel, and the Tate was a glamorous client to work for. It might even be fun.

Right from the beginning, the Tate said that they were looking for an architect and not a scheme. What they meant by this was that, although the competition process involved submitting ideas about what the entrant would do with Bankside, the winner would not necessarily be chosen solely on the basis of those ideas. A wonderful scheme that the Tate felt was beyond the ability of the architect to complete could be passed over in favour of an architect who was clearly master of his craft but needed more work to design a finished masterpiece. In fact the selection process itself would eventually involve much more than just looking over plans and renderings and reading about the competitors' previous buildings. The group of assessors appointed by the Tate would visit architects in their firms, talk to their employees, consult other clients and visit their buildings, all in an attempt to find a safe pair of hands as well as a brilliant designer. In the words of Ricky Burdett, who was one of the assessors,

'We're selecting a person that a number of people at the Tate are going to be seeing for about ten years maybe once a month, twice a month, five times a month probably in the first stages of this important project.'

There were 149 initial applications. Sixty-five were European, American or Japanese, and eighty or so were British. As the assessors began the task of whittling down, they knew that there was an expectation among many observers that they would choose a British architect. Serota was aware of this expectation but had no intention of pandering to it. 'I thought when the lottery and the Millennium Commission were first announced that there was a possibility that national – or even political – sentiment would determine a wish to see most of the projects being built by British architects. We've not been especially good at employing our best architects and one could imagine very good reasons for saying "on this occasion we're going to make it British architects and we're going to show the world what we can do". I think it's fortunate that that sentiment hasn't prevailed because, of course, we know that these British architects are good architects because of what they've built abroad. British architects have been given extraordinary opportunities to build abroad and it would be nice to think that European or American or Japanese architects could be given similar opportunities here. There are really no buildings by major European or American or Japanese architects in this country yet. So for the Tate to consider the possibility of that is very healthy. And that's not to say I'm prejudiced in favour of a foreign architect. As it happens, most of the Millennium projects that have so far declared themselves, particularly in the arts field, turn out to have British architects, whether it's the British Museum and Norman Foster, or the Opera House with Jeremy Dickson and Ed Jones, or now the South Bank with Richard Rogers or even the Cardiff Opera House with Zaha Hadid who is represented as an Iraqi architect by certain parts of the press but has been working here for twenty years and in my book is really British. And it does actually, in a strange way, give us a certain licence to look at the field and choose the person who we think is the best for this particular project, whether they be British or foreign.'

In deciding to base a new museum in an old building, the Tate was throwing out a challenge to the architects of the late twentieth century, a challenge it didn't have to face itself. The building had a unique status – although of considerable architectural merit, it had not been listed by the Department of the Environment, as might have happened if there had been a desire to preserve every detail of its design. In fact, the Twentieth Century Society had lobbied to get it listed, but in spite of the recommendation of English Heritage, the government had refused, bowing to the view that listing would have made it impossible for Bankside's owners, Nuclear Electric, to sell the power station. If the building was left unlisted, the way was open for a purchaser to knock it down and use the site much more profitably. As it has turned out, the building's new life will expose many more millions of visitors to a version of Giles Gilbert Scott's vision than would have seen it if it had been left to become increasingly derelict on its back lot in Southwark.

By an early stage in the process, the Tate had made a number of key decisions that were to determine the future progress of the gallery. With such a large and complex project, Serota was determined that the Tate would behave like an informed and sure-footed client in a situation where there would be many opportunities for things to go wrong with budget, schedule or management. No one at the Tate wanted a repeat of their experience with their new Clore Gallery, built to house the Turner Bequest and completed almost a year behind schedule. It had been an unhappy experience for all parties, with Tate and architect at loggerheads over the smallest details such as wall colour and lighting. To help smooth the decision-making process, Serota had enlisted the help of Stanhope Properties, a property development company run by Stuart Lipton, a developer with fingers in many pies, some of them culturally or socially significant. Lipton and Serota had known each other since Serota had run the Whitechapel Gallery, where they developed a close working relationship during the completion of an improvement scheme in 1985. The Tate hired Stanhope to advise on a number of issues as they looked at sites, and when they found one, the company played a major role in taking the project through to completion. Two Stanhope staff, Peter Rogers and Ron German, were to supply design and construction expertise to the Tate team over the next five or six years.

In summer 1994, the following notice was published electronically in the *European Architecture Journal*, the place where, by European law, international architecture competitions have to be publicized:

The Trustees of the Tate Gallery plan to convert the redundant Bankside Power Station in London into a new Gallery of Modern Art of national and international significance on a scale similar to the Museum of Modern Art, New York and Centre Georges Pompidou, Paris.

The grand scale of the power station and its spectacular site on the south bank of the River Thames, opposite St Paul's Cathedral, requires an architectural approach of boldness and imagination.

The gallery will be developed in phases, this first phase providing 6 suites of galleries each of 2,000 m² together with public facilities totalling 21,500 m² of accommodation.

The competition is intended to select an architect rather than a specific design solution.

Awarding authority: The Trustees of the Tate Gallery, Millbank, UK – London SW1P 4RG

Among the couple of hundred applications for preliminary information, there were 149 architecture firms who applied to enter the competition, and Serota and his board of assessors sat down to sift through them. After rejecting obviously inappropriate applicants they still ended up with a list of forty or so and went through them one by one, looking at slides of their buildings and reading their preliminary submissions.

'The number and range and quality of architects who were interested in the project was absolutely overwhelming,' said Ricky Burdett during the judging process. 'I would say that there were something like thirty or forty of the best architects in the world and I stress *in the world*. There were some omissions from this country because they were otherwise engaged or felt that they shouldn't really be involved in this project, but the calibre of people at the international level is extraordinary and I think the shortlist reflects that. And it means one thing – the spotlight is very much on London at the moment to set the standard of buildings which will take us forward and I think that is quite unique and the profession is very excited about that.'

Eventually the assessors arrived at a long shortlist of thirteen architects. They would each be given a sum of money and a month to come up with a more detailed submission. The Tate would then compile a final shortlist of six to assess through a series of site visits, meetings, workshops and informal discussions.

This process of considering carefully the ideas of a huge range of international architects had one interesting side effect, as Serota described on 23 September 1994: 'Without wanting to necessarily plunder the ideas of the hundred and forty-nine architects who submitted, having been obliged to look at [such] material . . . causes you to rethink what you're doing. It's tremendously easy in a project of this kind to start narrowing options at too early a stage. After all, the Trustees and the staff here have been talking about this project for quite a long time, and their starting point, however ambitious they might be, is the existing Tate and the existing collection and the existing patterns of behaviour. To have first of all a group of assessors and then a group of architects coming at us and saying, "Well, hold on a moment, you shouldn't take that as given", is very helpful, and will help to make this a project that many people share in.'

The long shortlist of thirteen consisted of:

Will Alsop, UK
Tadao Ando, Japan
David Chipperfield, UK
Future Systems, UK
Nicholas Grimshaw, UK
Herzog and de Meuron, Switzerland
Michael and Patty Hopkins, UK
Arato Isozaki, Japan
Rem Koolhaas, Holland
Rick Mather, UK
Rafael Moneo, Spain
Renzo Piano, Italy
Claudio Silvestrin with Rolfe Judd, UK

On 7 October 1994, as the autumn sun streamed through the tall windows of the Duffield Room at Millbank, representatives of the thirteen architecture firms gathered to hear about the Tate competition for Bankside. In some cases the principals of the firms had managed to clear their diaries for the hurriedly organized day's events; otherwise, other architects from the firms had substituted for their more distinguished colleagues.

The foreigners were more likely to be represented by substitutes. Arato Isozaki, Tadao Ando, and Rafael Moneo were all absent, but Renzo Piano had made it from Genoa, along with a colleague; Jacques Herzog was there, but slipped in late; and Rem Koolhaas, the Dutch architect, had come (but he is a London resident). Michael and Patty Hopkins hadn't been able to make it but there was otherwise a strong British contingent.

Nick Grimshaw was among the first to arrive, checking his watch and his invitation to make sure he'd got the time right. Piano and a colleague arrived and immediately began making arrangements to fly out again the following morning. Coffee and biscuits were handed around and knots of people stood about making polite conversation. Fred Manson was there from the Borough of Southwark, chatting with Rick Mather and describing his responsibilities – 'All of environmental health for the borough along with the mortuary and cemeteries, and the crematorium.' There was a brief discussion about the vote-catching potential of Bankside among a knot of architects and engineers, including Grimshaw and the pair of architects who called themselves Future Systems – Jan Kaplicky and Amanda Levete.

'Bankside's the thing for the people,' said Mark Whitby, a structural engineer.

'Sounds like a socialist project to me,' said Nick Grimshaw.

'These are socialist times,' said Whitby – this was three years before Labour's landslide.

'We'll have a socialist government by the time this opens,' said Levete.

'We'll have *had* one,' replied Whitby, inaccurately as it turned out.

In another part of the room, Peter Rogers from Stanhope Properties was chatting to David Chipperfield. 'I've told Nick I want the concession for the top of the chimney,' Rogers joked. (Ironically, if Chipperfield had won the competition, there would have been no chimney.)

There was a ripple of interest as Serota swept into the room. This was the sort of occasion at which he excels. He was on first-name terms with most of the 'signature' architects and worked the crowd, shaking each architect by the hand and, often, making a personal reference to some project of theirs. 'The sycamores are dropping outside your house,' he said, referring to a recent Future Systems project that had received some publicity. 'You should get them to change the trees.' 'They're all protected,' said Jan Kaplicky, gloomily. Serota seemed particularly jovial with Renzo Piano. Piano was probably the biggest 'name' in the room anyway, and his height and bearded dignity set him slightly apart. While at this stage in the competition there were no firm favourites, Serota liked Piano's architecture and if a bookmaker had been quoting odds he'd have put Piano among the top three.

The day was to kick off with the Tate team giving a series of presentations, starting with Serota. Alongside him were Stuart Lipton and Michael Craig-Martin.

Serota spoke in a relaxed way, fluent and inconsequentially humorous. For instance, in introducing Peter Rogers he said: 'This is Peter Rogers, no relation of Richard Rogers – he's just his brother.' It was the sort of remark that didn't bear inspection but puzzled the foreigners and amused the British. He told the architects to ask questions whenever they felt like it, even though he understood that people might be hesitant to do so in public in case it gave away their intentions. But he urged the British architects, at least, to overcome any such inhibition and help the foreign architects understand some of the nuances of Bankside and its urban site. He said two significant things. One was to emphasize that the competition was to select an architect and not a design. 'We're looking for a partner with whom we can work to develop a design,' he said. 'We don't have enough confidence to produce a brief that develops every single detail, and ask you then to design it. Of course we have our own ideas but we want to work collectively with all of you and then with one person. It's important that we work as a collaborative project.'

'Working collectively with all of them' would have the advantage, already exploited in the initial assessment, of coming across ideas from one architect which might then get incorporated into the design of the winning architect. No one at the Tate seemed to think this particularly unusual, although in any other profession it might have seemed like industrial espionage.

Serota's other interesting point reflected what must have gone on in the competition assessors' deliberations behind closed doors. 'We have not set up a beauty contest,' he said. 'If we have, we've chosen a fairly narrow spectrum to look at. We have not put on this list an architect who works in one way, then an architect who works in another and then an architect who works in a third way, so as to have a big debate about whether this should be a conservationist solution or a modernist solution or a post-modernist solution. We're interested in getting the right solution for this building and I think it's fairly clear from the people who are in this room that we are looking for a radical solution.'

Michael Craig-Martin, one of three Tate Trustees who was also a working artist, fired the group with his enthusiasm for the project. 'The building is potentially the most important museum of modern art in the world – it's an immensely large building and it will represent something about a view of contemporary art. The lack of a great museum dedicated to modern art in London has symbolized some sort of refusal of the twentieth century in Britain, and to open a new museum of this importance in the beginning of the new millennium and the new century could be seen as a symbolic way of accepting the present and the future. In looking at other museums, there seem to be certain problems in many of them that are avoidable. There's a tendency for the public spaces to be over-designed and the galleries underdesigned – in the sense that the public spaces become architectural wonders and the galleries become unitized and repeated, and it's very important to say that this is not what we want. This is a big building and it's going to house a collection that has very different needs. I go into some museums and I feel that the rooms were designed to be empty – perfect with nothing in them at all.'

As the thirteen hopeful architects set off on a coach tour of Southwark, finishing up inside Bankside, they had plenty to think about. The morning's speeches had given them only a glimpse of what the Tate wanted and in any case, in the end, the Tate could change its mind at any time in the light of a particularly imaginative or innovative proposal. And the aspect of the briefing that was to cause most puzzlement to the competitors was the phrase 'we're looking for an architect and not a scheme'. This was certainly a case of having your cake and eating it, since no architect believed that his presentation could merely extol the virtues of his practice, nor that he'd have much chance of winning if any scheme he presented was seen as entirely misconceived or inappropriate. And the biggest challenge facing the thirteen on that bright autumn day was the fact that they had about thirty days to produce a detailed, consistent, achievable proposal for the way forward in order to get to the final stage of the best architectural competition in the world at the time.

3

Competition

On the 14th and 15th of November 1994, the thirteen shortlisted architects were each given twenty minutes to present themselves, followed by forty minutes of questions from the jury. There were ten assessors appointed by the Tate to choose the winner. Apart from Nick Serota, there were a handful of Trustees and several architects, including Ricky Burdett. There was also an American museum director, Richard Koshalek, and the broadcaster Joan Bakewell, representing the Friends of the Tate. The architects had been asked to submit four A1-size boards responding to three issues – the setting of the building in the context of its urban location and site; planning the general layout of the building; and ideas for the display spaces. Between their visit to the building on 7 October and the date to submit their boards there was just over a month. The practices were given an honorarium of £3,000 and expenses of £1,500 to do the work. Few of them can have worked shorter than twelve-hour days during that month. Whatever their opinions of competitions – and some were very dismissive of this method of choosing an architect – the chosen thirteen couldn't afford to miss an opportunity like this. When they turned up at Millbank, some carrying their boards under their arms after a midnight push the previous night, they were like nervous candidates for an A-level exam, rather than some of the world's leading architects.

After the event they described the process of meeting the jury, and it was clear that some felt they hadn't done their best and that the situation had intimidated them. First in and first out were Michael and Patty Hopkins, the husband and wife team whose design for Glyndebourne Opera House was also a competition entry and who had more recently designed the new Houses of Parliament office building. They felt they had suffered, if only in frayed nerves, by being first.

'It's very difficult being the first one,' said Michael Hopkins, 'you know, the projector doesn't work properly and so on. I think we had a few minutes extra because of that.' They had obviously felt uncertain about the best strategy to adopt with a jury which, whatever the brief said, would inevitably expect more detailed answers than they could provide. 'People say, "Well, what are you going to do about this, that and the other?" or "That doesn't work", and you say, "I know it doesn't work!"'

'It's a "no win" situation, a competition,' said Patty Hopkins with a nervous laugh, 'except that, obviously, somebody does.'

For Renzo Piano, the Italian architect, detailed questions about a scheme that could only be rudimentary at this stage had to be taken in his stride. 'It's very difficult when somebody says to you, "Yes, great, but what will happen if you don't do the bridge on the river?" Or, "What happens if you cannot cross the Switch House to make the internal street?" And this is delicate, because after one month's work, you cannot give a precise answer; you don't know. But you guess, you feel. In my experience, it never happens that if you have a good solution, it doesn't work. Sooner or later it will work. At my age I start to recognize what is possible, and what is not, and for me those are things perfectly possible, and they will happen.'

For Claudio Silvestrin, displaying just a hint of paranoia, at least one of the questioners had an ulterior motive. 'I said I was going to achieve a concealed light fitting, and his question was: "How are you going to do it?" That means, "I want to know so I can use it for my own job" – obviously. So I said, "I'm not going to tell you."'

Rick Mather dealt slightly more tactfully with questions that were, perhaps, a little too detailed. 'The jury today did ask me if maybe one of the landings for the escalators was a little bit small, and then they apologized and said, "Well, we know it's diagrammatic", and I said, "Yes, it is", and that I felt the same way: we could make it a little bigger. But it's really the big idea and the flexibility within that big idea to conform to the existing building that we were trying to get across today.'

Don Hands, who co-presented with Claudio Silvestrin, saw it as a sign of success that the questioning mainly dealt with broad matters. 'We didn't do too badly,' he said, 'because only one person asked about the toilets.'

David Chipperfield was one of several who just felt they hadn't been given enough time. 'We had to hurry so fast through our description of what we'd done that I'm not quite sure it made any sense.'

And Nicholas Grimshaw found it all rather intimidating: 'I've done it dozens of times before but, still, it was a breakneck-speed job. You go in, there's a U-shape of people sitting there, and they say, "Right, we haven't got time to introduce ourselves: go!" and you're thrown in absolutely at the deep end, but we were ready. I think we got a bit twitchy halfway through, wondering whether we were going to do it in time. But I think we were almost absolutely dead on our twenty minutes.'

Rem Koolhaas was guarded about the events of the previous hour: 'I have just had an experience which is fairly elaborate, which means that any impression I might have at this moment is completely insignificant.'

And Amanda Levete seemed relieved that it was all over: 'After two weeks of euphoria, thinking that we had a very good idea, we had two and a half weeks of complete despair where we were struggling with the spatial problems to try and get it to work.'

That the Tate were looking for an architect and not a scheme had become a kind of mantra. Nevertheless, as many of the shortlisted thirteen were aware, the scheme they presented to the jury, however much they said it was one of many possibilities, would be bound to have some impact on the jury as an indication of how they thought architecturally. And some architects felt that the jury themselves didn't really play it by the rules.

'They all were talking about the solution rather than the business of appointing an architect,' said Michael Hopkins, and Patty added, 'Inevitably.' 'One knew that they would,' Michael Hopkins went on, 'you can't help yourself.'

'No,' said Patty, 'they constantly react to what they see, and we were first, therefore they were learning about things, weren't they?'

'Practising,' said Michael.

Nicholas Grimshaw also felt that the jury's approach presented him with problems: 'I think that this has been a very difficult process. We're being consistently told not to design a building, and yet really one is longing to get one's hands on it.'

Renzo Piano actually found it a relief not to have to go to town on a design. 'I think it's great,' he said. 'I think it's very good. Everything is happening in a very good atmosphere and I think it's good not to ask for a scheme. I only hope that the assessors will never forget that they didn't ask for a scheme, because if you don't ask for the scheme then you have to understand that the architect doesn't bring a scheme, but brings advice.'

Rick Mather sensibly had his cake and ate it. 'I thought it was pretty pointless just to do a few magic marker diagrams,' he said, 'because what the architect who's chosen needs to be able to do is actually to make the most of what's there, and the only way to judge that is really to see an architect's proposals that had gone into that in a lot of detail, and really thought about it.'

Rem Koolhaas saw the value of the Tate approach: 'As far as I can tell, their claim to be more interested in an architect than in a scheme is entirely sincere and, personally, I also think it is very intelligent because there is something rather painful sometimes when you win a competition and suddenly you confront the group of potential users with an edict in which they had no involvement, and it frequently creates at the beginning of an operation a kind of tension that can be very negative.'

But Jan Kaplicky of Future Systems took a cynical view of the whole idea of 'architect rather than scheme'. 'I think that's forgotten a long, long time ago. I think that's what they say to the public or whatever. We were talking with them only five minutes ago about absolute details, at the level of what sort of door hinges you will have. So I think that's history.'

Amanda Levete added her view: 'There's a complete dilemma expressed in the brief that they're looking for an architect, and then they tell you what the budget is. Well, you can't design an idea to a budget. You have to have an idea for a scheme, and then the difficulty is, how do you pare down your idea to make it look diagrammatic enough, to make it loose and open-ended enough that you haven't actually thought that you solved all the problems?'

Future Systems were among several of the thirteen who showed a barely concealed irritation about the whole competition. Perhaps because of inexperience, perhaps because of overconfidence, they spoke as if the scales had been weighted against them by an 'Establishment' client. Claudio Silvestrin – he who thought his ideas would be pinched by the jury – also came out of the presentation very irritated. '*Nobody* has asked us questions concerning the architect's role. All the questions were, "Are there enough lifts?" "How many loos?" "Is the depth of the approach enough for the expected visitors?" So it was absolutely contrary to what the original brief stated, and I think perhaps only Nicholas Serota asked questions which were really concerning the world of art. All the others were kind of strange questions about nonsense details.'

David Chipperfield felt that there was a financial reason for the Tate's approach at this stage. 'I think that the Tate suggested that we weren't to design a project at this point partly as a way of justifying that they give you such a small amount of money that you don't come back with a full set of plans. And if you don't come back with anything then they say, "Well, where's the door?", "Where's the entrance?", which is of course what they asked us.'

Jacques Herzog was uncharacteristically diffident as he looked back at the presentation he had just made. 'I don't think I was so good today at the presentation,' he said thoughtfully. 'If you say they choose an architect, I think this is a very good method to choose someone that you can trust, that you have a certain relationship with, or that you can have a certain communication with also, and so this personal level is very important, very nice, I think.'

Regardless of the brief, each architect did present some kind of scheme, ranging from sketchy outlines to detailed plans. Looking back afterwards, Serota divided the thirteen into two groups – those who went with the grain and those who went against it. That any went against the grain at all was surprising. The Tate was sending a pretty big signal to the competitors merely by choosing Bankside Power Station. Even if the architects had not read any of the interviews with Serota about Bankside that preceded the competition, they only had to read the competition brief to understand that the Tate team was not looking for a total mutilation of the building, and that by choosing to convert it they were, on the whole, happy to base their new gallery on a monumental piece of fifties architecture.

In the days after the presentation, the jury and their advisers had a whirlwind programme of visits and workshops and technical assessments designed to whittle the thirteen down to six. Ricky Burdett described how they approached their task: 'Remember that there were two dimensions to the decision: one was ideas in the form of schemes which they did in models or drawings on boards which were seen by everyone in the jury; but then the other side was actually going to see some of these architects, seeing them work in their office, seeing them think about the project, seeing them talk to some of us on the jury, and getting a feel of what they felt about the building. And I'd say that second dimension was as important as the first. Then, a lot depended how people performed on the day.'

The six finalists still reflected some of Serota's 'with and against the grain' division. Tadao Ando, the only Japanese architect in the final six, presented a scheme which seemed to defy the 'grain' of Bankside in several different ways. Two dramatic glass structures containing gallery spaces fought the right angles of the old power station by slanting across the main east–west axis of the building. They both protruded on the river side of the building and provided dramatic views of the City of London. Inside the building, above and below the level of the glazed beams, the interior spaces were organized into more galleries and other public facilities, but again, not paying much attention to the traditional lines of the power station. Ando's landscape design was a very structured and layered area that brought elements of the building out on to the riverside area at ground level in the same way that his glass shafts hovered over the ground three storeys up, and he carried the idea of different levels on his external plaza into the building, where visitors would go down below ground level at the base of the chimney before ascending into the building by way of interior ramps.

Ricky Burdett was very familiar with Ando's work. 'If you showed me a magazine I could tell you this was a Tadao Ando building. They tend to be in concrete, so beautifully produced that it feels and looks like marble. In fact it's sand-papered by his students – that's why it's so smooth. He was able to impress me by the sense of the quality of light that he was imagining could come through this building into the galleries. That's what he is well known for with his buildings in Japan: quality of light which actually penetrates the deep interior spaces, and his understanding of that is quite exceptional. Not surprisingly, maybe, the other side of the coin is that the relationship of his building to the surroundings is less sophisticated.'

Michael Craig-Martin, one of the Tate's Trustees and also a member of the assessors, was very excited by Ando's scheme. 'I thought it was poetically brilliant, because one of the shafts lines up with the route up to St Paul's on the other side of the river. So what he's doing is connecting one side of the river with the other side, and then by having the shafts go through this vast building – which actually acts as a barrier, and there's a terrible feeling about the difference between the front and the back of this building – by putting the shafts right through the building he is uniting the back of the building with the front of the building. And so they aren't just something to do to the building to make it more interesting, they have a very clear function in locating the building with its site and then re-defining the building in itself, and I thought that was very clever. Now, whether it's technically possible, because it does involve going through the electricity sub-station, these are slight practical problems, but in terms of the poetry of vision about what a major intervention could be, I thought that was brilliant. And also, although it is a massive intervention, it leaves the building completely intact. You can read the building exactly as it was before, and yet see that something extraordinary has been done to it.'

Interestingly, in spite of his great enthusiasm for the aesthetics of Ando's proposal, Craig-Martin saw some drawbacks in having Ando as the Tate's architect – back to 'the architect not the scheme'. 'I read sometimes in the press that he is considered the favourite,' Craig-Martin said. 'I was amazed that people can say such things, it seems very intrusive to say that, and I have no sense of that at all. He is one of the world's great architects, but he's also a really difficult architect. And it would never be easy to do a building with a Japanese architect who didn't speak English terribly well. And I would never suggest that we did something on that scale purely on poetic grounds.'

David Chipperfield was the only British architect in the final six.

When Serota was criticized for including so many foreign architects among the finalists he pointed out that as many British architects had major projects abroad, why shouldn't foreign architects design major British projects? Chipperfield was one of those British architects, with prestigious (but small) buildings in Germany and Japan.

His scheme for Bankside incorporated the daring – and possibly unwise – idea of doing away with the power station's chimney. This proved fatal to his chances of winning the competition. It was perhaps another of Serota's 'against the grain' ideas. In place of the chimney, on the middle of the north side, Chipperfield had designed a wide glazed tower that rose some way above the roof level but still appeared squat compared with the soaring height of the old chimney. The tower contained a restaurant and some gallery spaces, but the main galleries were built in concrete and filled both the Boiler House volume and the Turbine Hall, around interior courtyards. His scheme was described as a small city of streets, courts and buildings under a glazed roof.

Ricky Burdett described Chipperfield's scheme as an open umbrella, 'and everything under it is protected. You leave the building exactly as it is, so you leave the skin one brick deep, and then you create a series of boxes inside and those boxes could have wonderful galleries, jewels for modern art, you know – that's where the Picassos and the Kandinskys can go, and then you have leftover spaces in between, which can be for much rougher, much grander, more unknown contemporary art, and that seemed to be an interesting approach which needs of course to be proven in the next stage. Will it work for a museum? Can you channel two million people through it?'

Chipperfield, like the other five finalists, had presented improved versions of their schemes to a Tate workshop in the final stages of the assessment. After that workshop, Burdett picked three things about Chipperfield's scheme that he liked: 'One is that he leaves the shell of the building, the envelope, the roof and the brick skin intact and all the new building stands away from it so that you can actually walk round in the new Tate in ten years' time and look up and you'll be able to see the old building and you'll be able to see the new building. That leads to the second point, which is by doing that there's a very exciting dynamic tension between old and new which one warmed to in the way that David was presenting it – the images we've seen of projecting boxes which are clearly new which sit against this cavernous space – that tension is good and exciting and to be commended. The third good thing, the thing which has an interesting potential, is that if you break up the volumes inside the shape you have great possibility of bringing in natural light, deep down into the building.'

Michael Craig-Martin said, 'I thought that the way David Chipperfield had looked at the entire nature of the building, and the entire nature of the site, and the way he had broken it down in a certain kind of way, was more thorough than anybody else. And also the idea of using the building as a shell within which something of a free-form nature could actually take place. From what I know of his work, he is very good at dealing with mass and interval in architecture. And the opportunity with this great space, of doing something of that kind, of building something virtually free-standing within this shell seemed to me to be a real possibility.'

Renzo Piano was perhaps the favourite from the beginning. He was one of the most distinguished of the competitors, a senior figure in the architectural world with a number of major projects, some of them museums, around the world. His scheme for Bankside definitely went with the grain, as it reflected the axes of Bankside through its internal and external use of rectangles. He kept the southern Turbine Hall as an open public concourse and concentrated the gallery spaces on several floors of the Boiler House. Piano also designed two pavilions extending from the north and south sides of the building, creating a north–south route for visitors as well as east–west.

'Piano understands London well because of his past partnership with Richard Rogers,' said Ricky Burdett, 'and he grabbed everyone's attention by his rather bold urban approach. He understood the problem of penetrating the building from the south, from Southwark, and just taking people all the way through this amazing space into the gallery and then shooting them out on the other side. I'd say, of Renzo Piano's fundamental concept, that aspect grabbed my attention and other people's attention. That doesn't mean to say he didn't think about the other parts – galleries and public spaces and how they work – but that was the one element that struck us.'

Serota was impressed by Piano's solution to some of the urban problems presented by the site, but less convinced by some of his early ideas about treating the building itself. 'There was a certain moment,' Serota said, 'when one just felt that Renzo was answering all the questions by painting it all white.'

Of the six finalists, Rem Koolhaas's design was the most unconventional, and created spaces and elements that seemed deliberately to fight the design of the power station. Koolhaas is known for challenging received conventions and he certainly did that with Bankside. In his competition entry the north (river) face of the building had a huge transparent wall across the middle, leaving sections of the old brick walls and their windows at either end as apparently free-standing elements only tenuously connected with the interior of the building. This was filled with three vertical blocks, made of different materials, creating spaces on different scales for the display of art of different periods and styles. With dotted lines and solid arrows, his submission charted the paths of exploration through a highly complex interior. The chimney was retained but stripped of its brick cladding, leaving a steel skeleton containing a transparent lift shaft. And in a *jeu d'esprit*, on the model he submitted there is what looks like a giant radio dial across the top of the north side, with marked out grades of no apparent significance at all.

Burdett said, 'Koolhaas took the approach that you bring people in under the building and up through the Turbine Hall in a sequence of incredibly dynamic spaces, stairs winding round, escalators zooming up, so that this vast building becomes a tour de force of movement, which is an interesting approach to a building which is fundamentally static. So here is a building which just sits on the ground, it's heavy, it's brick, and he comes through it in a rather dynamic way.'

Michael Craig-Martin compared Koolhaas with Rafael Moneo, the Spanish architect. Moneo's entry had an entrance hall at the west end of the building but then filled in the Turbine Hall and the Boiler House from floor to roof with galleries and public areas, playing down the vertical element of the old power station. He also pushed the north face of the building out towards the river with three extensions, fanning out at angles, which housed restaurants and cafés. The roof of the Boiler House was an architectural feature that channelled light through vertical 'scoops' to various levels of galleries via gaps in the gallery layouts at each level.

Herzog and de Meuron submitted a scheme where the Turbine Hall was kept unencumbered by additions so that it formed a kind of interior street, running from a gentle ramp the width of the hall at the west through to the east end, with the only sign that it was an art gallery being large sculptures or installations. Their computer graphics showed Rachel Whiteread's *House* dwarfed by the proportions of the Turbine Hall. Then the Boiler House was turned into seven storeys, with three floors of galleries above public spaces such as a shop and auditorium. Surmounting the whole building was a glazed structure, which became known as the Light Beam, that would be illuminated at night along the entire length of the building. It carried two more floors which included space for a restaurant and plant rooms, and was also a way of getting daylight into the top floor of galleries. They left much of the external façade untouched, apart from stripping away some of the extensions and outhouses that had been added since the power station was first constructed.

Ricky Burdett, who had suggested to Herzog and de Meuron that they enter the competition, was impressed by their entry. 'Jacques Herzog is recognized by many as being one of the most talented designers in the world today. He's in his mid forties, so he still needs to prove himself – architects at least until fifty-five, often till sixty, consider themselves young. (Louis Kahn didn't start building his greatest building until he was sixty-seven, so one should take history into account.) Jacques Herzog came up with a very simple, rational approach to the building, which is: you divide it up so that everything between the Turbine Hall and the river is galleries, three floors of them; some of them get top light, some of them have side light: very straightforward. The Turbine Hall is a sort of public space also for installations of art. What was interesting – and we need to see what it's like – is that the wall between the two – the galleries on one side and the Turbine Hall on the other – becomes an enigmatic sort of fluctuating, translucent *something*, which gives this building another dimension of life.'

Janet de Botton, one of the Tate Trustees and a noted contemporary art collector, was impressed by Herzog himself as much as by his scheme: 'We all had the feeling that Jacques really loved the building and that he wanted to alter it enough to make a difference, but not enough to ruin the original statement of Bankside, which is a very powerful one. For instance they've got their circulation in a very intelligent and easy way. They're very interested in meeting places and how people can get into the building with the greatest ease, where they could meet, where they can eat if they want to, how they can best enjoy the river view, how they can best get from whatever station that they're landing at or whatever bus stop or car park, how they can find their way to the museum – which is quite complicated – in a way that's going to be clear and easy. I think that one of their great strengths is that they are very involved in the public perception of the building and how to make it simple and friendly and not one of those things where you're looking around thinking, "Crikey, where do I go from here?"'

Peter Wilson, who attended the Herzog and de Meuron workshop, was impressed by their approach: 'Of all the practices that we had workshops with, they were the one who responded to the workshop in a way that you could go and look at their scheme afterwards and recognize things that had happened as a result of the workshop. A lot of the planning of the entrance for groups and for the art-handling entrances came out of our workshops. They responded very quickly and were obviously very agile in terms of their planning. They could rearrange the building, see good reasons why things might be different, and then make suggestions.'

It was Herzog and de Meuron who were awarded the contract, and it seemed with hindsight as if they were rarely out of the first two or three during the long competition process. Nick Serota summed up the changing fortunes among the final six, where it seemed that the final choice had something to do with age.

'In the second stage of the competition, Koolhaas, Chipperfield and Herzog moved forward, and Moneo, Piano and Ando stood still. It was an interesting generation question. I don't think it had to do with the way in which the workshops developed. I don't think it was a question of simply the younger architects feeling more in tune with me or with the Tate staff and therefore giving more. Maybe they were more hungry. In some cases I think they were more in tune with some of the art that we will be showing there. Renzo came with this tremendous idea at the outset (the north–south route through the building), which of course has changed the whole way in which everyone looks at the building and there's an irony now in that it will move forward in a new light from the thrust that he has given it and we will all owe him an enormous debt, which he recognizes. There was a steady movement forward of the younger practices and yet Renzo evidently wanted this job and was passionate about it. Even at the final stage the model came in and they suddenly realized that they'd got the scale of the piazzas in front of the building wrong. So they sent someone over to modify the model just so we wouldn't be misled. It was just that he just didn't continue to move forward. Every time we talked to Herzog and de Meuron we sensed that we had moved forward, and this became a very powerful argument in their favour.'

Janet de Botton summed up why the assessors finally chose Herzog and de Meuron. 'At the last stage all six architects presented schemes, all of which were capable of being built. One of them was too expensive for our budget, so maybe that would have been the first to be discounted because of the cost. Of the other five, all of them had good points, bad points, things that we learned about the building. But at the end of the second day, we all felt that Herzog and de Meuron were capable of building us a museum that was going to be the first of the next generation of museums. What I was very keen to avoid was a museum that was going to be the end of the last generation of museums. I think it would just be a shame to do that.'

4

Serota and Herzog

The architectural practice of Herzog and de Meuron is spread between two buildings on the bank of the Rhine just north of the centre of Basel in Switzerland. One building, where the four partners have their offices, is an elegant nineteenth-century house with creaking floorboards, narrow wooden staircase and a top floor peeping out from under the mansard roof. The other, where about twenty architects and students work, is a long, three-storey building which looks as if it might have been a light engineering workshop or a school, probably built in the thirties. Between the two buildings is a low structure, little more than a shed, which is called by everyone 'the cafeteria'. Here, at ten o'clock on a Friday morning in February 1995, everyone in the company is gathered for the daily ritual of morning coffee or tea, plus cake and – today – a chocolate replica of Big Ben, donated to the practice by an engineering company on hearing that they had won the competition to design the new Tate Gallery of Modern Art in London.

Herzog and de Meuron was an unexpected practice to choose. They were very much the dark horse of the contest. Some people at the Tate involved with the selection process had never heard of them when they entered the competition. And they very nearly didn't enter. Christine Binswanger, one of the four partners, had recommended against it because of the tightness of the competition schedule and the amount of work the company had on its books already.

In the way that often happens, everything seemed to be coming together in 1994–5 for this unusual practice. Since the company was founded in 1978, they had designed 130 buildings. An exhibition of their projects was planned at the Pompidou Centre in Paris, and now a new display had to be hastily organized for it featuring their Tate design. A major book of photographic 'portraits' of their buildings had been produced in New York, and they were in the middle of designing a £200 million development in Munich and an £80 million project in Frankfurt. With the Tate and a range of other projects, from railway signal boxes upwards, the total value of the schemes they were designing was almost half a billion pounds.

And yet they stand out from the usual run of major international architects. Their premises are spartan: whitewashed walls devoid – for the most part – of any decoration, plain wooden tables on trestles, a long wooden dining table in the cafeteria. Most extraordinary of all, the partners appear to place a considerable amount of importance on the mental and physical well-being of their employees and themselves. With large projects, most architectural companies will find themselves working into the night and through weekends as the pressure builds up to meet deadlines or solve tricky problems of detailing or construction. But at Herzog and de Meuron work is punctuated by frequent intervals of compulsory pleasure, relaxation and amusement. At ten o'clock and four o'clock every day, the whole company assembles in the cafeteria for half an hour or so of unorganized conversation and refreshment. At lunchtime the premises are deserted as everyone leaves for lunch. Every Wednesday a group of the architects goes off to play football in a sports stadium designed by the practice. Twice a week, one of the founding partners, Pierre de Meuron, dresses up in running gear and sets off for a run along the Rhine.

All of this is perfectly natural to Herzog. 'In England people very often have sandwiches and that's a cultural phenomenon. I personally wouldn't like staying in the office and having sandwiches, I think it's terrible to do that. I think it's very good for the brains, for the body to go out, to move a bit and to forget about things. To mix everything, to eat and drink and watch TV and work, this is a disaster.'

If a hallmark of the Tate – indeed of contemporary art in general – is surprise, then Herzog and de Meuron were the obvious firm to appoint. They were not exactly unconventional. Their decor and attitudes to work would have been unsurprising in a firm of solicitors. It's just that they were outside the mould of the world-class architects who had been candidates in the competition.

For the judges in the Tate Gallery competition, and in particular for Nick Serota, the key event that probably gave Herzog and de Meuron the prize was a visit by a Tate selection team to the practice in late December. There seems to have been a sea change in the judges as they toured Herzog and de Meuron and visited some of the firm's buildings in and around Basel. A copper-clad signal box, a sports stadium, a factory and store for a company making small jellied sweets – each of them is very different in scale and purpose from the major transformation of Bankside Power Station and yet the judges found in each of them a design feature, a use of space or an innovative decorative technique that they had not seen elsewhere.

'One of the things that undoubtedly turned us towards Herzog and de Meuron,' Serota said, 'was the realization that no two of their buildings are the same. Each of them embodied certain principles which are consistent, but the expression of them is very different according to the function and use of the building. Equally, seeing buildings working at different scales was also important. It's conceivable that they had a slight advantage in the final stages because some of the jury had seen their buildings over a day and a half, in a sweep. Although they had visited the buildings of Koolhaas or Piano or even Chipperfield, that was an assembly of fragmented images.'

Serota and the jury had actually gone to Basel with another purpose. 'The prime motive for the visit was that I wanted everyone to see an Ando building because I thought there was no way that they could begin to appreciate what he was doing without having experienced one building, and very few of the jury had ever seen a building by Ando. Tacked on to this was the idea that we might see some Herzog and de Meuron buildings, and I thought it very likely that when the jury saw those buildings they wouldn't respond. And on that first day I had thought that we shouldn't show the jury Herzog and de Meuron's "apartment building along a party wall", because although it embodied some of their principles it was a slightly atypical building, designed when they were a relatively young practice. I thought if the jury see that first they'll think, "Oh, this is just a young team", and maybe they would feel, "These people are only capable of building apartment houses". As it happened, we were walking down the street going to see another building and I realized that we were within a hundred metres of this apartment house, and I thought, "This is ridiculous, I must take them to see it". And so we went in and saw it and they responded very positively. That was actually the first building that they saw.'

The partners in this unusual practice were Jacques Herzog, Pierre de Meuron, Harry Gugger and Christine Binswanger. The firm had been founded by Pierre and Jacques, who had known each other since childhood.

'With Pierre and myself,' Herzog said, 'because we know each other since we are children, it's like having another brain, like a computer where you have more power because the communication goes faster, so that's the ideal thing. Sometimes you do not even know where an idea comes from, and very interesting things come from a discussion and you don't know exactly who brought that in.'

With the Tate project Pierre de Meuron played a less visible role – although one that Herzog still saw as vital – contributing through regular Sunday afternoon meetings in Basel when Herzog and Gugger returned from London, and often paying attention to the business side of the project. But the public face of the company as far as Bankside was concerned was Herzog, a man who was ambitious, driven, and quietly obstinate about the principles of his architecture. He was also an enigma, particularly on first meeting. Shaven-headed, neatly dressed, outwardly polite and seeming a little anxious, he would puzzle the Tate people from time to time by sticking when they thought he should yield and yielding when they were convinced he would resist. Rem Koolhaas, the Dutch architect and co-competitor, described Herzog as having 'an explosive temperament, rigidly controlled', and he's one of Herzog's friends.

Even his partner, Harry Gugger, found Herzog difficult to 'read' when he first met him: 'I was a student when I first met Jacques, and he bothered me a lot by his person and by the work he showed. I think it was in my first year that I met him first. He gave a lecture and he showed this really weird building, a house for a vet. And we'd been training in the first year to set up nice elevations, very well structured, and he showed this elevation that had windows here and there and I just thought, "Well, this is not properly done. There's something wrong with this." Plus he was speaking not to the audience, but to the wall where he had his slides projected, and so his back was always turned to the audience and talking to his slides. That was the first time I met him, and since then they (Pierre and Jacques) always bother me by what they are doing. It was always like a challenge – there was something unexpected, something which maybe I hadn't seen, or at least which made me think, "What is it about and why are they doing it?"'

In spite of his bewilderment, Gugger ended up working with the puzzling pair, and eventually become de facto the partner who ran the Bankside project on a day-to-day basis. He explained their initial doubts about entering the Tate competition: 'We were very surprised that we were asked to enter the competition. And this was an issue that we had to discuss, because we thought that there was no need to enter the competition if we didn't have any chance. For us it's always very important to work with art, and it's very interesting as well, and this was the reason we went on, because we thought it's quite a challenge, because we have to deal with art and to deal with an old building.'

Even when they were down to the final six, Gugger and his colleagues were convinced that they would not be picked. 'We often said it's evident that they would choose Renzo Piano. He has done similar things. He has lots of experience in museums and he has worked on the refurbishment of the Fiat building in Turin. So we thought he would be a natural choice.'

Although it was Burdett who drew Herzog and de Meuron into the competition, it was when Serota saw their work and met them that the momentum began to build. Serota himself is an enigma to some. Not the least puzzling thing about the way he is perceived is that newspaper profiles of him quoted stories circulating among staff at Millbank that Serota had suddenly asked staff to address him as 'Director', a throwback to civil service practices of former decades. To observe him in action at meetings, social events and staff functions, where everyone appears to be calling him 'Nick' without retribution, contradicts that image.

His office at Millbank is above the classical portico where the 'football crowds' swarm into the gallery. He sits at a plain, light-coloured wooden table with neatly arranged papers and the occasional votive object such as a shell or a piece of wood. Sometimes he will take a phone call standing by the window, looking out at the queues down below or at the Thames flowing past the gallery's front door. He is tall and thin, with rimless spectacles and an angular, peaky face. He can seem a severe, ascetic individual when he is preoccupied, and a menacing one when things are going wrong, but when he is embroiled in the nuts and bolts of an interesting situation he can clearly be seen to be enjoying himself like anyone else, and happy to share that enjoyment with others.

One of Serota's major achievements since becoming Director of the Tate was to have created a mass audience for modern and contemporary art. That's not to say that he made everyone like it, but the kinds of things that were seen at the Tate and the kind of artists who were promoted or commissioned by the gallery were talked about both positively and negatively by the quality press, the broadcast media and even the tabloids in a way that could only increase the numbers of visitors to Millbank. Most important of all – since it fitted the views of Serota and his colleagues – the Tate's policies led to a continuing discussion about what art is, in addition to stimulating comment on particular works of art and artists.

He saw Bankside as an extension of that dialogue, shorn as it would be of the Turners and Pre-Raphaelites, Hogarths and Constables. But he saw it as more than a place to display the art he loved – he and the Trustees also had a specifically social ambition for the new gallery:

'We've always had the ambition of building not only a Museum of Modern Art but also a great civic building. A building that would actually add something to the city. And obviously it's the characteristic of such a building that it does draw its own audience. It's a place that people feel they can share in. It's a place that people will want to go and meet others, and then perhaps go and look at some modern or contemporary art. It's a place that should become part of the social fabric as well as the cultural fabric. In selecting sites for a possible museum of modern art in London, we always looked at sites that could give something back to the city as well as being a fortress of modern art in its own building, firing outwards.'

Certainly as the Herzog and de Meuron design evolved, it emerged as a building that would work in a fundamentally different way from the Tate at Millbank. You go to the Tate because you want to go to the Tate. If Bankside could attract people by the social amenities of the building it might bring a wider group of people face to face with the modern and contemporary art which Serota saw as a desirable part of everyone's cultural life, rather than an interest of the intellectual few.

'There isn't a priesthood of artists that's grown over centuries along with a sort of caste system that provides artists to do a certain thing for us in society. Most artists are first generation artists from an extraordinarily diverse range of backgrounds. Something in them has led them through a path which has given them the opportunity to express that creativity. But they're drawing on experiences that we all share in differing degrees.'

No director of the Tate would be able to avoid the snipings and tabloid criticisms that modern art receives at regular intervals, but of all recent incumbents Serota seemed best able to handle them, or to remain unfazed by them. On a day when he had been on the phone with the editor of the *Sun*, trying to deflect criticism of the Bankside project, he was able to discuss the matter with logic and equanimity: 'He was saying what one would expect him and others to say, namely that if you ask an individual on the street to choose between a new hospital and a new art gallery which will he choose? Of course it's going to be the new hospital because he immediately sees himself with his kids who've been knocked over in a road accident, needing treatment. But actually that's a rather false polarity. One of the things I asked him was "how many new hospitals have been built in Britain since the war, and how many new art galleries?" And the answers are self-evident. We have to make some investment in our cultural fabric as well as in other parts of the fabric of society. In the late nineteenth century all those great northern cities had art galleries built within them, and those galleries fundamentally helped to change the way in which people saw their place in society. And we should be investing in a similar manner.'

There was another Tate individual who was to play an important and continuing role in the Bankside project. He was Peter Wilson, the Tate's Head of Gallery Services, a man who at Millbank was responsible for everything from lavatories and warders to gallery refurbishments and major new extensions. As bulky as Serota is slender, and as hairy as Serota is smooth, Wilson was to prove a tower of strength on the Bankside project through the years of interesting, frustrating and exhilarating events. He always appeared to maintain a sense of perspective and, to use a favourite word of his, pragmatism. But behind his straightforward manner was a subtle and Machiavellian mind. Now he was to acquire a second set of responsibilities without relinquishing the old ones, as he contemplated a regular series of meetings stretching off over the next five years to monitor, plan and manage a brand-new gallery. Wilson would have to work closely with Serota – as he had done often in the past – but the two men would also have to ensure that their responsibilities, hardly yet defined, did not overlap.

'That's something that we're trying to work out at the moment,' said Wilson in January 1995, 'and I don't think I can give a definitive answer. But I think I tend to lead on technical and logistic matters and Nick tends to lead on the curatorial and aesthetic matters. And rather like the relationship between architects in a practice, we both understand what the other person's concerns are going to be and so we work fairly well as a team. I think both of us are agonizing about how much time we personally will be able to give to the project and who it is who's going to be the day-to-day liaison between us and the design team. In an ideal world, both of us would like to do the liaison ourselves but we realize it isn't practicable.'

And that liaison had to begin almost immediately, as the Tate got down to the task of taking Herzog and de Meuron's design and making it match a brief for the gallery that they had hardly had time to draw up, and, more important, for which they had no money.

To create the Tate Gallery of Modern Art the Trustees needed to raise £130 million. Fifty million pounds of this would go on construction costs and the rest would be needed to cover site purchase, consultants' and architects' fees, fund-raising and PR costs, and recruiting and training staff. They were unworried by this target. As Serota described in September 1994, when not a penny had been raised apart from project development funding, the most important factor in the decision was not its feasibility but the *necessity* – as he and the Trustees saw it – that there should be such a gallery.

'We've taken the initiative to do this,' he said. 'It isn't as though government has come to us and said "it appears that the nation needs a museum of modern art". And it isn't as though an individual has said, "I would like to establish a museum of modern art bearing my name", which is the way in which such institutions have frequently been established abroad. After all, the Tate itself was established rather against government interests as a result of Henry Tate giving a group of pictures and then also paying for the building. We've taken an initiative because we believe it is necessary and timely. And we have to marshal the support that will realize it. Now support is going to be a combination of public and private. "Public" – in the sense of money coming from the taxpayer in one form or another – is an essential component of this project, not least because I think that it has to be a project that enjoys a wide measure of support in the community rather than simply something which is either an individual's plaything or has been imposed on people.'

The factor that had transformed the fund-raising possibilities and kicked the project into a higher gear was the creation by the then Conservative government of a national lottery (announced in 1992 and active in 1994), with the profits going to a number of worthy causes. And one of those worthy causes was to be a clutch of projects designed to mark the new millennium. The Tate Trustees and Serota immediately saw the funding opportunity presented by the Millennium Fund, as it was called, for their new gallery, provided it could be achieved in time to open in the year 2000, which was somewhat earlier than their original thinking.

'I think it unlikely that we would be anticipating completion by the year 2000 were it not for the existence of the Lottery,' Serota said. 'But for us to be successful in getting money from the Lottery, we're going to need to demonstrate private sector support. And that will come from people interested in art. It will come from people who are interested in London. It will come from people who are interested in the culture. And they won't necessarily be British, because I think this is a project that has international significance. We have to spend the next year trying to find private sector money in the run-up to making an application to the Millennium Commission for Lottery funds.'

In spite of the Tate team's protestations that, up to the last minute, they weren't sure whether they would get Millennium Commission money, the whole exercise worked like a dream. By the time the Tate prepared its submission they had a project that was almost an identikit picture of an ideal Millennium Project. For Jennie Page, head of the Millennium Commission, it pressed a number of other buttons that the Commission would be expected to respond to favourably. 'The first thing to say is we're all very conscious that the Tate's collection is a very popular one. If you try to get there on a Sunday afternoon, you're pushing and shoving in the rush hour. And there's quite clearly a demand from a lot of people, including a lot of very young people, to see more of that art. So that was an example of how the Commission were aware of the broader interest in it. There is a sense also in which the Commission are very impressed by what the Pompidou Centre managed to do for that part of Paris and it can be expressed in terms of the impact on the economy, how a run-down area can suddenly find a new focus for activity which brings in new jobs where there's the sense of a buzz which lifts a quarter. And the public can benefit from that. More broadly, I think that people simply benefit from having good, interesting, exciting places that are aesthetically challenging and pleasant to go to. What we're talking about is the art of the whole of the twentieth century, which is certainly marking the end of the second millennium, and a playing field from which you can move forward into the third millennium. The exciting and innovative ideas of the architects and the use of that power station, which stands on one side of the Thames looking a little like a cathedral of power facing the cathedral of St Paul's on the other side of the river, and which is, in a sense, being turned into a cathedral of art for the twenty-first century was also exciting.'

With such a glowing testimonial it was surprising that anyone at the Tate should lose a moment's sleep over the question of whether or not they would get the £50 million they were applying for. But there were a number of causes for concern. For one thing, the Commission only had £350 million altogether for landmark Millennium Projects and the Tate was asking for a seventh of that. There was also the fact that Bankside was in London and there had been a lot of press comment that the Lottery was resulting in grants to too many London projects, while being able to fund only a limited number of projects overall.

Complacency in a situation like this can lead to falling at the last hurdle and Serota seems to have taken no chances: 'I think the politics at that moment were to do largely with the debate that has been continuing about whether too much Lottery money is going to London and whether too much Lottery money is going towards so-called elitist arts projects. And I think we managed to persuade the commissioners of the strength of our case. But during the last three or four weeks both Dennis Stevenson and I seriously doubted whether we would get the money, although I spent the time walking round London meeting people who kept saying, "Oh, it's a certainty". And it plainly wasn't a certainty.'

When Serota was asked at what point he felt sure that the Bankside project would get the Millennium money he said, 'At 8:01 on 30 October 1995, when we got the fax confirming it.' With £50 million in the bag, there was still a long way to go. There were other public bodies that could also be approached – the Arts Council, for example, and English Partnerships, a regeneration body for England. But the bulk of the rest would have to come from private donors.

The Tate has lived for a long time with what some would see as the necessary evil of relying on private funding for many of its activities. Serota's own fund-raising activities have been extremely successful in the past, but the Bankside project was his biggest challenge in this area. One of the first obstacles he came across was the fact that the Tate had chosen to build its new gallery in an old building. In early 1996, as he worked his way through his Rich People address book, he consulted and cajoled and schmoozed but found that his charm was not always working. Some people were unwilling to contribute because of the Bankside factor. They felt the Tate should be building its new gallery somewhere else, in a new building.

Serota knew that the gallery could astonish the doubters if it was allowed to fulfil its potential. But he was afraid of what would happen if the fund-raising went badly and they just scraped together enough to fund what he called pejoratively a 'British project'.

'There's a danger that we'll end up doing this in a rather British way by the year 2000. People will walk in and they'll all look at it and they'll say, "Oh, if only we'd known, we've have given you a bit more money and you could have done that bit and that bit." My job now is to try and persuade people to come up with the money so that we can deliver a full project by the year 2000, rather than a British project. If we can do it in a really proper way, it will be that much more extraordinary.'

When Serota talked later about his attempts to raise the £80 million the Tate needed to add to the Millennium Commission's £50 million, he couldn't conceal his impatience and irritation at the unreasonableness of some of the people he had approached. He compared the way American donors give money to big arts projects with the reluctance of the British. 'I have been surprised by the willingness of some Americans to make a commitment to a project in London. And I've been surprised, on the other hand, by the reluctance of some of those people who regard themselves as great patrons of art in this country to make the commitment of money that is required to create this institution. There really isn't the tradition of giving here that we see in America and elsewhere. I had lunch with someone today who lives in San Francisco, and they've offered us money for a gallery here. There are people who live in London who've been coming and having dinners at the Tate for the last ten years who haven't yet put their hand in their pocket. That's shaming. And I've got to do something about that. It's the one time, not just in our generation, but in several generations, when there will be an opportunity to create something really remarkable. And from where I see it, it's slightly surprising that some people aren't running forward to commit, rather than holding back.'

5

The Design Evolves

On 23 March 1995 the main players met for the first time formally at the first of a series of fortnightly design meetings. Jacques Herzog was there with Christine Binswanger and Harry Gugger, and the Tate party consisted of Serota, Peter Wilson, Ron German of Stanhope Properties and Ricky Burdett. For the first two months or so after the competition announcement, the relationship between the two main parties – now tied together for the next five years – got off to a faltering start. Serota described Herzog and de Meuron as being 'in shock', and the Tate itself had to change tack rather suddenly. 'We were working out what it meant to build the building rather than run a competition.'

But in informal meetings with the architects, Serota had begun to formulate two main worries, and as the group settled into their meeting, he articulated them. First he reiterated the mantra of the competition – 'Your competition entry was a brilliant proposal and it helped you win the competition but *it* didn't win the competition. We chose an architect and not a scheme. You have the freedom to make changes and so do we.' Serota quickly moved to the other point that was giving him some concern. 'I need to be clear now which of you are to be working on TGMA.' Serota and the Tate team had rather enjoyed working during the competition with Christine Binswanger, who had worked closely with Herzog on the scheme. Now they'd heard that she would not continue on the project and they needed the new arrangement to be made explicit so they could understand the implications.

This shifting of personnel occurs often with the bigger 'name' architects. Everybody wants Foster or Rogers to design their building personally when their firm gets a contract. Clearly this is impossible, and the more famous companies have to convince clients that they are still worth employing because their project will have the stamp of the 'name' even if he doesn't work on it on a day-to-day basis. Herzog and de Meuron in 1995 wasn't yet seen as up in the big league, and therefore the Tate expected the senior partners to play a hands-on role. Furthermore, the idea that the moment they won the competition one of the partners who had been closely involved in the winning design should be taken off the project and another partner substituted struck the Tate as a little cavalier.

'I stay with the project,' said Herzog, 'that's my main job. Instead of Christine it will be Harry. Harry's more experienced than Christine.' Binswanger's strengths were seen as design and Gugger's as technological, but Herzog hastened to add, in his free-wheeling style of English, 'It's not that we go from a design genius to a technocratical stupid person. Harry is a very strong designer also.'

Herzog's statement that he would stay with the project was to acquire a hollow ring as the project proceeded. Paradoxically, it was the very success of the firm in designing the Tate project that generated huge demands on Herzog and pulled him away from day-to-day work on Bankside. But it left Harry Gugger more in control, a situation that Serota eventually accepted. 'I think we've actually come to welcome it, in the sense that I think Jacques and Harry complement each other very well. Jacques can only dip into this project on a regular basis, but he isn't giving it his full-time attention, whereas Harry can. Harry's incredibly rational, logical, rigorous. He forces the issue on questions where they need to be resolved, whether it's with the design team or whether it's with the client. And he's a really powerful motor in this project.'

In fact everyone who met Gugger liked him, and the projects he had worked on for Herzog and de Meuron, such as a railway shed and the signal box in Basel, had all been seen as possessing the distinctive and innovative use of design, technology, and materials that was their hallmark.

Serota's second point at the first design meeting was that he wanted Herzog and de Meuron to work with a British architect who would compensate for their lack of experience of working in a UK context.

'You're making a kind of architecture which is very different from British architecture,' Serota said, 'that's why it's exciting to have you.' But this made it all the more necessary – and all the more difficult – to find a British partner.

Herzog was unwilling. 'This is the first time we hear Nick say this so clearly,' he said to the meeting, with a worried expression on his face.

But Serota, too, was aware of the dangers and difficulties and hastened to reassure him. 'I wouldn't feel more comfortable with a solution that said, OK, Herzog and de Meuron appoint Richard Rogers, say, as the associate, but what we know in practice is that it will never be Rogers but a very junior person in Rogers – I'm more interested that they should find someone in whom they have confidence who in effect becomes a junior partner.'

Underlying these concerns of the Tate's was the growing realization of the hugeness of the task that faced them all, and their knowledge that as the transformation of Bankside got under way the need for daily or hourly decisions would come thick and fast. Serota and Wilson really weren't sure that a company five hundred miles away in Switzerland could make those decisions as effectively as they would need to.

Ricky Burdett raised another factor – the possibility that the success of Herzog and de Meuron at Bankside would lead to other projects which could further dilute their work on Bankside. He then dropped a small bombshell into the meeting. He spent a lot of time as an architectural guru and this led to him being involved in other competitions. To Herzog he said: 'You were excluded from a project yesterday in Stuttgart because you were too busy with the Tate.' He turned to Serota and added, 'Daimler-Benz wanted them to build a tiny little museum.'

Binswanger was astonished. 'Oh, come on Ricky, you're kidding,' she said.

'That was part of the discussion,' Burdett said.

'You agreed?' asked Serota.

'Absolutely,' said Burdett. 'We can't have them playing around.'

It was a sign of Herzog's lack of concern on this issue that a year later an example of 'playing around' was to create the greatest friction between Herzog and de Meuron and the Tate.

On the whole, the tone of this first meeting was light. No one wanted to rock the boat at this early stage and there was plenty of easy banter which suggested that the individuals liked and respected each other enough to be able to discuss problems as they arose openly and honestly.

The group got up from the meeting table and set off on a bright, sunny spring morning to walk around the site. The main design issues to be discussed this morning were to do with the exterior of the building and the surrounding area. For Herzog, the transformation was not going to be an easy one. 'When we drop off by cab,' he said, 'the immediate neighbourhood is architecturally terrible.' He was right. Indeed, it was hardly surprising. Power stations, even designed by a distinguished architect like Giles Gilbert Scott, are not usually sited in architecturally distinguished areas, and for decades this part of Southwark had been a backwater. Drab office buildings surrounded the power station on the southern approaches and hardly more exciting blocks of flats stood on the north-west corner by the river. The only buildings of any architectural merit were the seventeenth-century houses that stood in a row on the north-east corner of the site, whose residents were to take a keen interest in the new Tate as it developed.

There were three layers to Bankside, working outwards. First there was the building itself. Then there was the land around the building that would be the Tate's responsibility. And finally there was the immediate neighbourhood, including nearby buildings, the riverside walk and the local streets, owned by the Borough of Southwark. The building itself was not a simple structure built at one time to a unified design. The power station had acquired several accretions during the years after its initial construction, and the architects used this fact to try to understand what Gilbert Scott's basic concept had been and how to reflect it in the changes they now planned to make. Harry Gugger summed up their approach: 'It was a very early decision to take everything away which hides the main body of the building and hides the relation of the ground with the main body of the building.'

This approach presented a dilemma on the south side of the site, where London Electricity needed to hold on to the Switch House with its humming transformers. They would need access to those transformers and so the buildings on the south, used by the Tate as its visitor centre during construction, would be kept initially to form a courtyard for that access, although Herzog and de Meuron would have loved to get rid of them.

As the group turned the corner and walked down the east side of the building towards the river, they unfolded the site plan and looked at the outbuildings on the south-east corner. The Tate had decided that they couldn't afford to demolish all the outbuildings. They would need office space for their staff who would work at Bankside and the budget wouldn't allow for all that square footage to be built from scratch as part of the main gallery. So they decided to hold on to one low building on the south-east corner and upgrade it to create that office space.

But they still retained a vision of creating a strong form that reflected Gilbert Scott's original intentions, while adding their own complementary contribution. 'The form was always there,' explained Gugger, 'and I think it was destroyed when other buildings were added to the main building. What we are recreating is what Scott was imagining. Like every industrial complex, it was amended all over the place and the strong big form was lost and I think we basically went back to what his initial design was.'

Around the base of the chimney tower was an extension that had been added later as part of a district heating scheme. Herzog and de Meuron decided to remove that structure and Gugger explained why: 'The chimney was much more incorporated in the main body of the building and we now do the opposite. We will make the chimney a more free-standing element. It's as if the chimney would have grown by another hundred metres – much more dynamic and almost higher. Then once the Light Beam is on top it will create this cross and get in discourse with the chimney.'

There were several points of interest to be addressed as they walked on towards the river. On the east side of the site was the growing structure of the new replica of Shakespeare's Globe Theatre. 'It's Disneyland,' said Burdett dismissively to Herzog. But Disneyland draws crowds and the Globe was an asset to the whole Tate project because of its contribution to the crowd-drawing power of the whole area. Whatever the attractions of the new Tate itself, people would be more willing to come to this urban backwater if there were other attractions too, and by all accounts it looked as if the Globe people had had a good idea and were going to be very popular. 'We need to think about a connection here,' said Serota. As part of the urban landscape, the architects would have to plan pedestrian traffic routes and pay some attention to where people would be coming from and going to. Serota and the Tate team were also very keen to ensure that there was some kind of passage from the south side of the site to the river, down the east side of the building. At the moment this looked difficult. If the east side was mainly for loading and for employee access, it might present security problems if there was also a route through the area for crowds of visitors.

The group stood and looked at the back of the seventeenth-century houses. In one of them lived the Reverend Colin Slee and his family. He was Provost of Southwark Cathedral, and from his first-floor living room at the front of the house he had one of the most desirable views in London, across the river to St Paul's Cathedral. But at the back he had what was soon to be one of London's biggest building sites, with all the noise and dirt that that implied. He and his neighbours, including the cathedral organist and a psychiatrist, formed a small subgroup of residents who made their own particular needs felt to the Tate very early on and because of their class, status and articulacy were probably listened to more than the inhabitants of the block of flats the other side of Bankside, numerically a much larger group. But it wasn't really a case of the empty pot making the most noise in this case. Combined with an agenda that suited their own personal needs, Slee and his neighbours felt that they had also identified one or two concerns of general benefit to the neighbourhood that the architects and the Tate might have overlooked.

It was their personal agenda that Serota drew attention to as he stood with the architects looking at two garages that were embedded in the existing landscape between the power station and the river. 'The Provost of the cathedral and his neighbours have the use of these garages,' he said to Herzog, 'and they would like to do a deal – new parking in return for taking away these garages. I think they also want a slightly longer garden.'

He and Ron German laughed. 'They've got a shopping list,' German said, drily.

In fact, Slee and his neighbours had even grander ideas than that. One of the group was also an architect/developer and they had taken advice on the feasibility of acquiring a small area of the Tate site to build new houses on, in return for fitting in with the Tate's need to redesign the whole north-east corner; but that idea was quashed very early on by the Tate.

Everywhere they looked, the group found issues that needed to be resolved, and the three architects and four Tate team members broke up into knots of animated conversation.

Serota and Herzog looked up gloomily at the brickwork on the north side of the power station. 'The first immediate response to the building,' Serota said later that day, 'is to scrub it down, make it clean and shiny, and it'll be bright and beautiful. But actually when you look into it you find the building was built in two stages, that there are slightly different bricks on the upstream side from the downstream side. If you clean it you're going to expose that. You're going to wash away a certain sense of the patina of history. And there's a danger that we'll get the whole thing so cleaned up it'll no longer be the building that we wanted or that we saw or that we were inspired by. Now, on the other hand, at the moment its message is somewhat gloomy, austere, dirty. How do we strike a balance between those two? At this moment we don't have a solution.'

Herzog and Serota were also concerned about an engineer's report that had indicated that sulphur in the mortar joints might damage the brickwork and then eventually damage the underlying steel. 'We can't get ourselves into a position where we completely rebuild the building because of an engineer's report,' Serota said. 'We need to put money inside the building, and also we don't want to change the aesthetic.' For admirers of Gilbert Scott's building, the brick detailing was one of its highlights.

Serota then suggested that he or Herzog get another opinion, from an engineer who had been involved in David Chipperfield's competition entry. 'Either you or I should ring David,' Serota said. 'He's calmed down a bit.' It was no secret that Chipperfield, the only British architect in the final six, had felt a little bitter about not winning the competition.

Having talked about the immediate envelope of the building, the group then went on to the river walk. This was partly on Tate land and partly on land belonging to the Borough of Southwark, who had made valiant attempts to provide a pleasant walkway between Southwark Bridge and Blackfriars Bridge. But their attempts were not good enough for Jacques Herzog. 'All that shit goes away?' he asked, meaning the concrete benches and other street furniture.

By now the group had circumnavigated half the site and in addition to discussing the envelope of the building and its landscaping possibilities they had begun to get a sense of the different approaches to the site. The architects' competition entry had designed the main entrance down a huge ramp at the west side of the building, and the group finished their walkabout by approaching the building from that side. There they found their view of Bankside blocked by a nineteenth-century light industrial building now used as a paper merchant's. It stood in the middle of the route that would bring visitors to the Tate from the direction of Blackfriars Bridge, and concealed much of Bankside from view.

'This building doesn't belong to us?' Gugger asked, and he was told that it didn't. The paper merchant's windows stood out from the dull grey-brown brick because they were picked out in bright red paint. There were shudders from the architects at this sight. 'There's only one solution,' said Harry Gugger. 'We'll have to paint *our* windows red as well.'

Sotto voce, Serota, Peter Wilson and Ron German discussed whether there was any way the Tate might acquire the building in order to demolish it. 'I tell you what,' said German, 'it won't get any cheaper.'

'I think we should think about it,' Serota decided. 'Someone should find out how much this building would cost.'

'Someone who's got nothing to do with us,' Peter Wilson added. (It was later to transpire that it would cost £2 million to acquire and deal with the rundown establishment, far more than it was worth, and certainly more than the Tate was willing to pay.)

It was now one o'clock and the group set off to continue their discussions over lunch. This first down-to-earth exploration of the Bankside site by all of them together had consolidated some of the ideas that Herzog and de Meuron had built into their competition entry and raised new ones. They had confirmed in Serota's mind the belief that, philosophically, the architects had what he felt was a sympathetic attitude to the old building.

On the whole Serota felt that they had done a good morning's work. 'I thought we achieved a great deal today. We talked about four or five different entry points to the site and what the needs would be with those. I think we began to develop a sense of what the hierarchy will be for the visitors as they approach the building from, say, the tube station or from Blackfriars Bridge. Their final destination is Giles Gilbert Scott, modified by Herzog and de Meuron. On the boundary of the site I think they are likely to encounter not Giles Gilbert Scott but Herzog and de Meuron, whether it's a question of a pavilion which is erected on the site of the oil tanks; some form of entry or gateway on the north side, overt or rather subtle; or where they're dropped off from a coach on the south-east corner. Then as they step back further in their approach, the next level will be as they leave the tube station, as they approach from Blackfriars Bridge or from some remote car park: what kind of marker or signal will there be at that point? So there'll be these three levels of immediate recognition that you're in the vicinity of the gallery.'

Meanwhile, what of the inside? There was one major design feature that had been a key part of the competition proposal and that very early on had dropped out of the scheme. Herzog and de Meuron had proposed that the gallery floors should be hung from the Light Beam. A normal steel-framed building would have steel columns rising from the ground, thick and strong at the base and slimmer as they rose, supporting all the weight of the floors and walls that were attached to them. Herzog and de Meuron proposed to invert this pattern, by making the Light Beam structure strong enough to support vertical steel members hanging down, to which the lower floors would be attached. In their view this would allow the gallery to have some display spaces that were column-free, so that it would be the needs of the display spaces themselves that would determine where walls would go, rather than some spatial pattern that was a function of where the columns had to be to support the loads.

For Harry Gugger, this use of the Light Beam represented an ingenious combination of a design feature and a functional asset. 'It's not just a light sculpture on top of the building, but the same piece has also a structural function. We want to tie in function to form. We are always aiming for that and I think this would have been the major issue, to give another reason to an element we are designing. And of course it would have been nice to have one floor without any columns, with the freedom to have the gallery spaces arranged in whatever way you want.'

There were a couple of reasons why this elegant and adventurous design feature didn't survive the competition entry. First, it was an engineering nightmare. As Harry Gugger explained: 'We had interviews with several engineering companies and they all went mad about this. They said it's impossible.'

The second reason the upside-down structure disappeared was that, actually, the Tate weren't really bothered about column-free spaces. Peter Wilson explained why. 'Although it's an elegant notion, it was based on a slight misconception of what we as a client wanted. The architect had a feeling that we would need column-free space over the entire area of the galleries, and when he began to talk to us it became evident that we were a bit more relaxed about that than he'd thought, and without that imperative it became an expensive option. We've had column-free space in large measure at Millbank since the late nineteen-seventies, and in my experience, which stretches back that far, we've never ever used a space that big. There's been a certain amount of disenchantment with the notion that absolutely flexible space is a good thing, because curators generally like to have some kind of hard architectural notion to relate to and to hang on.'

This was just one issue that emerged in a kind of shaking-down period during the first half of 1995. Each of the design features that had been in the competition entry was scrutinized much more closely in the light of the fact that the Herzog and de Meuron competition entry now had to be turned into a real, functioning building. Most of them survived, though not always without a fight. One feature that Gugger and Herzog clung to, in spite of questions raised by the Tate people who were used to running public buildings, was the ramp at the west end and the fact that it took people down into the basement before they could go up into the galleries. This was part of the overall concept of the Turbine Hall as a huge public space from floor to ceiling. If there had been any major entrance that brought people in at ground level, many visitors would bypass the floor of the Turbine Hall, which was at basement level, and miss out on the experience that had been so carefully designed for them – the moment of revelation on the threshold of the gallery as visitors came through what seemed, because of the scale of the west end, a modest horizontal slit and found before them a soaring space lit from above by daylight through the rooflights and from the side by illuminated bays into the gallery floors.

The final scheme for the interior of the building was not to be fixed until a year after Herzog and de Meuron won the competition. On the left of the ramp, at the basement level (Level 1) of the Boiler House, there was to be a shop, an essential part of any modern museum. No longer a corner of the main lobby, carrying a few postcards and guide books, museum shops can be big business and contribute significant revenue to a museum like the Tate that has to think creatively to make the most of the buying power of its non-paying customers. Around other parts of the basement there would be offices and education project rooms, as well as cloakrooms and information desks.

On Level 2 there were various options for seminar rooms and auditoria that still needed to be addressed, as well as some form of eating area, again with decisions that had yet to be made and were to take several years to sort out.

Levels 3, 4 and 5 were to be occupied by the galleries, with some form of concourse outside each one, where people could wander and make their decisions about where to go next, and also look into the Turbine Hall at the vista below. Level 3 had another imaginative feature – a double-height gallery that benefited from the full majesty of one of Giles Gilbert Scott's 'cathedral windows' and was expected to provide a breathtaking experience for the visitor because of its size, although no one was quite sure what would eventually be put in it. The double-height gallery took up space on Level 3 and Level 4, cutting down the available display space on Level 4. Even Serota had hesitated before agreeing to this bold move, although Peter Wilson, familiar with the value of unusual spaces in other Tate buildings – the circular gallery at Tate St Ives, for example – felt that this was an example of where less really is more.

The galleries were designed with certain walls that would be permanent and others that could be changed every few years if the curators felt that new display policies required it. Some of the walls became what were called 'fat walls' – double thicknesses of walling that allowed staff to enter and access extra equipment, such as video monitors or power supplies, for example, as well as to hang tricky pieces of art that required complex fastenings through the walls to support them.

The floor materials of many of the galleries were not specified at this stage. They might be wood, they might be concrete, although it had been decided that Level 5 would have a concrete floor. The galleries at this level would benefit from daylight coming through the lower part of the Light Beam, which would act like a clerestory, the high-level arched windows of a Gothic cathedral.

Level 6 would contain some private rooms for Trustees and VIPs to use and then Level 7, the top level of the Light Beam, would have a second eating area, conceived early on as a rather expensive dining facility, although ideas about this were to change.

Even in the early days, Serota grasped and identified with the architects' vision of the building – then only existing in detailed drawings and a few artist's impressions. He saw it as his personal quest to achieve that vision by staying close to the project, although this closeness was to provide a number of headaches for his colleagues as they worked day after day to control the design, costs and schedule of a project that was more complex than any of them had been prepared for.

Part Two

1996–7

Demolishing
and
Constructing

6

Managing the Architects

Once it had been decided that Stanhope Properties would play some continuing role in the project, one of Stanhope's senior managers, Ron German, was assigned to work with the Tate team to provide project management expertise. Serota could deal with big design and policy decisions, and Peter Wilson with a whole range of cost, construction and design issues, but neither of them had the kind of regular, detailed experience that German had of managing a succession of large construction projects. In fact the Tate had appointed a major construction management company called Schal to supervise the dozens of contractors that would be required at every phase of the project – but then, who would manage the construction managers?

German is a quiet-spoken northerner, trim and grey-bearded, and he brought to his task of representing the Tate's interests a canny and meticulous mind, experienced in project management and in how to deal with the sort of crises that could arise at any time in a complex project such as Bankside. His title was Project Manager and in the early days of the project he described what that meant: 'My role is to help the Tate deliver the project. Stanhope as a company has a wider role – we deal with the acquisition of the site and peripheral property issues, and we've been dealing with appointing all the consultants and so on – and now it's a question of managing the design process, and going and buying the construction and making sure the project actually gets built.'

German would chair many of the regular meetings that were to infest the diaries of the main participants for five years or more. Often his skill was in injecting common sense into a fraught situation and using his wide experience of the construction industry to tell the Tate when to worry and when not. His main task was to keep an eye on Schal and ensure that they were doing what the Tate was paying them to do, and that usually meant dealing with Schal's senior on-site manager, Ian Blake.

Blake had been on the project since June 1995, when he was told that he was going to be managing the construction of one of the most complex and unusual buildings in his career. He had been involved with the proposal document Schal prepared for the Tate, describing why they thought they were the best company to manage the construction of the new Tate Gallery of Modern Art. Now he had been told that he was to be in daily charge of the project.

Blake is a round-faced man in his thirties, with a lock of fair hair that he brushes away from his face when he is harassed, which was often on this project. But he retained a cheery South London matter-of-factness about the daily surprises the project threw up. He had no pretensions, and occasionally identified himself as a philistine when discussion of art topics came up, but was clearly very good at holding the increasing complexities of the project in his head, even though it presented him with choices and decisions he had not been faced with before. There was to be a lot of chopping and changing in the construction methodology in the early months of the project as the team coped with the challenges presented by the hidden interior of Bankside. Their task was essentially to build a building within a building, keeping the outside shell of the power station and constructing an art gallery inside. Blake liked to point out, as a way of indicating the scale of the task, that you could fit St Paul's Cathedral inside the volume of Bankside.

Schal's duties on this project were to supervise every aspect of the construction. They planned how it was going to be done, sending out to contractors documents describing each of the hundreds of types of work that would have to be carried out; supervised the tendering process that identified the companies that would do the work; monitored those contractors as they did the work; dealt with the effects of changes in one contractor's schedule that might affect the overall programme; worked with the quantity surveyors to keep the costs within budget; and – as important as anything else – stayed in close contact with the architects' intentions to make sure that what was designed was buildable and fitted in with what the Tate wanted.

Blake and his team were installed in open-plan offices on the south-west corner of Bankside, refurbished after a decade or more of disuse. Blake's own office was little more than a glazed cubby-hole with a desk, one chair for visitors, a filing cabinet and a whiteboard. The board was usually covered with rough sketches of the site, showing the position of a crane and an indication of how far its arm would swing, or an elevation of the Light Beam showing some detail of the window-cleaning apparatus. In addition to the actual construction work, every aspect of site activity was controlled by Schal, from catering and toilets to employment policy and safety.

Blake and his colleagues started looking at the best way of constructing the 'building within a building' that was at the heart of Herzog and de Meuron's design, while the 'deplanting' work – the removal of all heavy equipment and steelwork – was in progress inside the old power station. The Schal team had decided to keep the existing roof in place for as long as possible to give stability to the whole structure. If they took it off too soon it would leave the original steel exterior framework holding the brick walls and windows in a very unstable state. But with the roof in place there would be some quite complex manoeuvring to be done to get heavy materials into and out of the building, using mobile cranes inside the structure. Only when the new interior steel structure was in place to give support to the old walls could the roof be removed. This would then mean that Schal could use bigger, more flexible, tower cranes to lift material through the roof from outside.

At this stage, the planning was based on the architects' early schematic designs, giving numbers of floors, general layout of spaces, and rough positions for stairs, escalators and so on. This was adequate for Schal to make their initial plans for how to construct the building, but Blake needed to be sure that no major changes were made in the design that would affect what Schal had to build, or that if they were, he knew about them. This wasn't always easy as the architects were not used to the kind of timescale and information flow that a project of this scope, run by a construction manager, required. Schal and the Tate had allocated set design targets – dates by which certain phases of design work had to be done so that the drawings could then be analysed and the information broken down to provide costing and schedule information.

As a result of the concerns Serota expressed to Herzog and de Meuron at their first design meeting, a British firm of architects called Sheppard Robson had been appointed to work with the Swiss architects, and Ian Blake welcomed this. 'Until Sheppard Robson came on board, there was a problem caused by the difference between what we wanted and what Herzog and de Meuron have tried to preserve as part of their culture. So the whole thing has been a growing up process really for them.'

But Herzog and de Meuron were not at all convinced that they needed the help of a British architect. In fact, Sheppard Robson's appointment disrupted what Harry Gugger saw as a key part of their design process. 'It's a matter of control. Since we don't have a kind of "Herzog and de Meuron architecture" which we can impose on every site and every employer, our employees tend not to know what we would like to do, and we don't want them to do what *they* want to do, so there is still this wish to control the design. But unlike Richard Meier or Mario Botta or other architects – where it's pretty clear what the outcome has to be – we don't have this language that we just can make someone aware of and then let him go and he does a Herzog and de Meuron building. That's why we wanted the team to be in Basel and to be close to us. All of a sudden something strikes your mind and it's nice then to just walk over, discuss it with the team and see if it works or not. It's important to control not only your team but also your ideas, which can appear when you are bicycling through the city, for example, and then you turn around, go back and discuss them.'

For Ian Blake, of course, the ability of the architect to have an idea on his bicycle and rush back to change some feature already designed was a problem, not an advantage. 'One of the things that is important, is that we don't let the designers go so far on a design that it becomes a fait accompli and we end up with a problem where we can't afford it, we can't build it, we've got a maintenance problem, all sorts of issues like that. And construction management in all its glory tends to restrict that happening to some extent. We recognize that there is this conceptual stage when you have to give designers space to be able to think without too many interruptions, but it's also fundamental that we're guiding them along a particular route that doesn't get so crazily out of hand that you can't deal with it. And what's important for us is not to see a detail for the first time once it appears on a computer screen or a computer worktop drawing. We like to be involved with the development of the design when it's really sketches or drawings. I do think it's important for us to understand their way of thinking, but equally they need to understand that there is a budget for this job, there is a programme for this job, and there are client brief requirements that have to be maintained, and that's where our role really starts to come into its own.'

Part of the problem in the early design phase of the project was due to the fact that the architects were continually learning new things about the old building. Unlike a new building, conceived on a blank piece of paper, and progressing from the general to the specific, Bankside Power Station had a way of presenting new faces and triggering new ideas every time the architects visited it.

Speaking in mid 1995, Harry Gugger explained why he and Herzog were refining their ideas as they came to understand the building better: 'The whole building is a very delicate building. To lots of people it has an austere or even a brutal expression, but if one really works with this building, with the skin, with the elevations, one recognizes that it is very delicately done. It's a very fine design. And we have realized that we really have a big problem because it's not an ordinary elevation, it's brick, and we see the brick as if it was a cloth covering for the steel frame. Once you start working on the elevations it's as if you would hurt the building, it's as if it would start bleeding. It's really difficult to insert new openings and I think it's interesting, now that we look back at the competition, that there were some architects who really had a brutal attitude towards the building. They almost destroyed, it, or they would have had to destroy it to build what they intended to build. And this is the big challenge, that we want to keep the building, we want to keep its expression, but still we have to do something with it, and it's very difficult.'

While the architects were still thinking in these very philosophical terms about the exterior of the building and what to do with it, Ian Blake was having to make quite practical plans for the first phases of construction, due to begin in August 1996. Schal's role was a vital one, and a key to its success in maintaining the schedule and budget that the Tate saw as essential would lie in the ability of Schal's man on-site to be everywhere, see everything and maintain good relationships with the bewildering number of people and parties who seemed to have a say in the Bankside project: Stuart Lipton, Peter Rogers and Ron German at Stanhope Properties; Nick Serota and Peter Wilson at the Tate, along with Dawn Austwick who had been appointed by the Tate as its Project Director; Jacques Herzog and Harry Gugger; employees of Ove Arup, the consulting engineers for the whole project; the newly appointed associate architects Sheppard Robson – the list went on and on. It might have seemed a superhuman task to stay on good terms with all those participants, and, as Blake was eventually to find out, it was.

He was experienced enough in construction management to know that he was in for several years' hard grind – and that was acceptable, it went with the territory. But the thing he found more difficult to accept – and he suspected it would happen with Bankside – was the possibility that all the work of the construction management team might not be appreciated. 'The one big frustration about what we do is that all the hard work and all the blood, sweat and tears that goes into a project – all the hours spent outside of normal working hours, all the weekends, all the time when you're not seeing your family – that never really gets thought about at the end of the day. It's really how the job finishes – that's what people remember. It's the last three months of a job. They don't remember the heavy rainfall and tremendously icy conditions and what happens when people don't think they can do what we want them to do and we motivate them to raise their game beyond levels they don't think they can achieve. All those sorts of things that go into a project, the human aspect, just gets lost and if there's any frustration and loss of sleep it's really as a result of those sorts of things, not because we didn't do a good job. It's the recognition that should have been there that perhaps won't be for reasons beyond your control.'

The group that assembled in the Tate's boardroom at Millbank on the morning of 22 June 1995 was largely made up of people who expected to work together in a close but not necessarily harmonious relationship for the next few years as their skills combined to design, construct, engineer, and control the costs of the new Tate Gallery of Modern Art.

The participants in the first joint Project and Design Review met around a large boardroom table and under a couple of aggressively modern paintings. At one corner sat Jacques Herzog and Harry Gugger, Gugger sporting an unexplained black eye. Then around the table were Ricky Burdett, the man who suggested to Herzog and de Meuron that it might be worth them entering the competition; an American landscape consultant, Laurie Olins; John Hirst, a structural engineer working for Ove Arup; Mohsen Zikri, an Egyptian mechanical engineer who also worked for Arup; Ron German from Stanhope, who was chairing the meeting; Peter Wilson and Nick Serota; Paul Morrell, a quantity surveyor from Davis Langdon Everest, the company that would monitor the costs of the project, and Ian Blake.

The agenda for this meeting was largely technical, addressing such issues as fire escapes, building services, options for rehousing London Electricity's facilities, and how much space would be needed for the plant rooms. This last issue was fundamental to a whole lot of other issues in the building, including something as basic as how much space there would be for galleries.

Behind the scenes in any large building is the machinery that is needed to heat and ventilate the building. And the need for that machinery generates demands for dedicated volumes of space in the building. Those volumes consist not only of rooms to house the equipment itself but also paths through the building to carry large pipes that will carry the heated or cooled air to where it is needed and other pipes to take the used air to the outside. Then there has to be a water supply, again carried in pipes throughout the building to the lavatories and washrooms, and to the sprinkler systems that are mandatory in public buildings. The rooms that house the plant, as all this heavy equipment is called, can't just be put anywhere in the building. Engineers have raised to a fine art the process of working out the best compromise between one central plant room from which huge air ducts and water pipes have to spread out all over the building, taking up valuable space, and the situation where every room has its own associated plant room, thus removing the need for all the ducts but multiplying needlessly the equipment for heating and cooling the air.

Mohsen Zikri, round-faced with crinkled hair, is a master of mechanical engineering. He oozes confidence in his engineering recommendations, given in precise and fluent Egyptian-accented English. Today he was to present to the meeting his first set of recommendations for how best to deal with the mechanical engineering need for space in this new 12,000m² art gallery. John Hirst would then tell the team how many fire staircases would be necessary for a building with the throughput that Bankside would expect. And then, if there was any space left in the building for galleries, Herzog and Gugger would be allowed a word at the end. In fact, Ron German in a joking announcement at the beginning of the meeting said, 'Reports first, playtime later.' It was a light-hearted remark that seemed unintentionally to put the architects in their place.

German asked John Hirst and Mohsen Zikri to present the results of an analysis they had been doing of the current Herzog and de Meuron design, in an attempt to work out the number and positions of fire stairs and plant rooms. At this stage – preserving the arrangement in the competition entry – the building had six floors – below the Light Beam. Level 1 was the basement level; then Level 2, inserted between the basement and ground levels, had art-handling facilities; Level 3, at ground level, had cafeteria and auditorium facilities. Then Levels 4, 5, and 6 were gallery spaces for six 2,000m² galleries. Then above them all was the Light Beam, housing plant rooms and a restaurant.

This had all looked fine on a Herzog and de Meuron sectional drawing, but Hirst had some bad news for the group. He and his colleagues had tried and tried but they could not see any way of fitting all the necessary building services into the building as currently laid out. They needed rooms with more height than the current design allowed for, to provide room for the large heating and refrigeration units that would be needed. He had looked at the idea of lowering the basement, but the extra work involved would be expensive. They had looked at perhaps raising the parapet of the building to add a little height, but that would then block off light to the Light Beam.

Now it was Zikri's turn to explain how the need for all this plant and the space it needed had been calculated. Where Hirst's manner had been disarmingly matter-of-fact, take-it-or-leave-it, Zikri was eager to show the basis for his reasoning and to demonstrate the unavoidability of his conclusions. Presenting a series of charts with the various plant room arrangements outlined in yellow, his hands flew back and forth as he described different assumptions of lighting levels and occupancy, which led to calculations of heating and cooling load which, in turn, led the engineer inexorably to the amount of plant machinery and the size of plant rooms. Whichever way you looked at it, the current design didn't have enough space. 'We've tried to push as much as possible to the roof level,' Zikri said. At this point he showed an engineering drawing that had air exhaust louvres along one of the Light Beam walls. Herzog sat up, alert where before he had seemed bored, and asked about this sudden interpolation of an apparent design feature that had not been drawn by Herzog and de Meuron.

'Jacques,' said John Hirst, wearily, 'it's a *diagram*.'

'I hope so,' said Herzog. 'It's like a contract – we have to read the small print.'

'It's to give you an indication of how much air exhaust capacity we're talking about,' Hirst went on.

'But this is only half the problem,' Zikri butted in, 'because at that level you need to bring fresh air in as well as exhaust it.'

Zikri's undoubtedly correct observations seemed like a red rag to a bull, as it began to look to the architects as if they would have to lose some of their beloved gallery space. 'It's just impossible to fit everything in and maintain gallery height,' said Gugger despondently.

There was more bad news on the way. John Hirst gave a rundown of the current fire escape requirements for Bankside. These are calculated by working out the expected occupancy of the building and providing enough staircases to evacuate everyone in a specified time, with a safety margin in case some stairs are blocked. The rule of thumb for the art gallery was considered to be one person per 3.5 square metres, and the group spent a happy ten minutes or so dealing with the paradox that if you set a certain level of occupancy and work out the number of staircases to allow people to escape in a fire, the stairs might take up so much space that there wouldn't then be enough room left for the people you had made the staircases for.

Whatever the final calculation, the staircases, too, were proving too much for the architects to stomach. 'I now know why the Pompidou Centre consists only of pipes and no pieces of art,' Herzog said.

At mid-morning there was a coffee break and Herzog wandered over to the boardroom window that looked out over the front portico where the daily visitors were crowding into the gallery. As he leaned over a small balcony he looked for all the world as if he was about to throw himself off.

After the break, the torment continued for Herzog and Gugger. John Hirst discussed the plan for getting daylight into the top floor of galleries through the sides of the Light Beam. 'We're going to be fighting over the same space in the plant area,' he said to the architects, since some of the plant had to be installed in plant rooms in the Beam itself.

When it was finally the architects' turn to present their current thinking on the overall layout of the building ('playtime') it was clear that both they and the Tate were still working with a fluid brief, in spite of the Tate having had six months after the competition to flesh out their initial needs. This wasn't just indolence on their part. There was going to have to be a lot of give and take, as it turned out to be impossible to accommodate the Tate's full shopping list in the building. This problem would get worse as the team explored the option of losing a floor to accommodate the vertical space problem highlighted by Hirst and Zikri. At one point Ron German started to say, 'We have an auditorium and a seminar room . . .'

Harry Gugger interrupted him, 'The seminar room is not in the brief, I swear you.'

'I swear you it is,' said German, adopting Gugger's Swiss-English.

'If there is, the problem gets bigger,' Gugger replied.

One of the elements that had been introduced into the brief after the Tate's earliest ideas on Bankside was what the Tate called the Black Box. This had emerged as a result of what some curators had seen in other museums. Indeed, from time to time at Millbank the curatorial staff had converted an existing room into a Black Box in order to show a piece of video art. In Bankside it was conceived as a large space that could be entirely enclosed and isolated acoustically, with services to serve the needs of a wide range of artists who liked to work with video, film, sound, machinery, water or any of a range of less conventional ingredients. Desirable as this Black Box was, nobody had worked out where to put it yet.

'Could it be a temporary pavilion in the Turbine Hall?' Herzog asked.

'If it's in the Turbine Hall,' Gugger said, 'it brings down the scale – it's a huge piece.'

Herzog then ventured a small joke. 'We suspect the Black Box is Arup's Trojan horse to put all the plant in that they can't find a place for anywhere else.'

As the list of facilities and services that had to be fitted in grew longer and longer – stairs, escalators, ticketing area, toilets – Herzog again expressed his frustration through a flippant remark. 'About the problem with the additional stair and the toilets – maybe we can use the tower as a shithouse – psshtt,' and he made a swift downward movement with his hand.

A month after this meeting the accumulated demands for space, height and volume came to a head, and it was finally confirmed that Herzog and de Meuron's design had too many floors to accommodate all the plant needs *and* allow a generous height for the galleries.

Like motorists and traffic wardens, architects and engineers are constantly in situations where each has reasons for resenting the other. In reality, of course, motorists in search of legitimate parking spaces won't find them if there's no one to prevent illegal parking; and no architect's building is going to be loved and admired if it is too hot or cold, lets in rainwater, or leads to many people burning to death in a fire because there are not enough escape stairs.

Herzog and Gugger's barely concealed irritation with Mohsen Zikri and John Hirst at the June meeting was perhaps no more than might have been expected. The irritation focused on plant rooms and staircases, but almost every aspect of the building's mechanical engineering came under fire from the architects, either in an open forum like the design meeting or in private grumbles and snide remarks. For Herzog and de Meuron, design came first and everything else a poor second. Jacques Herzog wanted each of his galleries to be clean, white, pure and uncluttered: 'Any technical equipment should be as invisible as possible. We don't like to see intake grilles or outlets or air supply or cameras or sprinklers. There are so many things which are very active visually. In an art space I would like to have a very calm and very discreet and very concentrated kind of atmosphere. So that anything which takes your attention away from the piece of art disturbs me, because today many artists are dealing with things like grilles or signs like these running men saying "this is the emergency exit". These are very often part of what is art today, so we try to clean the space from all these things, to make them very strong. If you have grilles everywhere you have the impression that you are standing on some technical installation. It's also a problem as soon as an artist like Carl Andre or Richard Long puts some sculpture on one of these floor grilles.'

In fact, like it or not, Herzog's beloved galleries did end up with floor grilles, as a result of a much wider discussion that raged back and forth for some months over what sort of air conditioning the new Tate should have. In the end, for reasons of economy and 'greenness', the Tate opted for a 'displacement' system which required conditioned air – heated or cooled – to enter the galleries through grilles in the floor and leave through slots in the ceiling. And it wasn't only Herzog who disliked grilles. The curators were not too keen on them either.

Jeremy Lewison is one of the Tate's modern art curators who found himself firmly on the other side of the grilles from Wilson and the engineers, but as he described his concerns after one of a series of 'consultation meetings' held at Millbank, it was clear that he felt his views counted for very little: 'I accept the view that we have to go for the displacement system, but I continue to be worried about the grilles on the floor and how they will look and how they will determine what we can put where, especially in terms of sculpture. That is a big issue for me and it's one which, although a design has been accepted, I don't feel the issue has been resolved. But what else can I do?' Lewison's objections were not purely theoretical. He had lived with floor grilles at the Tate's Millbank gallery. 'We have grilles here down the middle of the gallery, and they're totally unsatisfactory. It means you can't put sculpture in the middle, you have to put it towards the walls. They are intrusive – what more can I say?'

When the fight against grilles was lost, and they were firmly built into the gallery designs, it was a sign of Herzog and de Meuron's ingenuity that, instead of saying 'What else can I do?' and wringing their hands about it, they actually seized the issue as a design challenge.

They might have thought that, to make the best of a bad job, they should design light-coloured, thin-metalled delicate floor grilles, made of brass, say, or stainless steel. What they in fact came up with was chunky, heavy floor grilles that looked as if they might have been part of the original building. And yet, as Peter Wilson pointed out, although they were not invisible, they were unobtrusive because they were consistent with the rest of the building. 'Unobtrusive always means consistent, it never means invisible, because even minimalist architects produce things that are quite visible.'

7

Basement to Roof

When the Tate negotiated with the original owners of the Bankside Power Station, Nuclear Electric, they insisted on Nuclear Electric handing over a decontaminated building, one that was safe for the construction team to work in. Essentially that meant asbestos-free, since the major contaminant of the old building was the asbestos that had been used throughout to insulate various items of plant, ducts, pipes and internal walls. It's only comparatively recently – in the last twenty years or so – that the hazards of asbestos have become apparent. Old construction hands tell stories of workers sitting on beams covered with asbestos dust while eating their sandwiches. Now it's accepted that even a single fibre of certain types of asbestos can initiate a cancer if it lodges in some bodily tissues.

The Tate's agreement with Nuclear Electric required compensation to be paid if any asbestos was later discovered once the building was handed over, since such a discovery was bound to delay the works. The deplanting team sent air samples off on a daily basis and received reassuring answers, but unfortunately there was asbestos that no one suspected lurking like a time bomb behind columns, in corners of the chimney and high in the roof.

As more and more of the contents were removed, it was possible to see the Turbine Hall evolving into the space that Herzog and de Meuron had so wanted to preserve and that had led them to put all the galleries into the Boiler House. On an autumn afternoon with the sun slanting down into the Turbine Hall from the south-west, the whole scene was a picture in shades of yellow and orange. The gantry cranes high up in the roof that had been used to lift supplies and equipment in the functioning power station were now working again to lift out the mangled pieces of rusting metal as the machinery and equipment were torn limb from limb by men with fiery oxyacetylene torches. The whole operation released a cacophony of noise and a haze of dust and rust, a haze that was pierced through and through by the sharply delineated shafts of light that came through the cathedral windows at the west end and through the grid of rooflights above the Turbine Hall.

The rooflights were solid glass blocks about fifteen centimetres square embedded in a diagonal pattern throughout a gently arched concrete surface. Viewed from the floor of the Turbine Hall they merged into a tight criss-cross pattern, almost like a fabric. When the architects had first toured the power station they had been struck by these rooflights and early on in their scheme they had proposed to retain them if at all possible.

'Right from the beginning,' Harry Gugger said, 'we were very much aware that whatever we do there we won't achieve the quality of the rooflights which were installed in the Turbine Hall. There was light coming in that was like a material which was weaving together the two sides of the building.'

Ian Blake summarized very well the emotions roused by the 1950s feature. 'The architect and just about everybody else fell in love with these existing rooflights. They're very nice to look at, good old-fashioned elements which were originally actually cast in situ.'

Unfortunately the one group who didn't fall in love with them – their feet are firmly on the ground in these matters – were the engineers who had surveyed Bankside when the Tate was considering taking it over. Ron German, of Stanhope, described their conclusions: 'The very first report that we had Arup's prepare before we purchased the building said, "These rooflights are in pretty poor condition. We think they should be taken off." And we've had that position almost from the beginning of the project. What has happened, however, is that everybody has been emotionally attached to them and thought, "I really like those rooflights. Is there no way of keeping them?" And so the prolongation of this debate has been, "Is there any way at all we can think of, of keeping those rooflights, knowing that they're in very poor condition?"'

'When you look at the rooflights in their current form,' Ian Blake explained, 'to the untrained eye it would appear that there's very little work to be done to bring them up to standard, and we pursued that dream for as long as we could. What turned it on its head was the inspection of the works from the inside in a bit more detail, when we could see that there's quite substantial problems developing – there's obvious signs of cracking. We got to the stage where there were contractors who were prepared to say, "Yes, we can repair it." Of course, when we said, "Well how long are you going to guarantee your works?" then you start to find yourself with a problem, because we'd be very lucky to get anything beyond fifteen years, and that's no good to someone like the Tate.'

It was one of those issues where it can seem as if the architects think only about design when you might expect them to be more aware of the practical issues. As Harry Gugger put it: 'Of course, I'm not an engineer, and sometimes I don't want to care for this kind of thing. If the rooflights are rotten or whatever I don't see it as immediately as an engineer does.'

There is a faux naivety about this attitude. Herzog and Gugger clearly knew that the weight of engineering opinion was against them but were 'pushing the envelope', as engineers themselves say, trying to see how far the Tate and Schal and Stanhope would go in adopting extraordinary measures to retain the rooflights.

Serota – the client – understood very well this tension the architects felt between clinging to what they couldn't have and helping wholeheartedly to find a solution: 'For a long time the architects have been running on two tracks. There's been a track which has said, "Preserve the rooflights as they are, keep the character of that space as far as possible as designed by Giles Gilbert Scott." There's been a safety-net position where in many of the drawings you will see a small rooflight which runs the full length of the Turbine Hall, which has a very simple, almost glasshouse structure with a slight incline on the roof held up by a metal structure. I think that they've designed that in the belief that really the preferred solution would be to maintain the existing rooflights. It's now become clear that we cannot retain the existing rooflights unless we want to run the risk that two or three years after the opening of the museum we would have to close the Turbine Hall and do major repairs to the rooflights. They clearly don't have a long life. We can patch them up, but they're not going to last for ten or twenty years.'

The rooflight issue was the first of many indications of Herzog and de Meuron's philosophical approach to Bankside. Their attachment to this feature was born of a respect for the architecture of the building and of a more general respect for simplicity of design, a type of simplicity that was apparent in many of the buildings they had designed from scratch. The way the problem was solved also showed how they thought about design issues.

There were various options, and for the sake of ease of construction Ian Blake was in favour of the simplest possible solution: a pitched glass roof rather like a greenhouse, bought ready designed. 'Certainly I would prefer to go that route,' he said, a little weary of architects, 'but then I'm a philistine.' The architects would have preferred a 'like for like' solution, where they replaced the old glass blocks with new ones embedded in a more modern and durable material. But the Tate team were adamant – this would be too expensive, and they favoured the pitched roof which could be bought 'off the shelf' for a fraction of the cost of 'like for like'.

Since it was the light quality of the original rooflights that the architects liked, they then thought about how to recreate that effect by some kind of grating underneath the cheaper pitched roof, which as a design feature Gugger hated. By skilful manipulation of budgets, incorporating some money that had been set aside to provide access to the roof for cleaning and maintenance, they designed a grid under the glass roof that could combine two functions – diffusing light and supporting cleaners. And this grid had one other function. As Gugger said, it meant that 'you don't see what a silly double pitched rooflight there is up there'.

During a meeting to discuss how to erect this new structure, Michael Casey, a British member of the Herzog and de Meuron team, described the architects' ingenious ideas for the combined light-diffuser and cleaning access platform. Ian Fraser, one of the quantity surveyors, ever on the lookout for cost savings, pointed out that if the grid was made more cosmetic and a simpler, cheaper means of access installed above it, they could save some money.

Casey and his colleagues were shocked. To separate the two would be like sticking polystyrene cornices round the ceiling of an eighteenth-century room. For them, form and function went hand in hand, and the beauty of their solution was that a feature that had a necessary function in the building achieved an aesthetic role as well. To make a separate element to imitate the effect of the original rooflights was just not on. 'We don't do that,' said Casey rather primly, and the architects eventually had their way.

It was surprising how often – as in this case – the drive to achieve a cost-effective solution led to something that in many ways was better than the more expensive alternative. Replacing the rooflights in this way turned out to solve three problems in one. It provided the light conditions the architects wanted, a means of cleaning the new rooflights, and – it turned out – a means of reducing the reverberation time of the Turbine Hall so that it was not too echoey. The whole discussion showed that good architecture could come out of the client's financial and engineering constraints. 'You need the client,' said Gugger, 'and so someone else makes you move and you're not working out of yourself, but you have your spirit and your own expectations and so by facing these limits they provoke us to move on.'

There was one other issue that was affected by the final rooflight design, and it was an issue that was part of an ongoing concern of Serota's. 'I think generally speaking we want to have more light in the Turbine Hall than was originally anticipated using the existing rooflights, and that will inevitably affect the final decision about the colour of the walls on the north and south faces.'

Decisions about colour in Bankside were to worry Serota almost up to opening day, and they were to be the subject of a daily or weekly battle of wills between Herzog and Serota, as the architects continually pushed the palette of the big public spaces in the building towards the darker end of the spectrum and Serota continually worried about the possibility that visitors to his new gallery would find the place gloomy.

There was probably no design issue that Nick Serota worried about more – or for longer – than the possibility that the new Tate Gallery of Modern Art might seem too dark and gloomy to the visitors who would pour into the building in the weeks after opening day. From the moment the Tate announced that it was going to build an art gallery in a building that on a dull day looked like a prison or a crematorium, there were rumblings of concern about the general gloominess of the exterior, and the issue of the colours to be used inside became all the more important once it became clear that there was no point in cleaning the exterior brickwork.

From the earliest versions of the Herzog and de Meuron design it was apparent that the decision to reflect and respect the industrial origins of the building carried with it basic implications for the palette of colours to be used in the building's public spaces. In the period shortly after Herzog and de Meuron won the competition, Serota looked back at some of the reasons that led him to prefer their scheme: 'I think that one of the things that drew us to their scheme was the realization that what they wanted to do was not to preserve in the sense of maintaining heritage, but to preserve in the sense of there being a building that was recognized as having had a life and having had a memory, but then to introduce these new elements and create a tension between the original and the new. I was slightly surprised when Jacques originally said that he wasn't sure that he'd take out the rooflights in the Turbine Hall. Not just because he liked glass blocks but because he wanted to maintain that feel. I think the issue will be whether we can maintain the sense, not of cobwebs quite, but of a building which is not just an industrial relic, but is exciting to visit in its own right. I'm talking about an aesthetic which is pretty rarefied, and you might say that a large part of the public coming to the Tate might not even recognize it and will just see the dust on the ledges. We've got to find a way of making sure that what we feel about that building is conveyed to those people who perhaps haven't encountered that aesthetic previously.'

The attention given to the colours in the Turbine Hall came into sharp focus as a result of a major design change between the competition entry and the more developed designs done once Herzog and de Meuron had won the competition. In the competition entry, the wall between the Boiler House and the Turbine Hall was conceived as all glass, to reveal the contrast between the industrial character of the Turbine Hall and the new galleries in the Boiler House. There were two problems with this. First, since the galleries backed on to the Turbine Hall – indeed it was seeing into these galleries that was part of the attraction of that early design – it meant that one whole wall of each gallery that abutted the Turbine Hall would be unable to have works of art hung on it. This was something the Tate were not prepared to accept and it was also something that perhaps the architects hadn't taken into account in their desire to produce what they saw as a unique public space. The second problem was to do with cost. The wall between the Boiler House and the Turbine Hall would have to act as a firewall that prevented the spread of fire from one side of the building to the other. It would be very expensive to achieve this with a wall that was largely glazed.

In the kind of dramatic back-to-the-drawing-board move Herzog and de Meuron were to demonstrate so successfully time and again, they came up with another design, one which gave the Tate solid gallery walls, but which pierced them at certain points with glazed bays. These bays could be positioned in the social spaces outside the galleries where they didn't interfere with picture hanging but still gave the effect the architects wanted of a world of light and colour and art visible to the crowds in the Turbine Hall. This new design, generally accepted by the Tate, raised a new issue. What colour would the wall be on the Turbine Hall side?

Here's where Jacques Herzog showed his true colours, as Serota described it: 'At certain moments Jacques has been suggesting that it would be black brick. I think we were all somewhat horrified, the thought of this massive black surface. He did a search for the sort of brick that he thought would be appropriate, couldn't find it, and then modified his thinking. And that's very much the way he works.'

Serota was describing these discussions in December 1996. He clearly thought that the final decision was well on the way to being made, although he showed signs of a type of thinking that became almost theological, as the issue wouldn't go away and people tried to find ways of describing exactly what shade of black or grey or white they would be happy with. 'I think it has to be a positive tone,' Serota said on this occasion, 'in the sense that I think it shouldn't be white and I don't think it should be a light grey. It needs to be lighter than the steelwork, and if it is lighter than the steelwork then it will appear lighter than it perhaps is.'

Herzog himself, whose preference continued to be for a dark-painted wall, dealt with the whole matter by explaining how the wall would hardly be visible at all: 'The wall is one thing and the glass is another. It has large openings and bay windows which are sticking out of this as well. So we decided to turn the façade of the wall into something materially not very substantial. There are basically these huge steel columns and the wall is just filling in between these columns, and the glass is flush with the front part of these columns. The visitor will see there's light up here, there's light up there, there is a gallery there, and it's like a screen. So *that* is the idea of the wall, rather than the greyish, blackish tone of the plaster or the stucco between the columns.'

In a corner of the Switch House area, in June 1997, a large area of wall was painted with one of the colours that Herzog and de Meuron were suggesting, and Tate group inspected it. 'I hate that colour,' said Serota. 'We talk of this building as having an industrial feel but that really *is* industrial.' In fact, the Tate design team were still staring and squinting at mock-ups of the Turbine Hall wall eighteen months later as they tried their hardest to imagine away the awful possibility that people might still think it was gloomy.

8

Building Relationships

When the Tate chose Bankside for their new gallery, they hoped they would be pushing at an open door as far as local acceptability was concerned. If someone had been proposing to turn an existing art gallery into a power station, that would have been another matter, but who could complain about the fact that a grimy, disused power station, surrounded by forbidding walls, would be turned into a high-class cultural attraction, with an improved landscape and possibly a footbridge across the river to the City of London? In fact, as had happened in the 1980s with the new Globe Theatre next door to the site, there were some Southwark councillors who were sceptical of the Tate project, and even hostile to it, so the Tate took no chances. They initiated a textbook example of community relations, organizing meetings, creating a newsletter, putting on fêtes and generally reassuring the people who lived around Bankside that they wanted to be good neighbours.

In the months leading up to their choice of Bankside the Tate had been left in no doubt that both the leader and the chief executive of Southwark Council wanted them there. It was a great coup for a deprived London borough to attract such a landmark scheme, and Southwark gave all the help it could during the period of development and investigation that the Tate team carried out in 1993 and 1994.

Cynics would say that all the Tate's wooing of the local residents was an insurance policy. Nimby (not in my back yard) campaigning was always a possibility even with such a worthwhile project. But the Tate's community activities were too widespread and went on too long for them to be just window-dressing. There was a genuine sense that from Serota downwards the Tate team were willing to give all the time necessary to reassure the Borough of Southwark that it was going to be a socially responsible organization rather than a cultural flying saucer landing on the riverside, with visitors beamed in from more fashionable parts of London without ever realizing quite where they were in the urban scene.

Of course, the same cynic who might have suspected the Tate's motives in wooing the residents could say that as far as working at relations with the borough as a whole were concerned, they had to, hadn't they? There were all sorts of conditions that were required as the price of Southwark's support for the project, either implicitly or explicitly, from providing employment on-site for local craftsmen to fostering artistic activities by artists, and anyone else, who lived in the borough.

There were two people who were charged with ensuring good relations between the Tate and Southwark. One of them was Dawn Austwick, appointed as Project Director by the Tate in March 1995. In a project which already had its fair share of people who thought they were managing or directing it, or some aspect of it, it might have seemed unnecessary to appoint yet another such figure. But Austwick's responsibilities were wider than any other individual's, apart from Serota's. 'My role is to make sure that in 2000 or thereabouts, the Tate has a new gallery, a new organization, and a new institution at Bankside.'

Austwick had overall responsibility for several different aspects of the project, including fund-raising, progress chasing, schedule and budget monitoring, and relations with the community. As far as the last was concerned, she displayed a degree of vocal enthusiasm which rarely flagged, even in the face of the sort of nitpicking the residents were reduced to when they couldn't find any big things to object to.

'In Southwark, we have a part of London that sits directly opposite the City,' said Austwick in 1995; 'St Paul's is just over the water. And yet Southwark has some of the worst social problems in the whole of this country and one has to feel, as someone who lives in London, that being able to help to revitalize that sort of area is an extraordinary contribution to be able to make. If I can look back in ten or fifteen years' time and go down the river and see the new gallery, there will be all sorts of reasons to feel very proud of the fact that it exists.'

Sometimes, to listen to Austwick, you would think that she was carrying the burden of the entire project on her shoulders, starting with the funding. 'We've got the Millennium Commission money, that's great, that's fifty million, but actually this is a project that's going to cost a hundred and a bit, so we have to identify the other sources of funding. We have to ensure that the building project is well developed, well conceived, and that we all agree on what's in it and what isn't in it. We have to finalize the outline design. And we also need to start building the team and the organization for the next five years, and looking at how we're going to start tackling some of the issues like how we're going to use technology in the future, how we're going to use the media in the new gallery, what really are we going to do for schools and young people who visit. We've had lots of aspirations, and we've been very good at articulating them. We now have to look at how we're going to deliver them. It's hard work now.'

In fact, of course, the details of this mammoth list of tasks were carried out by the teams that Austwick helped to appoint or to supervise. In the case of the day-to-day relationships with the residents, the Tate appointed George Cochrane as its community relations officer, and he started work on 1 April 1996.

'I'm not from an arts background at all,' Cochrane said, 'I've never worked in the Tate Gallery, or any gallery before. All of my experience is in community development work, regeneration work, working in small community organizations – community activism, really. It was a very interesting job for me to go for, and it has to be said, one that I didn't think I'd have any chance of getting. So I just went there with this agenda, saying, "These are the sort of things I think you ought to be doing." And luckily, Dawn and the rest of the interviewing panel felt the same.'

Cochrane is young and enthusiastic and fitted easily into the social setting that he was to work in over the next five years. Unpretentious and laid-back, he would act as a lightning conductor in those situations where local residents might be intimidated by the firepower of Serota or Herzog, who often seemed – whether intentionally or not – to descend *de haut en bas*. Even Dawn Austwick, with a professional jollity which was probably genuine, could leave the residents a little overwhelmed with her enthusiasm.

One area where this dialogue seems to have led the Tate and its architects to change their ideas was in the design of the landscape. This was, in any case, one of the more variable aspects of the overall plan during the first four years of the project. Laurie Olins, the original landscape consultant, was replaced by a new Swiss landscape architect, and because there were continuing doubts about how much money would actually be available, the plans and models that the residents saw over the years kept changing, and this provided an opportunity for them to exploit the Tate's own uncertainty and achieve improvements in an area of land that many of them knew better than the architects.

In facilitating this process, Cochrane seems to have identified with the residents and helped them achieve what they wanted rather than act as the Tate's man and try to preserve the architects' designs. In this he was, after all, doing what he was paid for.

'The power station closed in 1981,' Cochrane said, 'and this area's been basically public open space. In the bits of sunshine we have had this week [it was July], you get a hundred and twenty, hundred and fifty people picnicking out here, office workers. So it's very well used. And what we've been doing is bringing people together, to help inform the process by which we develop the landscaping, and making the landscape architects understand the current usage and the issues for people. And what we find – and I think this is a very important lesson for the Tate, but also for the community itself – is that they're not a homogenous group. You've got all sorts of different personalities, but you've also got different perspectives. You've got those that love to walk their dogs here, and those that don't want dogs walking here. You've got the cyclist lobby, who love cyclists, and those people who'd ban them from Southwark. And that's quite interesting because we're starting to explore the differences that exist within the community as well as helping to inform the process here.'

In Ian Blake, gearing himself up to inflict major noise and pollution within a radius of a hundred metres or more of Bankside, the residents had a surprisingly sympathetic project manager. 'It is a very important part of what we do. We *have* to bring the community into the job, we have to bring them along. After all, long after we're gone, they're going to be the neighbours to the client for many years, and it's unacceptable that we should be treating them with anything other than courtesy. What we have done on this job very early on is to let them know exactly how we're going to be building this building, how it's going to affect them, what the key issues are, what the programme issues are. Some people can make it quite difficult for you if you don't bring them along with the process, and don't tell them why you can't, for example, use the main entrance because British Gas have dug the road up, so you've got to use a different route, which means you've got to take lorries past their factory; or that you've got to suspend certain parking bays. You just have to tell people these very basic things. This is what affects their lifestyle and this is what's important to them.'

Blake's 'reasonable man' attitude was to pay off as serious construction began on-site and he and his team embarked on three years of dirty, messy, noisy construction without any major disruptions as a result of residents' complaints.

During 1995 and 1996 the Tate team arranged a programme of visits to Basel for some of their design meetings. To help their thought processes – and remind themselves what a finished Herzog and de Meuron building looked like – Dawn Austwick, Peter Wilson and Ron German visited the practice in Basel in July 1996 to see some of their completed buildings in or near the city. Although some of the team had visited Herzog and de Meuron buildings during the competition phase, they now had a different agenda. With some knowledge of what the architects were proposing for Bankside, they could now look with informed eyes at how they had carried out similar tasks in other buildings.

They knew they were getting a *simple* building from Herzog and de Meuron but, as Peter Wilson put it on the flight from Heathrow to Basel, 'It's a question of whether simple is cheap. We're going to go and look at some buildings and try and get some idea of what sort of finish and build quality Herzog and de Meuron's buildings have and to discuss with our cost consultant whether there's a match between the cost-plan and the architects' aspiration for the building. There are areas of doubt and concern about whether we're getting a simple building or an expensive building. In some respects we will, and in some we won't. Everyone needs to understand what "not an expensive building" means and, for example, making a building with concrete floors sounds like a warehouse, it sounds cheap, but a concrete floor by Herzog and de Meuron may not be as easy to build as a warehouse floor.'

To help judge issues like this, they would be visiting a factory with a Herzog and de Meuron trademark concrete floor; a small art gallery and workshop designed for a friend of Herzog's, the Swiss artist Rémy Zaugg; a small cartoon museum; and a private house. To help answer the question of whether simple was cheap, Paul Morrell, the quantity surveyor from Davis Langdon Everest, was on the trip. He is a bluff, no-nonsense man who sees walls, floors and windows as so many man-hours of work or pounds' worth of materials.

Ron German was there to look out for any untoward effects on cost or schedule; Peter Wilson to gauge the effect of some of the proposals on the Tate as a client; and Dawn Austwick to do a bit of both, as well as to ask, 'Are we sure we really want this?'

The pace had been so intense over the last few months that the team thought that some of the design issues relating to the final appearance of the building had been neglected. It might even be – perish the thought – that the architects were working away making some important decisions that the pressure of other work had prevented them passing on to the Tate.

'We've spent a lot of time talking about process,' Austwick said, 'about the mechanics of what we're doing. This is a moment when they want to share with us the quality of what it is that they're doing. And we haven't done that before. Our regular monthly meetings have become much more mechanistic, they're much more about how we do it. This is rather more reflective, very different.'

Jacques Herzog is fond of saying in interviews that all Herzog and de Meuron buildings are different. But there are certainly techniques and materials that they use over and over again, incorporating unconventional ideas that sometimes have almost philosophical origins. The first building the group saw was Rémy Zaugg's studio. It is a building with solid rectangular ends and a glazed front and back. Overhanging either side are canopies, also of concrete. The building has simple skylights to bring daylight into two gallery spaces, about the size of the smallest Bankside display spaces, and the architects had designed them while they were thinking about how to bring daylight into the Bankside galleries. The roof and side walls were designed so that rain would run down the walls, creating streaks and patterns. In Herzog and de Meuron's view this wetting process should lead over time to the growth of algae and lichens which would add colour and texture to the walls.

Harry Gugger had met the Tate group at the airport and led them straight off to Zaugg's studio. Unlike Herzog, Gugger seems eager to please and sometimes appears to be on the alert for adverse comment that is not really there. As Paul Morrell walked around the building, looking closely at the concrete floor that was laid inside the building and as a path around the edge, he said, 'You laid this all in situ? Single bay? Saw cut?'

'What's wrong with it?' said Gugger suspiciously.

'It's fantastic,' said Morrell.

Inside the gallery, the group looked at the floor-to-ceiling windows broken up by mullions, which Morrell fingered. He also inspected the workmanship where the windows joined the walls and was pleased with what he saw. 'It fits a different budget,' warned Ron German.

'But why?' Morrell turned to Gugger, 'Why would you go to a different part of your brain to do that at the Tate rather than the way you did it here?'

'It's just a different place from the museum at Bankside,' said Gugger apologetically.

There was a cleanness and simplicity about the building which the Tate team obviously liked. The walls met the floor neatly and without the gaps which Herzog so hated. And the skylight brought indirect daylight on to the white gallery walls in an even wash, although the day outside was sunny and bright.

Half an hour later the group were donning yellow baseball caps in a factory Herzog and de Meuron had designed for the Ricola company, who make small herbal lozenges with a brand image of all that is healthy and life-enhancing. The Ricola factory was similar in shape to Zaugg's studio, but several times larger. It had the same concrete walls, now stained with the algal deposits that Herzog and de Meuron intended, and a slightly more rugged concrete floor to support small forklift trucks and a more robust cleaning process. Peter Wilson closely inspected the drains in the floor, circles set in square frames. He was looking for signs of cracking where the concrete screed met the drain. The Tate was not averse to cracks in the concrete – they just wanted to be sure that they were consistent over the whole floor, not a function of variations in how the floors were laid.

At the first design meeting held in Basel, the Tate team had seen sample panels of stone lying outside to test the weathering ability of another Herzog and de Meuron technique – imprinting photographs on building materials. Now, in the Ricola factory, transparent panels of polycarbonate walls stretched from floor to ceiling in the front and back of the building with a repeated photograph imprinted across the panes, a monochrome leaf, that acquired an abstract quality by being repeated in several rows from one end of the wall to the other.

Several Herzog and de Meuron buildings – either actual, or designed but never built – involved this same photograph imprinting technique, sometimes a pattern of pebbles, as in a Basel sports centre, sometimes photographs of the interior of a building printed on the exterior walls that concealed it. The technique was to arise from time to time in Bankside design discussions, as a possible way of treating various glazed surfaces inside the building.

The next building on the whistle-stop tour was a museum of cartoons in Basel. The museum building was in two parts – a medieval house opening on to the street and behind it a new extension, consisting of three floors of gallery space. It was an illustration of Herzog and de Meuron's ability to reflect old architecture in new construction without imitating it. In the heart of the combined old and new buildings is a well of light, spilling daylight on to each floor of the new extension and through the old windows of the medieval house. And one wall of the new extension was the third example the visitors had seen that day of a wall washed by rainwater so that tiny plants could grow in the moist surface and eventually add colour to it.

On each floor there was a ramp joining the old building to the new one, and a small group gathered to test the gradient. This was to be a continuing concern of the Tate team: that their entry ramp might be too steep for wheelchair users. And they certainly felt that this gradient was too steep.

The gallery's current exhibition was of cartoons about architecture, including several about Bankside, one showing the invasion of Herzog and de Meuron architects on to the site, carrying a banner 'Swiss is More'.

The last building the Tate group visited was a private house for a family called Koechlin. Built on a slope, the house had rooms that were connected both vertically and horizontally by spaces that were sometimes exterior courtyards, sometimes interior wells or lobbies. Each space could find itself inside or outside the house depending on the current arrangement of sliding windows and doors.

It became clear as Gugger showed the group round the house that the Koechlins had been dream clients. Whatever the architects did or said seemed OK by them. Ron German looked down at the floor in the kitchen, a pigmented concrete screed. 'You left a lot of texture in this, Harry,' German said, a nice way of noting the irregularities in the surface treatment. 'Is it one of those situations where you've done it once and you won't do it again?'

'They accepted it,' Gugger said. 'They were aware of what they got, but they liked it.'

However, Herzog and de Meuron hadn't always had clients who were so obliging. When a similar problem had cropped up with the pigmented floor of the signal box for Swiss Railways, the client insisted that the whole floor was painted over.

Outside the back of the house, where an interior courtyard opened on to a lawn, Ron German and Paul Morrell closely inspected the rendered wall, a very smooth dark-coloured surface. A similar technique had been proposed for Bankside during the discussions about the Turbine Hall wall and German and Morrell were impressed by the high quality and hardness of the surface seen here.

On the way out, the Tate people crowded into a purpose-built nuclear shelter entered off the ground floor and built into the hillside. It was surprising to find such an old-fashioned element in a house owned by allegedly peace-loving Swiss, but it is required by law in new houses.

While every Herzog and de Meuron building was different, each of the buildings seen on this visit had provided – sometimes literally – concrete examples of elements that would be reflected in the floors, walls and roof of the new Tate as construction began in the now empty Bankside Power Station.

9

Guided Tours

By September 1996, Bankside Power Station was in a state no one had ever seen it in before. From north to south, east to west, floor to roof, it was one huge volume, 170,000 or so cubic metres of empty space. Only the line of columns running parallel with the river between the Boiler House and the Turbine Hall and a bridge at ground level joining the former south entrance to the Boiler House interrupted the space. This had been retained in the Herzog and de Meuron design as a viewing platform and would provide useful access to the Boiler House if the Tate reintroduced a south entrance after later acquiring the Switch House.

There was a lull between the demolition and deplanting and the beginning of the enabling work, and the Tate seized the opportunity to take two groups of people round the building. First, on 20 September twenty or so artists and journalists gathered outside the south entrance, looking uncomfortable in hard hats and reflective waistcoats. They were to be taken on a guided tour by Sandy Nairne, the Tate's Director of Regional and Public Services. He described one example of how the Tate had promoted itself recently: 'Many people told us that the thing that gave them the best image of the Tate was that poster on the tube that says "The Tate by tube", and it's a rather humorous relationship between an artist's oil paint squeezed out as the tube lines. They loved this because it made them feel that it wasn't a stuffy place, that it wasn't a place that was somehow cut off from them, and luckily when they came to the Tate they said that they found what they'd expected.'

Nairne's role in the early stages of the Bankside project was to supervise a group of people planning the various activities that would take place in the gallery, from displays and exhibitions to education and public information. He had joined the Tate in 1976, left in 1980, and returned at the time the Tate was acquiring Bankside. Some of his colleagues felt that he had high ambitions for his eventual role in the new gallery, perhaps even as its director. He is a fluent and articulate communicator, some would say 'smooth', and was clearly in his element as he led the artists in a crocodile around the shell of Bankside, a building which, when he first saw it two years beforehand, he had found rather forbidding, perhaps because of a slight misinterpretation of how power stations work. 'I think it's very daunting, I think it's very sombre, I think it's not at all welcoming as a building because a power station wouldn't be. A power station is where you get electrocuted. It's not a public place – you don't walk into power stations. What we have to do to it is turn it inside out as an idea.'

The reactions of the group of artists to their experience was one of universal astonishment. No one was blasé about what they were seeing; everyone had gasped as they had walked across the threshold between the tunnel-like approach to the interior bridge and the Turbine Hall.

Katherine Shonfield, an architecture lecturer and journalist, had an intriguing range of reactions. 'I felt complete relief that it was Herzog and de Meuron and not blown up by the likes of Will Alsop. That's the first reaction. Another thing that really strikes me about it is it's a kind of take on the Uffizi in Florence, and what's so enjoyable is the way it doesn't go all the way round a space, which is the usual way in which modern galleries work – lots of small spaces off a big open space in the middle. What's so enjoyable about this is its *sidedness*. You really get that feeling that you're right up against the river and the galleries are all going to be on the north side. The [Turbine Hall] space is going to be left to breathe. And a third reaction really is how these huge spaces make you want to dance.'

Julia Wood, an artist, said, 'With modern architecture we're getting used to art being large scale. When you're actually walking through it and upstairs, you realize someone's going to have to get going making some really big sculpture, because English sculptors generally aren't used to that scale. You think of the great American sixties and seventies sculptors when you're walking through here.'

Helene Fesenmaier, a painter and sculptor, said, 'I was a bit nervous that it was going to be an anti-art museum, with the scale so immense that the paintings would look like postage stamps in such a huge space. But I think as they've designed it, the plans will allow the paintings to look wonderful in these smaller sections. And the gantry crane, for lifting sculpture, is great. I can't think of a bigger space I've been in anywhere in the world.'

Several of the artists had visited the building at an earlier stage, as part of the programme the Tate organized for artists to come in and respond in whichever way they liked to the building. Terry Smith responded through a graffiti art-form on the walls of the offices at the east end of the power station. Here and there, engraved in the plaster to the level of the underlying breeze blocks, was a drawing of a schooner, a ladder, or the word 'VIEW' in carefully carved letters. Few people had seen these works of art apart from the workmen who passed through on their way in and out of the main building, and who perhaps suspected one of their own number of having hidden talents. For Smith, who actually saw them didn't really matter: 'I was invited to make some works on-site. The kind of work that I do is site-specific. It's made in the building, out of the building itself, so I've been taking plaster off the wall. There were eight pieces of work and I'm surprised they're still here, because this whole area of the building's going to be demolished, so they weren't meant to last. Today we're getting an audience of about twenty people to see it, which is the first time the work's been seen. I didn't expect that many. I just thought it would be me. Half of my works are in buildings or places which are dangerous to get to or there's some reason why there has to be some kind of secrecy involved. Other works are in museums and in public spaces, so I can alternate between those two things. In a way I prefer the secret works.'

Smith was as impressed as everyone else with the potential of the building. He also had a personal connection with it in its former life. 'It's odd because my uncle used to work in this power station and I'm familiar with power stations in terms of looking at them, and the smell of them, so I've no real nostalgia for it as a building. But it's going to be an incredible place to have art.'

One painter, Albert Irvin, while looking around the vast volume of the Turbine Hall hoped – rather plaintively – that there would still be a place for more conventional works of art. 'God only knows how they'll use this space. He [Nairne] talks about having big screens for projecting videos on to and so on. I'm an old man; it's for young people to forecast what's going to happen in the future. I go on doing my paintings and hope they'll find somewhere to hang them.'

For most of the people on this tour, the visit to Bankside was an almost visceral experience, generating a whole range of emotional responses. Once again, the Tate had got it right, producing a word-of-mouth reaction that was almost entirely positive among a group of people – artists and art commentators – who mattered a lot in its continuing efforts to maintain the support of the British artistic Establishment in its choice of Bankside Power Station for its new gallery.

Artist Richard Wentworth's response was intriguing. 'The funny thing about the visit today is that it's exhilarating not because it's going to be an art gallery, just because it's an exhilarating place to have a look at. There's an extraordinary sense of saying goodbye to the past. It's a little bit like being in a ship that's been broken up or a mine that's about to be closed, any of those English images. The problem for the English is always to do with the past and the future, and maybe what makes this an intriguing place is that it's actually saying rather vigorously goodbye to the past, and bravely trying to say hello to the future, and I think if you are English, that is its own exhilaration. There's a lot of past to try and say goodbye to.'

A week later, Ian Blake and his team from Schal were showing a very different group of visitors around the building. As the architects' designs evolved and Arup's turned them into structural and mechanical engineering drawings, Schal had to draw up detailed descriptions of the different types of work that would have to be done once the construction period began. These would then be used as a basis for the tendering process, a systematized method for deciding which of the companies that wanted to do each type of work should be given the contract. To help the range of potential contractors understand what the work might involve, Schal had invited representatives of the major companies likely to bid for the Bankside contracts to an open day at the site on 27 September. As the managing directors and sales directors of a hundred or so companies gathered in the visitor centre at Bankside, Ron German started out by disabusing them of any idea that they might make a lot of money out of the project. There was about £60 million available for construction but that had to be spread over a lot of contractors doing a lot of work.

'This is not an expensive building we're about to create,' he told the group. 'It might sound like a lot of money but it's a lot of building and the whole approach, right from the outset, has been one of simplicity. The impact is all going to be in the scale, in the nature of the spaces, but it's not going to be in gold taps and marble vanity units. It's all about simplicity but quality. So there's going to be an awful lot of exposed concrete, an awful lot of plasterboard, an awful lot of steelwork, and it's all been geared around this thinking that the way we're going to approach this has to be that way to make it work.'

Ian Blake then took them through the essential elements of the building – the three-part structure of Switch House, Turbine Hall and Boiler House – and described the 'building within a building' that had to be constructed in the Boiler House: 'In terms of structure it's relatively straightforward. We're going to be creating a raft across the whole of the basement, probably about 1.8 to 2 metres deep, for levelling out the whole basement level, and the structure and steel will be formed from that raft, right the way up through the building, eight levels in total, quite a considerable amount of steelwork and a very interesting prospect, given that the structure will have to be installed up to Level 5, that's up to the underside of the existing roof, before we take the roof off.'

The significance of this last fact was that most of the steel would have to be brought into the empty shell while the roof structure was still in place, a tricky operation involving careful placing of cranes in and around the building.

Blake then went on, 'We're hoping that this is going to mark the beginnings of a new era in the construction industry after some years of it being in the doldrums.'

This remark produced a murmur of fellow-feeling from some of the group and a loud 'Hear, hear' from one of the visitors, Geoffrey Taylor, sales director of a company called Watson Steel, based in Bolton.

Taylor was here because he had his eye on the structural steel contract, the largest-value contract that would be awarded by Schal, and one that his company was very keen to get. But then so was another steel contractor at the meeting, Peter Emerson and *his* company, Rowen Structures, along with four other major steel fabricators from Britain and the rest of Europe.

After the initial introduction, the hundred or so contractors, mainly men with a handful of women, gathered outside to put on their hard hats and waistcoats. To a question about the weight the floors would have to support, Blake replied 'We've got some really heavy exhibits. I'm not sure it you're familiar with what sort of things the Tate displays but there's some very, very heavy ones and we're having to create floors that are able to take 30 kilonewtons, *30 kilonewtons*. You get a normal office floor which is 4.1 kilonewtons or something – we're dealing with something substantially more than that. Size? I don't know, they've got some very big ones. I mean they can really display anything from a grand piano hanging off walls to a stuffed giraffe or something. There's all sorts of things that they can display and probably will do.'

On their tour of the building, the group's initial response was similar to that of the artists of a week before – amazement at the size. As Geoffrey Taylor leaned over the rail at the top of a temporary staircase at the east end of the building, he asked rhetorically of Colin Berry, a Schal construction manager who was showing the group around, 'Have I ever been in a bigger building than this in my life?'

Looking a little puzzled, Berry said, 'I wouldn't know – have you?'

As Taylor drank coffee in the visitor centre after the tour, he explained how his appetite for the contract had been whetted by the visit. 'I don't think the steel is too complicated in terms of the technological side of it. I think that there's an awful lot of it because it's such a big building. And I think that it's got to be large-span framing. I understand there's enormous sculptures – I don't think Barbara Hepworth and Henry Moore is all holes, you know; there's an awful lot of stone and marble. We've been through a bad time in construction in the last two or three years and there haven't been exciting jobs like Bankside, there haven't been exciting jobs like the Millennium is going to bring us, for some time now and we're getting excited again. There are five or six companies that could do this work. Not as well as we can of course.'

Peter Emerson, too, was very keen to get the contract for his company, Rowen, based in Nottingham. 'Current estimates are that there are somewhere in the order of about four thousand tonnes of new steelwork going into the gallery. That's a big contract and an attractive contract and there's a lot about this project that makes it more attractive than most, insomuch that working inside an existing structure you are at least protected from the elements and you can get on without too much worry about what the wind and the snow might be doing to you. So it's an attractive proposition. I've no doubt the Tate won't be short of people wanting to bid it.'

It turned out that one of these two companies – Watson and Rowen – *did* get the contract for the steel, seven months later. It also turned out that by the time the company had completed the work, they rather wished they'd failed to get the contract after all.

In mid December 1996 Nick Serota stood on the north bank of the Thames, just across the river from Bankside, and took some satisfaction in the way the museum was beginning to emerge from the power station: 'The power station is now without the district heating plant which was put on in the nineteen-seventies at the front; without some of the buildings that were added at the lower level and east end; and without the brick structure behind the chimney that housed the gas-washing plant. Demolition has now taken place and the steel structure is exposed. And for the first time, you can imagine what the Light Beam is going to be like running across the building, and you can also begin to get some sense of what the windows on either side of the chimney will do, and also what the openings at street level will do. I think that there will be a very dramatic transformation of that building as people have known it. The interesting thing is that probably people will forget what it looked like. They will simply see this new building as the Tate Gallery of Modern Art, which was formerly a power station. Jacques and Harry's transformation is quite subtle, but it's nevertheless very profound, and the whole presence of the building will be changed very dramatically by what they have done. I have no worries about it looking like a conversion. I don't think it will look like a conversion, I think it'll look like a new building.'

Serota was seen by some members of the team as being too 'pro-architect', and as he described the reactions of the Tate Trustees to Herzog and de Meuron's design of the building, he showed excitement about the continual evolution of their design, rather than concern about the effect of the changes on the schedule. 'One of the interesting things about Herzog and de Meuron's way of working is that they go to first principles: they establish a skeleton, they elaborate, they realize they've become too complicated, reduce again, but what they reduce back to is much richer than the original skeleton. So every time the Trustees look at these drawings there's a new element of complexity in the whole design. One of the frustrating things during the first year was that the fundamentals didn't change very much and everyone said, "Oh, are we simply going to get the competition design writ large with a few additional staircases to deal with the fire escape problems?" What's becoming apparent now is that within the building there are pockets of really dense activity. There's quite a complex stair which runs now from Level 1 to Level 7, right the way up through the building. The whole relationship between the auditorium, the café and a bar is becoming very interesting. But every time Jacques and Harry touch the building in one way or another, it becomes denser, more complex, richer and fundamentally more exciting for the potential visitor to the gallery.'

The trouble was, every time Herzog and de Meuron touched the building they also changed the design. And Ian Blake was very worried about progress with the design, which had been twelve weeks behind a year ago when Schal decided to take action to catch up. They had accepted a delay in the very earliest design schedule, moving the goalposts to make it easier for the architects to catch up, and instituted a series of design freezes. These were five stages, scheduled through the year, at which the architects were told they had to stop designing so the drawings could be handed over to other members of the team for detailed design work. When Blake looked back over 1996 at the beginning of 1997, he was gloomy about the situation. 'We find ourselves now, in the early part of January 97, where some aspects of our design freezes four and five have not been cleared and it means that we are in effect four weeks behind where we wanted to be, but in real terms it's twelve weeks. We've gone back [in terms of slippage] to where we were a year or so ago.'

Blake had spent a frustrating year of attending design meetings with the architects where he felt they could have been more open about their intentions and the state of their designs: 'I'm not so sure there has been as much honesty as there should have been, frankly,' Blake said. 'We've reached a crossroads in the job now where you simply can't change anything any more. We can't go back and sit in our offices and think too much about things that can change in the future. We need to have a clear understanding of the key issues and the way forward. OK, we may come up with some brilliant idea which would have been great. Unfortunately it's just too late, because we can't incorporate all of them. If we can, we will. But there's very few now that we can.'

There was a factor that Blake had never faced in his previous projects: working with a client for whom art and aesthetics are of supreme importance. 'They come from this arts background and their appreciation of the process is perhaps not as acute as, say, working for a developer in London who wants to develop a new business park or a new shopping mall or something. People like that are familiar with the problems. They know what the construction process means and they know their responsibility as a part of that process in terms of making quick decisions. In the Tate's mind that is not necessarily fully appreciated. For example, if we're talking about proposed changes to a building, they wouldn't necessarily realize the significance of saying, "Oh, why can't I have a room over here?", not necessarily appreciating that that's going to move a couple of columns, it's going to affect the design of the steelwork which I need to get out to tender next week to meet the programme period. Those sorts of things are not fully understood and it's something that we still have to work on to get across.'

This project had some of the most senior and powerful figures in the British construction industry working on it, from Schal itself to Stanhope Properties, Ove Arup, the engineers, and the cost consultants, along with the Tate itself, and in Blake's view they were all being too lenient on the up-and-coming architects from Switzerland. 'We're still sometimes suffering from a sort of "Emperor's New Clothes" approach, in my view. Some designs and issues have stayed around a lot longer than they should have done. They should have been kicked into touch much earlier.'

10
'Not in front of the architects'

Ian Blake's concerns about delays in the design process were shared by other members of the Tate team. Herzog and de Meuron, like all good architects, pushed for perfection and had to be reined back when time and money prevented that ideal state being reached. As the design schedule rolled on, and more and more areas of the building were fixed in some detail, it no longer became possible to allow some leeway in the programme to let the architects make things just a little better. As Peter Wilson, usually the point at which this particular buck stopped, said in January 1997, 'If the architect says now, "Give me another week and it will be better" I might well say – and have indeed, in recent weeks, said, – "Well, thank you for that interesting proposal but I'll stick with the one that's ninety-five per cent as good as that that you already had." I'm probably quite polite about it, but that doesn't mean to say that I entertain constant changes of design. And I think one has to face it, every architect of the kind we employ, the ones that are creative and interesting, is going to want to do that sort of thing.'

Ron German was actually too experienced to be unduly influenced by the architects, and in meetings and behind the scenes he could be firm with them. 'It's clear that Jacques Herzog and Harry Gugger see this as a major project for them, and it's a major project for the Tate, and their objective is to make this the best they ever can. To that extent they never stop thinking there's a better way of doing it. And so part of the tension at the moment is to say, "Well, fine, the building can always be better but we must never get ourselves into a situation where it was the best-designed building that was never built." And that's where the tension is. It's because there's always a frustration, an understandable one in a way, that says, "We're three years away from opening this gallery to the public. Surely we can make some changes? Surely we can make it better?", and we have to try and resist that, because there is a lot to do in the three years, and we have to actually build something.'

There were two types of trigger for the architects wanting to make changes and improvements. One was when Serota or another senior figure dropped the hint that he was unhappy with something, or had a better idea. This often seemed like permission to take some extra time to redesign. One unfortunate incident had occurred on a recent visit to Basel, where Serota had made a passing remark about some design feature that could be improved. As Ron German said later, 'I think that trip said something about what it means when you just happen to mention something.'

'Yes,' said Serota, 'that was terrible. I *wish* I'd never opened my mouth.'

The other trigger for the architects to consider new design work occurred whenever the Tate tried to look further ahead, to the areas of the building and its surroundings that had potential for further development, but that the Tate could not afford to tackle during what they called the first phase. They concentrated their initial efforts on the Boiler House and Turbine Hall, but from the beginning the Tate had been attracted by the spaces under the Switch House and out as far as the oil tanks. There was even the possibility that some exploitation of this area could occur in the first phase, although that depended on the availability of more money. The worry wasn't so much that the architects would drop everything to design the new areas if they thought the funds would eventually materialize, but that they would look at the current plans and want to redesign them to fit in as well as possible with future new areas of the gallery.

In late 1996 the Tate team were in the pleasant situation of having more money to spend than they had expected. This had come about because of the conservative way they had handled budgetary problems at an earlier stage in the project, as Ron German described: 'We had a scheme that was clearly over budget, it was clearly not affordable and we couldn't justify building that scheme, and what we tried to do was wind the scheme back to something that we knew was within budget, with a contingency. The aim of the contingency was always to say, "Can we build a building that we would all be very happy with if that were the budget?" but then allow ourselves some luxuries, or some little areas where we could have some additions and just make it that bit better in certain areas.'

In fact by late 1996 the team had a lot of confidence in the design and what it would cost, and it looked as if they might not need some of the contingency that had been set aside for unforeseen circumstances. They now wanted to decide ahead of time on a shopping list, arranged in order of priorities, that they would spend unused contingency on if they had it.

When the Tate team met to discuss what they might do with any spare contingency money, they kept the meeting a secret from the architects. They believed that the architects would not be able to control themselves if they were faced with hints that it might actually be possible to do something with the underside of the Switch House or the oil tanks, or improve some area that at the moment had some very basic design.

The group that gathered in the Duffield Room on 17 December 1996 was a cross-section of the decision-makers on the Bankside project. They had all in their different ways experienced the frustrations of the existing design situation and there was a conspiratorial air about the whole occasion. Two Trustees, Michael Craig-Martin and Janet de Botton, had been sitting in on design review meetings for the last year and had seen for themselves the difficulties of keeping Herzog and de Meuron focused. Alex Beard, the Tate's surprisingly young-looking Finance Director, was only too aware of the financial effects of late design decisions. Peter Wilson and Ron German resented the effects of design delays on what could otherwise be a very tightly controlled schedule and budget. Stuart Lipton, head of Stanhope Properties, who liked to wield a big stick, could hardly believe the way everybody – particularly Serota – seemed to be pandering to the architects' whims. Meanwhile, Sandy Nairne, representing the Tate staff who had helped draw up the brief, was extremely concerned that pressure on budgets from any direction would reduce even further some elements of the gallery that he had fought to have. And hovering over them all was Dawn Austwick. Where the others might have personal concerns about current aspects of the design process, her worries were professional – it was what she was paid to do.

The atmosphere at the meeting was good. The absence of Herzog and de Meuron and Schal made everyone more relaxed. This group had lived with this project for longer than the on-site team and there was a lot of shared history. The tone was also set by the bantering relationship between Stuart Lipton and Nick Serota, who had worked together for ten years or more. As Serota's de facto adviser, Lipton had no qualms about telling Serota when he thought he was being carried away by his enthusiasms to the detriment of the project.

Austwick's brisk 'head girl' approach meant that she was very efficient at keeping meetings focused, and she plunged the group straight into discussing a long list that she and Ron German had already drawn up of possible ways of spending more money. She felt it was important that people understood each item before they addressed the task of organizing them in order of priority.

The list of options was an indication of Serota's grand scheme for Bankside as a whole. The team had always talked of the currently committed project as Phase 1, showing that they believed the new gallery could be even grander and provide even more facilities if more money came along for what they called Phase 2. They were committed to a 2000 opening date, if only to qualify for it being a Millennium Project, but the more Serota looked at the potential of the undeveloped portions of building and landscape, the more his mouth watered at what could be done after 2000. There were the oil tanks; the southern landscape, largely undeveloped in existing plans; the chimney, denied now the ambitious observation gallery on top. And there was also the space under the Switch House that stretched off towards the south. This would be an attractive site for what they called 'project space' – educational areas opening on to the Turbine Hall where schoolchildren and others could get involved in some of the educational activities the Tate was planning for new gallery.

Ron German explained how this might help the appearance of the gallery as a whole. 'The Turbine Hall at the moment is enlivened by what we're doing in the Boiler House, but on the other side it's pretty static, where Phase 2 would be. And so there is an opportunity underneath London Electricity, which potentially could have project rooms, coming off the Turbine Hall, as individual spaces, and we've just shown six of those as a possible option to activate that site. And there are other options for animating that particular area.'

The Education staff at the Tate, including Sandy Nairne, who were responsible for the Tate's public services activities, sometimes felt that education got short shrift among the more glamorous priorities, and that this meeting could identify an opportunity to enhance the importance of these activities in the new building – if the money could be found. But further down the list these project spaces faced a lot of competition.

There was an old jetty that could be removed; the carbuncular paper merchant's that could be bought and demolished at an estimated cost of £2 million; the fit-out of gallery spaces on Level 4 which were currently left empty; a better treatment of the northern landscape; and the oil tanks.

When the meeting turned to the old oil tanks under the southern landscape, there was no disguising Serota's eagerness to turn them into display space, nor some of his colleagues' disagreement with him. Ron German set the tone when he said, half-jokingly, that the item was only on the list 'to keep Nick happy'. With an estimated price tag of £9 million, it would use a big chunk of contingency if they went ahead. And, as Stuart Lipton pointed out, if they wanted to build more display space it might not be the best use of £9 million. 'Frankly,' he said, 'for this amount of money you're going to be able to buy yourself a twenty-thousand-foot gallery, brand new, at ground level, which could be a little gem of a building, without any of these complications. I just wonder why . . .'

Serota had been listening, immobile, with his hand over his mouth. Now he swung into action. 'Right,' he said, 'is this the moment where I can say my bit?'

'Go on, Nick,' said Dawn Austwick, 'give it to us now.'

'Oh dear,' Serota started off, clearly feeling that his colleagues needed to be reminded of one or two home truths. 'Why did we go to Bankside? One of the reasons we went to Bankside was because it gave us the opportunity to do two very different things. One was to create very fine gallery spaces with one of the best architects in the world; the other was to make use of the industrial spaces within the building. We are going to get the first part of that equation – we're going to get extraordinary spaces on the north side of the building. I think that we should also have the objective of taking in some of these rougher spaces. They are very much the kind of spaces that artists would be interested in using. I think that if we were to be able to have both the fine spaces and these rougher spaces, by a given date – I'm not going to say what date at the moment – it would give the Tate an instrument that all the major museums of modern art in the world lack, but some of the more exciting and interesting smaller spaces have. And we know that the Pompidou Centre is about to be completely refurbished, and its appearance will be enormously improved inside. We know that the Museum of Modern Art in New York is about to create itself a four-hundred-million-dollar campaign to take over most of the space between the museum and Sixth Avenue, some of which will be retail, some of which will be gallery space, but it could potentially be a very exciting scheme. If we're going to maintain ourselves in the position where we're able to do something which is different from those institutions, we do need to take in spaces like the oil tanks and spaces below the Switch Station. And I actually think that it's more likely that we would get a donor who gave us nine million to do the oil tanks than that we get a donor who gave us nine million to build another perfect gallery space somewhere else in the building.'

For Dawn Austwick, the issue was more complicated than Serota seemed to appreciate. The oil tanks were directly beneath the Switch House, a building nobody had really paid a lot of attention to since they were concentrating all their attention on the Turbine Hall and the Boiler House, the parts of Bankside that they could work on now. In design terms the Switch House could wait. Austwick was worried that by treating the oil tanks separately, linking them directly to the Turbine Hall as they'd have to, they would be missing out on an opportunity to plan a whole new visionary complex – Switch House *and* oil tanks – in the future.

But Serota didn't want to wait. There seemed to be a greater sense of urgency. His mention of the Pompidou and MoMA in the same breath as the Tate's plans showed that he was looking over his shoulder at rival institutions and didn't want the opportunity to be ahead (or stay ahead) to slip from his grasp because his team wasn't visionary enough. His biggest fear was that if they weren't adventurous enough now, they'd never get a chance to be adventurous in the future. 'What I don't want to do,' Serota said with passion, 'is to get to a position where we open in the year 2000, and everyone collapses in exhaustion, and nothing happens on the site for five or six or eight or ten years. Because getting the whole thing going again, in that sense, will be a major undertaking.'

Lipton chipped in to point out that any future undertaking would be less major if the Tate had use of the Switch House as well and was converting that at the same time as the oil tanks, rather than doing the two projects entirely separately.

At this point Dawn Austwick felt she had to move on down the list. They were still in the phase of the meeting that was to help the group understand the different items rather than make decisions, and it was in danger of turning into a 'Serota versus the rest' argument about the oil tanks.

There was a standing joke among the Tate design team, and particularly Dawn Austwick, that they found themselves spending far too much time on toilets. Now, it happened again. The current design for the Boiler House included a private room for use by VIPs. But if the VIPs wanted to go to the lavatory they would have to leave the room and join the ordinary visitors in the public lavatories outside. Austwick wondered whether there should be a private lavatory just off the VIP room.

'The issue is that if you are a VIP and you have put in –' she hesitated, as if she had only just heard what she was saying. 'This is a wonderful conversation – if there is one thing we're going to do, we're *not* going to spend half an hour on this topic –'

'We've set you up brilliantly,' said Peter Wilson.

Austwick ploughed on. 'The thesis being, you've given two million pounds or whatever, you would expect to find that if you've got this room that's laid out for you, there would be some loos attached to it, rather than having to go and join the hoi polloi. Anyway, I think now we've got the picture, we'll pass on.'

But Serota didn't want to move on. 'Sorry, can I ask something else? Loos occupy space, and isn't a more urgent requirement in relation to this room, space to prepare and serve food? I mean I worry about the VIP who comes and says, "I'd like a sandwich before I go to the loo." '

In spite of Austwick's valiant efforts, the group were soon plunged into the minutiae of sandwich preparation areas and whether a sandwich would be enough or whether VIPs would require salads, which needed more preparation. But for Serota, small though the issue was, it indicated something about the broader planning of the gallery. 'I just think that this little incident just shows the enormous potential for getting things wrong in this building. I'm amazed at how many times we just manage to avoid getting things wrong. But, you know, you go on and on. The number of decisions that have to be made . . .'

'We need to think about making people comfortable,' said Janet de Botton, one of the people who, as a major donor to the Tate's activities, would be likely to use the VIP room and, perhaps, want to go to the loo. 'And there's no doubt that they're going to be more comfortable having a loo nearby than having to wander up or down floors. And if we have to compromise a bit on space and not give a suite of loos but two or three, it's what we're there for.'

It seemed as if they'd never get off the topic. A moment later, Serota showed once more his inability to resist rolling up his sleeves and actually designing things himself. He looked at the plan with the VIP room and thought he spotted an opportunity. 'I don't want to design them,' he said, and then hesitated. 'Well, I *do* want to design them. I can see a space where they wouldn't interfere too much.'

Valiantly Austwick tried again. 'It's very dangerous when Nick starts coming up with plans quite so playfully. And we should therefore pass swiftly on to the next item.'

Now Lipton joined in the Do-It-Yourself Designathon. 'I think we can attach it to the core. Anyway, it doesn't matter, go on, not for this meeting, as the boss has instructed –'

'I'm being ignored,' Austwick said, 'but never mind.'

Lipton asked Ron German whether there was a 'wet column' by the core, a column carrying a water supply; German began to explain why there currently wasn't, and Austwick exploded, 'Don't answer him, don't answer him, just stop, stop! We've done enough on loos!'

'We're very interested in loos,' said Wilson.

'I *know* we are,' said Austwick.

'We can all relate to them,' said Janet de Botton, and the discussion finally moved on.

The group moved further down the list to a discussion of the finishes in the building. If there was contingency money to be spent, it could be used to improve some of the very basic finishes that were currently in the budget. Austwick tried to get the group away from the issue of the colours of the finishes, since she didn't see that as a cost issue. But Peter Wilson felt it important to pursue the topic a little more:

'Well, I think you can't escape from it, because the kind of notion that [the architects] have for the walls is, "If we can't spend any money on it, then let's make it black and not think about it." And we've come away from complete black, but we're still black-*ish*, aren't we?'

'We're into grey now, yes,' said Ron German.

'It's a dark grey that's sort of distinguishable from black,' Wilson went on, 'and I think if we did have the capability to spend more money on this, then we'll get the thing different, about the nature of those finishes. That's all.'

In Austwick's view they had now discussed the individual items enough – too much, perhaps – and she distributed lists to help them make firm decisions about priorities.

Rapidly, several items dropped out, including the jetty and the northern landscape. The paper merchant's also went from this list but kept a high priority in Serota's mind. But instead of using contingency money they decided to look elsewhere in the budget for money to deal with that problem.

The oil tanks became the subject of an 'either/or' discussion, as Michael Craig-Martin said that, for his money, he'd rather develop the space under the Switch House for education project rooms than create galleries in the oil tanks.

'If I'm being asked priorities, I would have said the project rooms were a higher priority than the more expensive oil tank development, which I think can occur later, although I know that Nick doesn't –'

Serota bided his time at this stage. He had something to say about the project rooms but was keeping it till later.

Fairly rapidly the team agreed that the preparatory work for the

Level 4 suites should go near the top of the list, along with one or two other items. At this point, Serota revealed an extra reason why more project spaces might deserve a higher priority.

'I think it's quite important we come to a firm view as to whether we want these things or we don't. And the only way that we're going to get additional money, beyond a hundred and thirty, is by having a scheme which people believe in, and you can't go to them and say, well, we'd like to do X if you give us some money. I mean, sorry, you've to be more convincing than that. And that's why one of the questions I wanted to ask about these project rooms is I'm pretty convinced that we have under-catered for our educational space in this project so that every time we look at the Level 1 plans, we find ourselves saying, "well, let's double up the use of those spaces". And we've lost the seminar rooms, have we, or have we not? And we've got workshops – well, those are OK, but what's happening about the infotech space? It's beginning to double with a welcoming space for groups and things of this kind. And I just think that at the moment, if you talked to the fund-raising people, they've got a lot of proposals going out for educational purposes, and they're all stacked up on top of each other for the same spaces. And yet, we know that we need more space. And it seems to me that this set of rooms underneath the Switch House potentially yields the option of (a) raising money, (b) dealing with the educational needs of the institution as a whole, and (c) providing some space for more project rooms.'

For Dawn Austwick, it was time to clarify a strategy for moving on, a strategy that might be endangered if Serota's strong belief in transforming the spaces under the Switch House leaked out to the architects. She wanted not only to make hard, sensible decisions about what 'cream' could be added to the building by improving or adding to the design, but also to keep the architectural team still focused on what had already been decided with the existing budget. These two had to be kept entirely separate or disaster would follow. And her biggest fear was that the architects would get wind of some of the new ideas before any decisions had been made, and lose more time from a schedule that was already weeks behind.

'I think it's absolutely fine,' Austwick said to the group, 'for us to set these priorities, and actually to mull this over, put it into a strategy and say, "These are the steps that we need to take". I think it's a completely different thing to actually open up those debates with the design team, at this point in time.'

'Well, that's why they're not here,' Serota pointed out.

'Exactly,' Austwick went on, 'and I think it's very important that we recognize that.'

'I couldn't say how strongly I support that, Dawn,' Stuart Lipton said. 'Because, for me, it's Jacques Herzog on tracks. He ain't gonna move off those tracks. And what worries me, Nick, is not that I disagree with any part of the sentiment of what you just said, it's that if we open up this southern building, we're going to open up a complete debate, which inevitably will leak to the north.'

'Sorry, can I be a bit more open?' said Serota, who had a piece of news up his sleeve that had coloured his passionate advocacy of giving a high priority to the project spaces.

'Why break with the habit of a lifetime?' said Peter Wilson to general laughter.

'Look,' said Serota, coming clean, 'there's a potential at the moment to get another big slug of money for this building. But we won't get it unless we open up a new possibility. Now, I'm not saying we have to share that possibility with the design team, but somewhere in the project we need to understand that that is part of our goal. There's a potential additional twenty million pounds to come into this project from a given source, ten of which can be used for the existing building as we stand, which will help to get us from a hundred to a hundred and ten. And ten of which can be used to bridge the gap between a hundred and thirty and a hundred and fifty. And it's that second part that we need to have some conception of in order to even bid for it. And it's sitting there and it's waiting for us to pick it up. But I don't think we should excite the architects at the thought that that money is available for, say, a glazed wall all the way up the staircase.'

'That's the difficulty,' Stuart Lipton said. 'Virtually every time we have this discussion we get what I might call leakage. And we're at a point now where we can go for gold with a reasonable degree of clarity and a good chance of success. So if you want to do that, Nick – and that's encouraging – then we should have a separate design team that works on this. In my view it should be completely ring-fenced from the existing team.' Before any further steps could be taken with project spaces, someone would have to put some design input into the matter, and that someone mustn't be Herzog and de Meuron. To ram this point home Lipton then said, 'I'd like a promise from you all. This south building should not be investigated by Jacques until we have a set of drawings [for the main building].'

'Yes, that's fine, that's fine, that's absolutely fine,' Serota said. 'I don't think we've got the money to pay Jacques to investigate the south side.'

'We haven't got the stamina,' Ron German said.

But the team would still need an architect's view of what areas of the building could house extra educational space. Or there was always Serota himself, of course, always happy to roll up his sleeves and try a bit of designing . . . Rather like Toad approaching the motor car he coveted, Serota said, 'I think we should just look, *in a very cautious way*, at the east end, and just see what opening up a bit of space might do for our education/information/project spaces, because I just think that it will give us the chance to pull in a lot more money.'

Lipton then got the designing bug. 'Is there anywhere that we could take more than the piece of basement?' he asked.

This Serota–Lipton dialogue was too much for Ron German. 'Don't *you* start,' he said to Lipton. 'I've got enough trouble with this man on your right-hand side.'

'I'm just thinking, in very simple terms,' Lipton continued, undeterred. 'As soon as you bite along that basement . . .'

German pointed out that there were problems going further into the basement.

'I'm thinking of going up,' said Lipton.

Ron German leapt in again. 'Oh, no you won't – you can't – go up . . . definitely not.'

'No space at all?' asked Lipton.

'None.'

'Nowhere?'

'No,' said German emphatically. 'Is that categoric enough?'

As the two-hour meeting began to wind down, Nick Serota summarized the funding position to make sure everybody realized that the project was still treading a narrow line between not enough cash and a small but comfortable contingency. 'The fact is that we've raised just over a hundred million so far, of which about fifteen is from the private sector. Even if we get ten from another source and pick up a bit more from the Millennium Commission, we've still got to double that fifteen to reach our target of a hundred and thirty. Even if we get the money I've spoken about as being hanging on trees and waiting to fall off into Dawn's mouth, that is another ten. On top of that we've still got to get another ten from the private sector. So the absolute minimum target from the private sector, to get to a hundred and fifty, is another twenty-five million, against the fifteen we've raised today.'

'It's a sobering thought to take away,' said Austwick, and the meeting broke up.

As Peter Wilson looked back at the meeting a month later, he explained the background to the decision not to involve the architects: 'It's not that the architects don't know that the oil tanks and the electricity sub-station are there to be developed one day, it's just that they don't need to know right now that we might find the money before they finish the rest of the project. If we were to tell them that today, then they would start changing the design of the bit they've done in anticipation that those changes will need to take place. And we can't afford that distraction. It is much better to manage that process when you know you've got the money and the resources to continue, than to have people trying to make a better building today. You've got to be pragmatic about it. It's quite hard sometimes, because I share the desire to play around with things until they're perfect. And one of the hardest roles you have to learn is to accept the eighty per cent rule: that it's better to settle for eighty per cent of what you wanted and get it delivered when you wanted it, than to wait for a hundred per cent delivered at some indeterminate time in the future that might be never.'

11

Landscape with Bridge

It's not often that two world-class architects are called upon to design the same piece of space. It got near to that situation with the end of the footbridge that would carry pedestrians from the St Paul's area on the north side of the river to the open space in front of Bankside on the south. From the early days of the Tate's involvement with Bankside there were plans for a footbridge across the Thames, to be funded by a Millennium Commission grant together with corporate donations. As the Tate started work on Bankside, there was a competition to find a designer for the footbridge. Jacques Herzog was one of the judges, to help ensure some kind of uniformity with his design, or at least avoid the worst clashes that might arise.

Norman Foster and Partners entered the competition in collaboration with engineers Ove Arup and sculptor Sir Anthony Caro, and the first design showed it. The span of the bridge was architecture and engineering and the ends were sculptures – of a sort. The main span was a delicate narrow white path from the steps that led down to the river from St Paul's, resting on the river banks at either end and on two silvery supports firmly rooted in the river bed a third of the way across the river from either bank. The supports split near the top like a letter Y and were joined at the tops of the Ys by taut cables from which the bridge span was suspended, shaped like a bow. In engineering terms it harked back to other Thames bridges in its use of thick eight-ply cables tethering the bridge to the river wall at either end. But unlike, say, the Albert Bridge, visible from the huge plate-glass windows of Foster's riverside offices, the cables were almost parallel to the span.

The bridge had to be high enough above the water to let ships pass beneath and the architects wanted a very gentle curve to make the walk across easy for pedestrians, as well as being aesthetically pleasing. The bridge started halfway up a flight of steps to St Paul's on the north side, so this meant that it ended 7.8 metres above the river bank at the south end and something fairly dramatic had to be done to get people down to the level of the river bank. So when the slim, light-coloured bridge met the bank by Bankside it turned into a chunky brick-red angular construction, a mixture of steps and ramps to carry pedestrians down to the riverside path. This was Caro's contribution.

The competition was held in two stages and Foster's got through the first stage with this design but were told by the judges that the design of the ends would have to change. They didn't like the contrast in materials and in design approach between the almost slim, light-coloured span and the red orthogonal, even brutal, steps and ramps at the end. For stage two of the competition, Caro took an entirely different approach. Instead of straight lines and right angles, the south end of the bridge was now to be made of concentric circles with wide sweeping ramps down to the riverside. The colour also harmonized with the bridge itself. It was huge, a sculpture in its own right, and a fine piece of design – as a sculpture. But for the people at the Tate it was not at all what they wanted, plonking itself on their northern flank.

In fact, at the time the competition winner was announced as Foster's, the landscaping of the Tate site was on hold, so nobody was even sure what the area between the north wall of the gallery and the river would look like. After a few months at the beginning of the design phase with landscape consultant Laurie Olins, the later plans of the site showed a few desultory clumps of trees and patches of grass while the team got on with designing the building. But Herzog and de Meuron's general intentions were clear enough. They and the Tate wanted a grand space on the riverside with unfussy landscaping that led people along the river walk and nudged them towards the entrance at the base of the tower. A large swirly bridge landing that pushed some twenty metres into their site would get in the way of their simple needs. But for Foster's the ramps and stairs had to be as large as they were on the design because of the need for a ramp that was shallow enough to allow people in wheelchairs to use it. If the ramp had been straight it would have run for over a hundred metres towards the gallery or along the river bank. By curving it round into a spiral it consumed less space, although still too much for the Tate.

In late 1996 a Swiss firm of landscape architects were appointed to look at the site afresh and come up with a new design. They were the firm of Kienast and Vögt, based in Zurich. Jacques Herzog knew of their work and felt that their approach would fit well with the design of the building. Kienast and Vögt's work had a regimented quality about it, with straight rows of trees and hedges and a disciplined use of materials such as gravel and stone. After a couple of meetings with Jacques and Harry the firm prepared two preliminary schemes to present to the Tate.

On 19 February 1997 some of the Tate group flew into Basel to discuss the design of the Bankside landscape drawn up by the Swiss landscape architects. Harry Gugger described why Herzog and de Meuron had suggested them. 'There's a robustness of ideas about planting and about layering, which I found quite attractive. It's going to be quite nice to see some continental landscaping influence in Southwark.'

Dieter Kienast is a tall, serious man with long grey hair and Gunther Vögt a thinner, shorter, more jovial man, with a quiet voice that sometimes got lost in traffic noise. They had used as their starting point the ideas Herzog and de Meuron had developed over the two years since they had drawn up their competition entry. Earlier, Nick Serota explained the evolution of those ideas. 'What a greater familiarity with the site has done is to make them conscious of the fact that the north, the south, the east and the west aspects of Bankside are all very different one from another. And so the development has taken the course of focusing on those four zones and developing them each with a slightly different language, and each to address different needs, and each to a degree working on a different scale. So that the west is clearly much more intimate, where they've suggested that we should have a courtyard close to the ramp down into the Turbine Hall. The south, at the moment, is still fairly bare and depends in the long term on us getting access to the oil tanks and opening them up and putting glass ceilings in and having light coming up from below. The east has now really been designated as a view through to St Paul's, but otherwise effectively it's a goods entrance, a staff entrance and so on. In the north they've taken a view about the way in which the existing landscape, that was put there in the early seventies to hide the power station, should be opened up to create on the one hand an urban park, and on the other hand a space, not unlike parts of the Tuileries Gardens in Paris, where we could show sculpture on a gravel base.'

As the group gathered for the landscape meeting in one of the first-floor rooms at Herzog and de Meuron's offices, Ron German opened up a brochure showing the details of the current design for the footbridge, and the two landscape architects leant over his shoulder to look at it. While trying to be polite, no one had a good word for it. They were clearly influenced by the large circular south end of the bridge, which seemed to take up an inordinate amount of the Tate's landscape and would dwarf any feature they proposed to put there. Also, Kienast and Vögt's design was very rectilinear, with areas of gravel (some bound in an asphalt substrate, others made up of loose stones), straight hedges as shelters for benches, and small groups of trees forming what the designers called 'bosques'.

Clearly a lot of thinking had gone into the northern landscape before the bridge plans were finalized, and now the team were worried. Gugger pointed out that the south end of the bridge was very different in style from the Tate's landscape plans, and even in a different style from the rest of the bridge: 'The bridge proves to be a delicate piece of engineering and I think it will be a nice bridge. I haven't seen a suspension bridge with such a shallow span as this one, so enormous forces will have to be held into the ground on the sides to make it work. But the landings seem in a completely different style, and I don't really understand this collaboration with an artist. It's more like putting two elements together, the landings created or designed by an artist and the bridge designed by an architect and an engineer.'

But he realized that designing an appropriate south end for the bridge was not easy, for engineering reasons. 'Norman Foster has left one of the most difficult problems to resolve to Anthony Caro. You have the line of the bridge drawn at a height for ships to move underneath and so it's just a matter of fact that you can't have the bridge coming right down to the level of the river bank. This leads to this complicated problem of having a landing which then must tie together the two levels.'

It was a requirement that the bridge should be accessible to people in wheelchairs, and so in getting people down from the height of the bridge to ground level, Caro also had to make sure that there was a ramp with a shallow enough gradient for them as part of his design. The mathematics of the situation meant that the ramp had to be 120 metres long, and there wasn't room for a straight ramp of that length heading from the end of the bridge right across the Tate's landscape. 'That's why Caro puts it in his sculpture by going forward and backwards, so it's a very understandable approach, but I think it's a bit over the top because you can't do this to disabled people. We would like to simplify the landings so that they are much more straightforward, with two stairs leading from the landing of the bridge down to the ground and an elevator for the disabled.'

(It so happened that Foster's had considered and rejected lifts: their maxim was 'Lifts in the public domain are a bad idea.' Experience had shown them that people desecrate them with graffiti and pee in them, and the architects wanted to avoid that if they could.)

'Caro has taken another approach,' Gugger said, 'so that he made this issue of the disabled ramp the driving factor for his design. It's a huge piece and it's loaded with other functions. They made a café underneath and I can understand why. Once you have this object and this volume you have to look for another function.'

The landscape plan that Kienast and Vögt had prepared had a sunken area with a lawn and trees surrounding it forming a 'bosque'. Then the rest of the northern landscape was more open, with a strip of lawn parallel to the river and hedges creating intimate spaces with benches. The team discussed the fact that the south landing of the bridge had to come down from a considerable height and therefore decided that a sunken area would not be a good idea. It would just add to the length of the drop, and Herzog and de Meuron decided to reverse the initial idea and have a mound instead of a pit. The next step would be to seek a meeting with the bridge team to see how the new idea could be integrated into an improved version of the south ending.

On 21 October 1997, Nick Serota and Jacques Herzog walked the length of Sir Norman Foster and Partners' huge open-plan design floor. The Foster offices are in a long white rectangular building on the south bank of the Thames in Battersea. The architects work in an open-plan area that is probably a hundred metres long, with a ceiling four storeys above their heads. Herzog and Serota had been trying for some time to organize a meeting to discuss the idea of turning the pit into a mound, so that Kienast and Vögt could get on with designing it. Foster, busy with projects from Berlin to Hong Kong, was a difficult man to pin down, but a date had finally been fixed.

The setting for the meeting was unpropitious. After the Long Walk past dozens of young architects huddled over their computers, Serota and Herzog arrived at a round table set out in an open area at the end of the design floor, within sight and earshot of a hundred or so Foster's employees. Through the window the setting sun shone on the ornate excrescences of the Albert Bridge nearby. Foster and Herzog had met before at a lunch at the Tate, set up by Serota to ensure that some kind of dialogue could take place about the Millennium Bridge and its south landing. Serota was doing his best to bring Herzog and de Meuron together with some senior figures in British architecture. He was surprised, and a little dismayed, by how little contact there had been between the profession in Britain and the Swiss architects, as he explained on the day of the first Foster–Herzog meeting back in March: 'I would say it's one of the interesting aspects of this whole exercise of bringing a Swiss architect to London that very few of the senior British architects have made any effort to be in contact with Jacques Herzog and Harry Gugger and Pierre du Meuron. I have found it rather strange that this competition ran, the winners were appointed, we're now two years on and we're arranging for the first time a meeting between Norman Foster and Jacques Herzog. I can't think of any other country in the world where the profession would have made the winners of a competition of this kind feel so much that they are outsiders. I'm not talking about them meeting ten thousand British architects. Maybe the President of the RIBA might have invited Jacques for lunch. I'm not saying Jacques hasn't met anyone, that's obviously untrue, he has met several people, but generally speaking it's been at his initiative and I think that seeing Norman today is part of the process of integrating Herzog and du Meuron into the British architectural world.'

That first meeting, on the Tate's home ground, had discussed the redesign of the bridge ending to make it less monumental. Now, on Sir Norman's territory, Jacques Herzog hoped to persuade Foster to accept Kienast and Vögt's redesign of the landscape to produce a mound rather than a pit for the bridge to land on. It seemed to have many advantages to the Herzog and de Meuron team, and Serota. It reduced further the distance between the end of the bridge pathway and the level of the ground where the pedestrian first set foot, allowing the bridge designers gentler slopes and smaller ramps.

After greetings and social niceties, the three men sat round the table, on which a model of the current bridge design had been placed. The southern ending was now like the eye of a needle, as the bridge path divided into two at the end and the left and right branches curved back on themselves to become one in a ramp that deposited people on the landscape facing back the way they had come. (This redesign had taken place in the preceding months, as it became clear that Caro's massive circular ramps weren't going to work. Harry Gugger had taken part in the discussions with Foster that led to this change, and at a meeting in June there were jokes about this. 'Harry should be paid by Foster's for redesigning it,' someone said. 'In future, Harry, when you're as famous as Norman Foster, you'll remember to listen to young up-and-coming architects.')

Jacques Herzog, a little nervous, unrolled a plan of the Tate's northern landscape and started to explain Herzog and de Meuron's current thinking. 'We use the fact that the bridge lands on this side to create more of a landscape piece. And the idea is to create a kind of a mound on which the bridge could land. And this mound is like a leftover from a landscape, which could be irregular, you know, and with this kind of artificial piece of landscape, we can also resolve other problems we have nearby. Because the drawing doesn't show that there is a level further down there with a garage, and the garage here on the side is a bit higher. So this landscape could weave in this as well as this area. It'd be one piece on which the bridge would land.'

At this point, Foster tried to intervene. But Herzog was now in his stride and wanted to have time to make his case. 'Let me just finish,' he said. 'The idea of this little mound would be that coming from the bridge, you could go down in different directions, and not need to go back in order to go there, for instance. So this little slope with trees on it would give the possibility to go in all directions.'

At this point Foster treated the director of one of the world's major art galleries and his architect to what appeared to be a lecture on the basic principles of architecture.

'Yes, well,' said Foster, 'I have had the opportunity to see that [a plan showing the mound], and if one goes through the sort of sequence of the thing, there is a certain continuity for me. I think I can try and explain that. It's like the connection between a tall building and the ground – in other words, if you really want an acid test of a tall building, it's the way that it finally connects with the ground. I think that it's the same with the bridge. You see that bridge over there?' He pointed over to the Albert Bridge, with its thick cables curving down to hold up the road surface. Serota and Herzog dutifully followed Foster's pointing finger. 'It connects with the hard horizontal of the surface,' Foster went on, turning back to the model of the Millennium Bridge, 'and every time I feel the need to bring this bridge down positively and to anchor it. With the forces which are holding every-thing back here, I feel very unhappy about it sitting on top of a mound. It looks as though it's going to be torn off. I'm very, very unhappy about that.'

Foster is someone who can say 'no' in ten different ways, none of them actually using the word. Herzog and Serota were a little stunned. Valiantly, Herzog tried to retrieve the situation. 'This is certainly not the final solution,' he said. 'We would want to geometrically define this, that's for the landscape architect to design –'

Foster continued with his lecture. 'But every bridge that I know that works in a satisfactory way connects positively. And this one more than any other, it's pulling, it's pulling. That base is actually leaning outwards against the force of the bridge. I'm unhappy about burying that into something which is greenery. I think it needs the continuity back into the ground, to be truly anchored. It is anchored, I think it needs to be seen to be anchored.'

'But in my view,' Herzog replied, 'the way I see this, having this mound is not actually hiding the structure, it just reduces the bridge to this ending, and then you land on earth.'

'No,' Foster persisted, 'I think it needs space. I think it needs to come down into the ground plane and the clearances here and the ramps have been worked and reworked now so many times and they're the absolute optimum.'

For the next half-hour or so Foster and Herzog talked at each other, neither shifting any ground. 'I'm not so sure that I agree, Jacques,' Foster would say, and, 'I would be less than honest if I said that I didn't have severe reservations about the core concept there.' And whether or not Herzog understood that Foster was saying 'no', 'no' and 'no again', he ploughed on in his attempt to reduce the impact of Foster's bridge end on his landscape.

But for Foster there was a matter of principle at stake, one that seemed to be embodied in the earliest origins of the bridge design, almost in an unchangeable *personality* the bridge had acquired as a result:

'I think that this bridge – which is highly sculptural – is a resolution of forces. In the end it cannot do everything, so it does what it does with integrity, with conviction and with total commitment. You can't spin off in all directions from this point. But in my view, like a Richard Serra sculpture, for example, it has to have a point of contact with the ground. It's the resolution of the forces. It's as fundamental to me in philosophical terms as a piece of design as that cliff edge of Bankside coming down into the urban pavement, although I don't dispute that somebody could come along and demonstrate a way of doing it, in the same way that I could argue that I could demonstrate that your cliff edge at Bankside could come down into a soft path. Of course it could, but you, with very personal feelings of deep-held conviction, would feel otherwise. And I feel otherwise about this, and I would be hypocritical if I didn't make everybody aware of that. It's a point of absolute fundamental conviction.'

At this point, Nick Serota injected a comment that, unfortunately, sent Foster racing off in precisely the wrong direction, as far as Jacques Herzog was concerned.

'I think there remains a feeling from our side,' Serota said, 'that the final exit or entry point from the bridge is in some way less substantial, and indeed to a degree almost apologetic. That you have this magnificent gesture across the river, but to get to it your means of access is via what feels like a very subsidiary route.'

Seizing his pen, Foster began to sketch on a roll of thin yellow architect's tracing paper.

'I think there is a way of responding to that,' he said, drawing rapidly. 'If at the moment we're looking at something that is coming like *this*, and then you're on the walk *here*, and you look through *that* hole . . . and what we perhaps should be doing is extending that ramp out so that it does become much more generous at that level . . . and again that would enable us to be more generous *here* . . .'

This was all too much for Herzog. He had to intervene and make his own views as forcefully as Foster, unfortunately without Foster's command of the nuances of English. 'I think to make it very clearly,' he said, 'my vision is different in terms of the landing. I think that we went a long way and it was a very good collaboration indeed, and there are obviously things that we disagree about, which is normal, but one thing, when you make it larger you would certainly not grow the agreement between us, because you make it even more a kind of a balcony from where you overlook the landing here . . .'

The meeting was beginning to run out of steam, as Foster pointed out the conflict between Serota wanting a landing that was less apologetic and Herzog resisting one that was larger. By doing so, he successfully deflected the meeting away from the original intention of Herzog and Serota, to fight for the mound.

Sometimes when great men meet, problems can be solved quickly, without the need to confer or consult with anyone else. In this case, for whatever reason, the great men left the meeting with their own positions intact. It was left to the subordinates – Foster's colleagues who were working day-to-day on the project – to work with Kienast and Vögt and Herzog and de Meuron to come up with the solution that was eventually adopted.

12

Tender Processes

The largest contract that Schal would be signing among the trade contractors on Bankside was for the structural steel, the framework of the 'building within a building' that would contain the galleries in the old Boiler House. Schal estimated that it would cost about £7 million and had set aside that amount in their cost-plan. The steel contract was put out to competitive tender in May 1997.

One of the companies that was keen to get the contract was Watson Steel of Bolton, whose sales director, Geoffrey Taylor, had been at the trade contractors' open day the previous September. Taylor and his colleagues were determined that Watson would do their best to get their hands on this contract, even if it meant shaving their profit margin down to a minimum. It was a good project to have, and Watson's needed a good project to ensure its continuing level of business over the next few months. In fact, the company had an even higher profile project at the time. It had built the huge steel supports for the Millennium Dome, which were the first structural elements the general public saw as construction began. But there was only one millennium every thousand years or so, and Watson needed to keep its order books full with other projects.

'By the year 2000,' Taylor said, 'the demand for structures for the millennium will have obviously abated, so we might well be entering the new millennium on a down-turn. As an industry we very much follow the *Joseph and His Amazing Technicolor Dreamcoat* principle of seven years of famine and seven years of feast. We have been bolstered in this feast period by the millennium. There has been a terrific demand because of the deadline effect. A lot of people – not only on Millennium Projects – want to get them ready for the millennium, so that has been a good opportunity for the industry.'

The steel contract was just one of a hundred or more contracts Schal had to organize by the tender process during 1996–8 and, like architectural competitions, this was not universally loved by contractors. The work involved in preparing the bid was all-consuming for several weeks before the submission date.

'The big weakness of construction is that you only do it once,' said Taylor, 'and it's like everything in life – the first time you do anything is not the best time you ever do it, and that's disappointing. And it's the same with the tender: it's terribly frustrating that not only have you not done it as well as you would if you had another chance, but you never have that chance, and ironically all the lessons you've learnt can never really directly benefit anything else, although you do get spin-off by learning from your mistakes.'

Even though Watson was one of the companies that had been invited to tender – showing that Schal thought they were certainly capable of doing the work – their chances statistically were still not very high, for all the work they would have to put into preparing the bid. But Taylor and his colleagues were determined to put their best efforts into the task. 'In Watson's, we tender for maybe seven jobs to get one. So this job is neither a million times more important or a million times less important than any of the other ones we're bidding. But we would view this as being substantial, high-profile and interesting, and therefore we will be going for it very hard.' Watson's also needed a big project fairly soon. 'It's absolutely vital,' said Taylor. 'It's absolutely vital to the well-being of this company. We desperately need a job of this size in the next three months. We're bidding four at this very moment, and we have to get one of them.'

Watson Steel is a large, sprawling steel fabrication plant a few miles to the north-west of the town of Bolton, ringed by hills on the edge of the Pennines. In late May 1997, a harassed Peter Gannon, one of Watson's senior managers, was wrestling with a pile of documents he'd received from Ove Arup giving a schematic view of the steel requirements for Bankside. Gannon's job was to manage a team of designers and steel fabricators as they took information from the drawings about every single piece of steel – thousands of them – and worked out how much each piece would weigh and how it would be attached to adjacent pieces. The weight was needed so that all the pieces could be added together and Gannon could work out how many tonnes of steel they would need.

Although you could see a structural steel framework as a giant version of a child's construction set, there's a major difference in how the pieces are connected to each other. A child's set has a standard kit of pieces and a collection of nuts and bolts. In a steel structure designed for any large building, the only standard 'off-the-shelf' parameter is the cross-section of the steel pieces. Columns and beams are generally designed using a range of standard cross-sections, usually shaped like the cross-section of a capital I. The thickness of the upright of the I and the width and thickness of the horizontal flanges are the dimensions that define a piece of steel. These pieces then come in standard lengths and the company buying them will order slightly longer pieces than it needs so it can cut them to exactly the right dimensions.

When the pieces arrive at the factory, it's the job of the steel contractor to prepare them, in a process called fabrication, so that when they are sent to the construction site, each piece will be ready to be bolted in place to the adjacent column or beam. It's not just a matter of drilling holes for the bolts. Even the simplest piece, say a section of a column, will require a flat plate to be welded to both ends, with holes drilled for attaching to the column above or below. And usually the attachments are more complex. Several different connection pieces will have to be designed, cut, drilled and attached to the basic steel section so that it can connect to other columns and beams that attach to both ends and sometimes across the middle; sometimes at right angles, sometimes at other angles.

With six or so companies all analysing and costing the Bankside drawings, there was a tremendous amount of duplication going on in late May, made worse by the fact that, although it would presumably have been possible for Ove Arup to press one button on their own design computers and get a figure for how much the steel would weigh, every company was making the same calculation for itself.

'It's quite a laborious process, unfortunately,' said Gannon, in mid-task at his drawing board in early June. 'We have several drawings, maybe fifty, a hundred drawings. We've literally got to count all the pieces. The column positions are shown either with circles or as an I-section. So we tend to list the columns first. Between the columns we have a number of beams, which are lines. So every black line you see is a beam, and on each beam you'll have a mark. So this one has B 1.1, and we look over here and it tells us the size of it. It's a 457 by 191 universal beam. So that's a standard beam, we can find it in the book, and we can write it down on the list. Every single piece is counted. On this job I think we've got maybe five thousand pieces. We then take the lists and somebody will go through the lists and compute the weight of the steel.'

It was that total weight in tonnes that was then used to calculate how much the actual materials would cost.

But Geoffrey Taylor explained that the price of the job was far more than the price of the steel. In fact, if they were aiming to be competitive, the cost of the plain steel was the least promising area for keeping the cost down, since everyone would have to pay roughly the same price. But in the other three areas, there might be some way the company could give the Tate a very competitive price. 'There's the engineering, which is design work and drawing office work. If we can somehow introduce a speedier means of communication between ourselves in producing the manufacturing drawings, and the engineering at the other end from Ove Arup, or the architect, that could save a lot of money and may be of interest not only to ourselves, but to themselves. The third element is in the manufacture, and if we can look at the elements, seeing whether by introducing cleverer manufacturing methods we can reduce the cost, by tinkering with the actual detail, then we can put that in our tender and that may prove attractive, to be researched further by the client to reduce his cost. The last element is the erection. The erection side is done by ourselves, and we have our own erection department. It could be that if we went to somebody else to do the erection, a company more local to London, or maybe more hungry, then maybe we could reduce the price there.'

If the Tate Gallery at Bankside had been an entirely new building constructed from scratch, the steel framework designed by Herzog and de Meuron and Ove Arup's would have presented few special problems. In plan, it was a grid of steel columns: about eighteen columns along the long side and four across the width, with five levels of steel between the basement and the roof. The Light Beam would then be a separate structure on top of the main steel skeleton. The individual elements of the steel framework were not unusual, nor were the connections between one piece and another.

But constructing such a framework inside an existing building, even if – as in the case of Bankside – much of the interior and quite a lot of the exterior elements had been removed, was to present bigger problems than anyone anticipated. There were two things that the contractors preparing their bids had to be careful to get right. One was the fact that the steel for the framework had to be taken into the building through an existing roof structure. If Schal had removed the entire roof it would have made it easier to bring steel into the heart of the Boiler House, but the surrounding brick walls would have had no support at the top and would have been very unstable. If they had left the entire roof on, it would have created a very stable box, as well as weather protection, around the steel erection, but would have meant that all the steel had to be brought into the building and lifted into position by cranes inside. By removing some of the roof slabs but leaving the large roof trusses that connected the riverside walls with the Turbine Hall wall structure, Schal could get the best of both worlds – a stable exterior shell with gaps for steel to be lowered from outside. But even this was not going to be easy, and Watson's, along with the other contractors, had to make some allowance in the schedule they offered for the extra complexity of getting the steel into position.

The second unusual element, by virtue of the fact that the new steel was to be erected in an old building, was a decision about providing a firm foundation for each of the columns on the north, east and west sides of the structure, the sides where the architects were retaining Giles Gilbert Scott's brick walls and windows. The ultimate support for these walls would be the new steel framework, built as a vertical layer just within them. But at the bottom of the old power station, below ground level, were massive retaining walls built of concrete, almost like the walls of a giant swimming pool, sloping steeply towards the basement so that they were thicker at the bottom than the top. These walls had originally supported all the steelwork of the old power station and Schal and Arup's now wanted to use them to support the new columns, by placing large steel baseplates on top of the retaining wall, on the narrowest part. But the engineers were concerned that the concrete in the retaining walls, now fifty years old or more, might spread under the weight of the columns, and so they had specified a series of measures to hold the walls together with huge steel plates either side of the wall, pulled together by huge bolts under tension.

There was one other element in the package of drawings from Schal which really had most of the contractors foxed. It was something that was called by everyone the Grand Staircase.

The Grand Staircase was designed to thread its way through the new museum from basement to roof. It was also destined to thread its way though the whole project from 1996 to 2000, causing a succession of problems – or *challenges* as the architects would prefer to see them – that no one anticipated when Herzog and de Meuron first dropped the feature into the early design discussions.

When Jacques Herzog looked back in 1999 at how the Grand Staircase came into the project, he seemed to believe from the start it had been an important part of Herzog and de Meuron's thinking about the personal experience of moving through the building. 'The [Grand Staircase] was there from the very beginning. Both the client and the architects believe that in looking at art in such a big building, moving the body from time to time to change the rhythm is very important. We often compare the building to a kind of artificial landscape – topographical architecture. And the stair is a very important element in that respect. Personally, I like to move my body rather than using escalators, also in airports and other big buildings where from time to time you get the understanding that you're still alive. And I think that's important. It will be important also in the future, especially when you walk in such a building to see these huge shows and maybe the lift brings you up and you walk down through the building – you have much more physical experience of the building and of the different levels, of the height, of the scale of everything.'

Nick Serota and Harry Gugger remember the early events rather differently. They don't remember the Grand Staircase being in the plans from the beginning. In the competition entry for the gallery, there *was* a large public staircase, in the chimney. But as serious design work began, that staircase disappeared. Serota described what happened then, making it sound a little less planned than Herzog's description: 'At a certain point it got squeezed out, and the main means of access through the building became the escalators and the lift; and there were then some subsidiary connecting stairs between floors, principally between gallery floors, so that you could move from Level 4 to Level 5 without necessarily coming back to the central concourse. And for a number of reasons those were taken out; in part to do with the cost, but also to do with fire restrictions and so on. And there came a point at which I and others felt that there was a need to reinstate an ability for a visitor to move between floors without getting into a mechanical means of conveyance. Especially someone who knew the building pretty well, who might well want to hop down quickly from Level 5 to Level 4. If they knew there was a staircase, they'd take it. And then Harry, I think it was, saw an opportunity to bring a slightly redundant space into use as a staircase.'

Gugger described how *he* remembered the events that led up to the Grand Staircase: 'For a long time, there was no Grand Staircase at all. For a long time we just had the escalators and the elevators and the escape stairs, but no Grand Staircase. And I remember very well, it was at one of those design meetings in Basel. I don't remember the exact reason, but I know that overnight I worked out the proposal of the Grand Staircase – it was linked into another design question: would the elevators face the concourse or would they create a kind of a lobby? And also, questions about accessing the restaurant, because the escalators stopped on Level 5. And I came along the next morning with this proposal, and everybody liked it.'

The 'slightly redundant space' Serota mentioned was an area slightly to the west of the centre of the Boiler House, part of one of the four cores of the building that carried essential services, emergency stairs, lavatories, and so on.

At the time, the architects were still in their 'Princes of Darkness' phase, and there was a lot of black concrete on various surfaces of the building, including the Turbine Hall wall. So their first thought about the design of the staircase was that it should be made of black concrete. From the way Gugger described what happened next, that idea was short-lived. 'That's when the engineers shouted at us that it would be far too heavy, since we are building to existing foundations;

that these foundations couldn't take the load of a concrete stair; and also that the construction industry wouldn't be prepared to build such an element in concrete, which would be the normal material in Switzerland to do it.'

So the material was changed to steel and the staircase had twenty-two flights, with solid steel sides made out of large plates. It also incorporated wood elements for the treads of the stairs and the handrails. But because the staircase was largely steel it was included in the steel contractors' package, something which was to puzzle the bidders for the contract, who found themselves having to deal with wood for perhaps the first time.

Joe Lock, managing director of Watson, identified another concern as his team looked at the plans more closely. It was clear to him that the architects wanted something that looked good. Unlike the steel framework, the staircase would not be hidden behind internal walls or ceiling. It would be on full view. In fact sometimes people at the Tate called it the Ceremonial Staircase. And this worried Lock. 'I am concerned when people look for architectural aspects from structural steelwork, because structural steelwork comes from plate that's obtained from the mills, and it's very easy for people to have the view that this is going to end up [having a perfectly smooth surface] like a filing cabinet, and of course it really isn't going to be like a filing cabinet, nor am I absolutely sure that structural steel is right for these exposed balustrades.' He didn't want to get into a situation where Watson's won the contract with a certain figure and then spent time and money trying to produce an unachievable appearance for a fussy architect.

The tender documents had to be in Schal's offices by 12 noon on Friday 13 June, and on the Wednesday before, Lock, Taylor, Peter Gannon and Dave Burnsall, who coordinated the whole tender process, gathered around a large table in Watson's offices. Burnsall's team had produced a mass of documentation, breaking down each of the four categories of work – materials, design, fabrication and erection – into numerous subcategories, each with a price. Adding them all up, the total came to just under £7 million, without any profit element being added.

There were several decisions that now had to be made, and everyone looked to Lock for guidance. It was his company, after all, that was being put on the line. The aim of those decisions was, of course, to win the contract. But not at any price. Although Taylor had said that it was 'vital' that they get a project of this size, it would clearly be doing no one in the company any favours if they came up with a price that got them the project but led to them losing money. But one purpose of the meeting was to go through the estimates and make absolutely sure that none of them was too high. One key determinant of the price was the schedule, part of the building 'programme' as it was called. Taylor knew that sometimes offering a shorter programme for the work could gain them an edge over a competitor.

'If somebody says, "I could do it in x weeks less," or somebody says, "No, I'm awfully sorry, I can't do it in the number of weeks you require, it would have to be another couple of weeks," then this enters the situation. But on a job of this prestige and quality, everybody on the tender list will have accepted what the programme is, and won't balk at that.' Taylor was right about not suggesting a longer programme for the work, but he didn't know how attractive a *shorter* schedule was beginning to look to the Schal team as they moved through 1996 and faced a number of delays in other aspects of the work.

Once the team had got the total costs of the project as low as was realistically achievable there was then the question of profit. Lock had to decide what percentage to add to the direct costs to supply the company's profit on this job. If they hadn't needed the project as much as they did, they might have added 5, 6 or 7 per cent to the total. In fact, the first total Lock was presented with included a 5 per cent mark-up.

With sleeves rolled up and a pot of tea to sustain them, Lock and his three colleagues set off down the list of items, a process that was sometimes conducted in silence, with an occasional remark from Lock such as, 'We need to take a big slug off that. Take a bit off again.'

There was a flurry of puzzlement when they came to the estimates for the staircase, and one of the fabricators was summoned to help.

'There's hardwood handrails the likes of which you've never seen in your life,' said Lock.

'I'm not very good with wood, you know,' the fabricator replied.

'I'm buying you a plane,' said Lock.

The group pondered the worrying matter of whether the welded steel panels the architect had drawn could ever be made smooth enough for his tastes. 'My big concern,' said someone, 'is as soon as you touch these things with weld they'll look absolutely horrendous.'

Peter Gannon said hesitantly, 'Those panels we made at Man United for the commentary box walls didn't look too bad to me.'

'Wait a minute,' said Joe Lock in an astonished voice, 'that's a *football stadium* – this is for the *Tate Gallery of Modern Art*. Come on Peter, bloody hell!' He returned to the Schal documents. 'I reckon this guy's thinking this looks like a slab of marble. Read that specification again.'

Gannon read it and then said, 'We can make it in a more exotic material if he wants that.'

However they looked at the Grand Staircase they couldn't really be sure that the figure the estimators had put in was an accurate forecast of how much it would cost. Then Lock made up his mind. 'Right,' he said, 'we'll put the number in but qualify it to hell.'

There was another issue that was to assume greater significance than the Watson team realized when Schal compared bids two days later. In the document Schal sent to the steel contractors there were a series of amendments to 'The National Steelwork Specification (Third Edition)', the starting point for all British structural steel contracts. Amendment 2.1 M said, 'ADD: the sulphur content of the steel shall not be greater than 0.015 per cent.'

At one point in the meeting Lock turned to Gannon and said, 'Anything stupid there?', pointing to the document.

'There's a note in the spec about the steel,' Gannon said. 'They want 0.015 per cent sulphur.'

'No way that we should get involved with that,' Lock said, 'No way, just write it out.'

Now presumably Schal had a reason for specifying low-sulphur steel. In fact the engineers believed that this type of steel withstands stress better. Lock struck it out because he knew that this type of steel was more expensive, but apparently it didn't occur to him that if Schal specified low-sulphur steel it meant that they wanted low-sulphur steel, and wouldn't necessarily take kindly to someone striking it out.

But it did help to keep Watson's bid lower. With 4,000 tonnes of steel in the contract, and an estimated price differential of £50 per tonne, Lock's decision was lowering their bid price by £200,000.

As they finished the process of accepting or adjusting each of the costs, there was one last decision to make: the profit percentage.

For Geoffrey Taylor, profit was too simple a word for quite a complex calculation that had to be made: 'We're not in the business of buying something and then selling it, in which case a profit is fairly predictable. Profit also includes a contingency in case something goes wrong – it isn't just a means of rewarding our shareholders. And the profit level is invariably linked to whether you feel that this is a straightforward job that will be engineered, manufactured and erected successfully without any problems; or whether we think there could be a problem along the way and we have to guard against that. Profit is a banal word, isn't it, really? I mean it doesn't really mean something you put in the back pocket and walk away with; it's something to guard against a rainy day really – in our industry, certainly.'

'I don't think we're going to get the opportunity for a negotiating margin,' Joe Lock said to the group, as he considered that crucial final percentage. He felt there was no point in putting in a higher margin than the lowest they were prepared to accept. 'My own view is that we shouldn't go for more than a three per cent margin. Let's put three per cent on. Agreed? Spit it out if you're not happy. No contingency. Bare minimum.'

On Wednesday afternoon, at the end of the meeting, Dave Burnsall took the figures off to prepare the final paperwork for Schal.

The final total for Watson's bid for the Tate Bankside steel contract was £6,085,285. If they had known that the Tate was expecting bids of about £6.5 million, and happy to pay that price, they would have been even more optimistic than they were after their intensive three weeks of hard work. Now they had to keep their fingers crossed that Friday the 13th would not be their unlucky day.

For Watson, Rowen and the other four companies who put in their bids that week, there was a lot resting on the final decision. But for Schal, too, this contract was a crucial one to get right. The steel contract was the largest, in monetary terms, in the whole project. It had to be carried out in a way that stayed within budget and, as important, within the programme – or schedule – that Schal had estimated. In fact there was a vital need for a schedule that was no longer than twenty weeks and that started on 1 December 1997, come what may. Not only was there no room for manoeuvre, recent discoveries and decisions to do with other parts of the building had put the whole programme under threat and the steel contract had to run smoothly to avoid worse problems.

Part Three

1997–8

Structures and Symbols

13

Ups and Downs

One event that had threatened the schedule was the discovery that areas of the concrete roof around the rooflights above the Turbine Hall were in a much poorer state than the engineers had originally thought – they were suffering from a type of concrete rot called carbonation. There had always been some worries, purely because of the possibility of deterioration with time. But the engineers had done tests in the early days of the project and in the areas they sampled they had found nothing to be concerned about. Making a leap of faith – as any engineer would be expected to do in that situation – Arup extrapolated from the samples they had taken and inferred that the rest of the roof was in similar condition. It was only as building work got under way and there was closer scrutiny of the roof that they made a nasty discovery.

At one of the regular project review meetings in mid 1997, John Hirst from Ove Arup described the results of a recent, and more thorough, survey. 'The system of protecting reinforcement against corrosion in some areas has effectively broken down, and therefore there is the potential for future corrosion, and with this being the main entrance to the building, the alternatives are to adopt various degrees of remedial works now to the existing concrete and accept that there will be further remedial works in the future; or to replace the existing roof with a new roof – those are basically the options that we have on the table.'

Hirst and the cost accountants had worked out that the situation could cost £400,000 to rectify. 'It's the net cost, as I understand it, of replacing the roof,' said Ron German, who had already been discussing the situation with the cost accountants and with Dawn Austwick. 'It doesn't necessarily yet incorporate some of the costs we'll be faced with – operational difficulties of actually cutting down the roof and setting back other trades and so on. And that's why . . .'

'. . . we shouldn't be reassured by it,' said Austwick, completing his sentence. As quickly as possible the team had to come up with a recommendation – to replace the roof or try to repair it. One thing they had to take into account was the risk of pieces of concrete dropping on visitors' heads, if they decided only to do remedial work.

'To quantify the risk of little bits of concrete flaking off – i.e., how much and when – is very, very hard,' said Tony Marriott, a senior Arup engineer. 'On a normal sort of building, if it was anything like a normal ceiling up there, you probably wouldn't worry too much about it. It's just the thought of it – (a) it's so difficult to get at, and (b) it being the main access – one really wants the risk to be nothing, and to say "nothing" is a very absolute sort of number. That's going to be hard. So it won't be an easy decision.'

Nick Serota had arrived in the middle of the discussion. 'Sorry, I arrived late,' he said, 'and you may have covered this earlier, but can I just ask when this came to light, and as a result of what investigation?'

'It came to light from surveys carried out as soon as we reasonably could,' said John Hirst, 'once they had access to the roof. Because up to the time that we had access up there, we really had very little opportunity to do surveys. The only surveys that we had were the initial surveys . . .'

'Before we bought the building,' said Serota.

'The initial ones showed areas with no carbonation, and some with some carbonation, but not approaching the reinforcement. But this more extensive survey, which could only be done when the scaffold was up there to get in there, shows a lot more areas, with a greater proportion showing carbonation, and also it's much deeper: it goes beyond the reinforcement.'

Schal's Ian Blake claimed to be less surprised than his colleagues about the discovery of the roof problems. 'They weren't much of a surprise to me, and it's disappointing that we addressed them now. We really saw the poor quality of the Boiler House roof some considerable time ago when we took that off. When we stripped the felt back there, it was clear that the planks of the eastern side had badly

When the Tate first acquired Bankside Power Station in 1994, the Boiler House – later to become five floors of galleries and public spaces – was full of rusting power generation equipment.

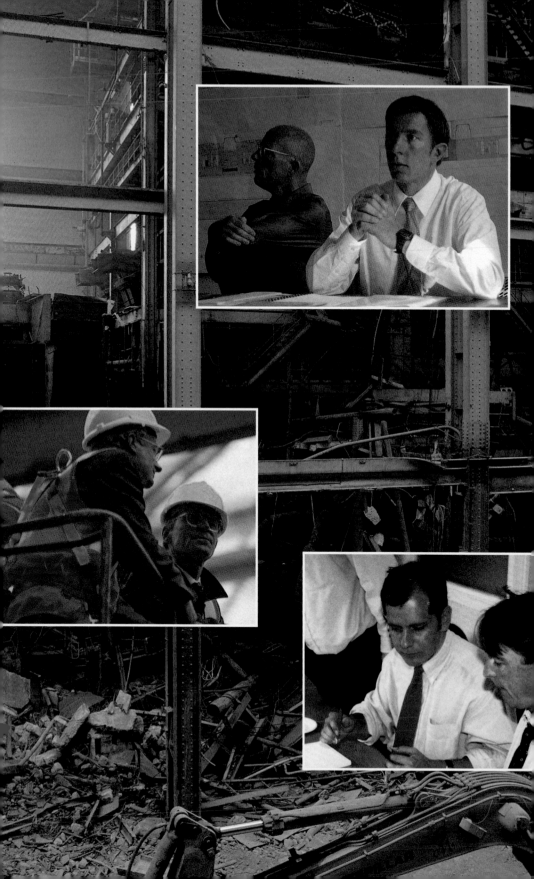

(*Above*) Once the interior of the Boiler House is stripped bare, a group of contractors tours the building to decide whether to bid for some of the twenty or more contracts to supply steel, concrete, floors and walls and the other essential elements.

(*Left*) As the interior of Bankside is dismantled (*background*), two of the partners of Herzog and de Meuron, Jacques Herzog (*top left*) and Harry Gugger (*top right*), are designing the new museum; Nicholas Serota (*middle left*, with Chris Smith, Secretary of State for Culture) is raising funds; and the director of the Schal construction team (Ian Blake, *bottom right*) is trying to devise a plan to build the museum on time and on budget.

(*Above*) Overlooked by St Paul's, the process of removing the original Boiler House rooflights is under way, to create space for Herzog and de Meuron's Light Beam.

(*Right*) As engineers investigate the roof, they discover corrosion in the old concrete, and the whole roof has to be removed and a new one constructed.

The most important aspects of the design are tested by building 'mockups' (*above*).

The first gallery walls and door mockup gets the thumbs down from the Tate design team, led by Nick Serota and three Trustees (*right*).

(*Below*) Concrete will fill the steel cage of reinforcing bars, once the team from Birse have installed the pipes and ducts in the correct positions.

(*Above*) As the steel skeleton rises, decking is laid across the beams, awaiting the concrete that will form a smooth, solid floor.

(*Top*) By 1998, the old power station has been stripped down to Herzog and de Meuron's basic design, with new windows either side of the chimney and the Light Beam skeleton rising above the parapet.

Jacques Herzog (*above, second from right*) visits the site regularly to monitor progress.

During 1998, two groups
of Tate staff visit other new
museums to compare notes.
In February, Frances Morris
and two colleagues visit the
Guggenheim in Bilbao (*top*)
and in November, Peter
Wilson and three other
members of the Tate team
visit the new Getty Museum
in Los Angeles (*bottom*).

As the Light Beam structure
is finished, teams of glaziers
fit the huge sheets of glass
that will bring light to
the Level 5 galleries, and
provide a stunning view for
restaurant goers.

The Grand Stair threads its way through the steel skeleton
during early 1998 (*left of large photo*). But Harry Gugger
(*inset right*) is unhappy about the small ledge (*inset left*)
– a mistake that it was too expensive to correct.

(*Above*) The major elements of the Turbine Hall are shrouded in scaffolding as the walls are installed and painted. On the left of the picture, the Switch House; above, the new rooflights; in the centre, the interior platform bridge, and on the right the wall between the Turbine Hall and the Boiler House.

Regular monthly meetings (*above right*) bring together the 'Tate team, Schal (the construction managers), Ove Arup (the engineers) and the architects to try to keep the project on target.

(*Below*) The early samples of frosted glass for the Turbine Hall bay windows fail to conceal the fluorescent light tubes and the Tate and the architects are unhappy.

(*Above*) As late as 1999, decisions are still being made about this area in the middle of the Turbine Hall on Level 1, where visitors will first arrive.

(*Top*) Outside the west end of Bankside, the concrete entrance ramp nears completion.

(*Bottom*) The ramp continues inside the building to carry people in a majestic sweep down to the basement level. The Boiler House wall is on the right, with one bay-window light-box partially completed.

The Turbine Hall from
the east end, with its bay
windows – making 'clouds
of light' – now completed.
The Level 2 bridge is in the
foreground, with the stairs
down to Level 1.

A gallery on Level 3, awaiting art, with its unpolished wooden
floor, 'unobtrusive' floor grilles, and no skirting boards.

'Tate accompli', with the Light Beam lit up at dusk.

deteriorated and would have been incapable of being salvaged anyway; so one could almost have assumed that what we would see on the Turbine Hall would have given similar results. We did carry out some initial core-drilling exploratory work some time ago. That didn't really indicate the problem of carbonation. It wasn't until relatively recently when we could get access up into the high spaces of the roof from the other side, which was done by means of cherry-pickers, quite large ones – there's only a couple in the country – about forty metres up in the air, that we could see what we were dealing with, and it became clear very quickly when the results came through that the carbonation was so bad that we really had to put plans in place to take the roof off.'

Blake's carefully choreographed programme of roof works was clearly going to have to go out of the window, while it looked as if the cost might go through the roof. 'Whilst they're demolishing the roof at the east end, we can probably only progress the substructure works on the west end, so we're having to juggle around with a series of contractors, but for obvious safety reasons there'll come an impasse when we get to the centre of the Turbine Hall roof, where we can't do any works in the adjacent Boiler House. So we're going to have to halt substructure works in total for about a week or so, and that's a major problem for us. It could be that the cost of the new roof demolition and the new roof construction is approaching £700,000.'

While the roof problems that had cropped up over the previous two years had all been dealt with satisfactorily, they had still been a blow to the project, and at a senior level there had been much behind the scenes work to minimize the impact on the schedule of each successive problem. At the centre of that process was Ron German, and as the solution to each problem was devised and put into operation, he had seen more and more of the 'float', the extra programme time that he kept up his sleeve for just this sort of problem, slip from his grasp, although he was determined to stick to the programme: 'All of the areas where there was the potential – "If we have another little hiccup somewhere along the line, we can overcome it" – it's much, much more difficult now. Everything is much, much more closely related in terms of trades. So I think – and obviously you wouldn't broadcast this in front of Schal just at this moment, but I think the answer is, we'll obviously work to the existing programme. But the risk to the end-date now is much greater and clearly we need to reflect that in our plans from the end of construction to the beginning of the opening of the gallery.'

On Friday 13 June 1997, the day the steel tenders were due to be opened, the Bankside site was unusually quiet. What was *meant* to be happening was the continuing treatment of the painted steelwork. Jacques Herzog would have liked to retain the green paint on the thick columns that rose from the Turbine Hall floor to the roof, but since the paint contained lead it all had to be blasted off and the columns repainted. It was Ian Blake's son's birthday that day, but he had had to leave home early, after a very brief celebration, and as he arrived at work he was given a piece of news that plunged him into gloom. 'Unfortunately, what we've found today is the presence of asbestos inside the building. We don't quite know how serious that is. Today's discovery was about six-thirty this morning. It's come about during the treatment of the existing steelwork, where we're blasting away at high level in the Turbine Hall and it's dislodged elements of asbestos that have been encapsulated in material and clogged behind existing framing at the top of the building. It's unfortunate because we've now had to clear the trades out of the building so we can do a proper analysis, and get down to the job of clearing the material. It's going to take what we estimate at the moment to be a good two to three weeks, and this is pretty bad news for us.'

It was a particularly unfortunate discovery, because the Schal team had thought things were going so well. The early removal of the Boiler House roof and the successful progress in removing the lead paint had all gone better than Blake had expected. Now they faced a delay which could be several weeks while they tried to find where the asbestos was coming from and decontaminate the building as quickly as possible.

For Blake, such a delay would just add to the problems they were already having with the programme, and as he went into the steel tenders meeting, he must have hoped that he wasn't going to find any unpleasant surprises when the bids were opened.

In a conference room that was part of Schal's offices on the south-west corner of the Bankside site, there were six packages lying on the table. One was a sizeable box and the rest were brown paper parcels. One by one, the team that was to assess these offers came into the room: Colin Berry, the Schal construction manager who would be concerned with the steel erection when the time came; Faith Wainwright, an engineer, and a colleague of hers who was a quantity surveyor from Ove Arup; and Ian Blake.

There was a well-tried system to the procedure that Schal followed during a meeting that lasted about three hours. They started by opening each package and making a note of the bottom-line figure on a summary sheet which each person then signed.

Opening the first one, Blake said, 'This one's from William Hare – £5,489,840.' There were looks around the table. This was a million pounds less than they had been prepared to pay. But no one was getting too excited yet.

'Hollandia – £6,455,195.' That was more like it.

'Watson –' Blake continued, opening the package Dave Burnsall had so carefully finished preparing the day before, 'elementary my dear – £6,085,285.'

'Ward Structures,' he went on, '£7,750,816.' Time for more puzzled looks, but this time because the figure was so high.

'Bit of a range, isn't it?' someone said.

'Rowen,' Blake ploughed on, '£6,094,154.' So now Watson was neck and neck with Rowen – Peter Emerson's company – but both were more than William Hare.

The final package, the large box, was from a company called Cleveland Bridge. 'My son's birthday today,' said Blake. 'This morning I was opening up things like this.' He ripped at the paper with some difficulty. '£6,491,514,' he announced, and the figure was filled into the summary sheet and then everyone signed it.

Now the first task was to find why the low bid was so low. The group suspected that William Hare's had missed something out, and Colin Berry and one or two of the others dug their way through the papers to see what they could find. It didn't take long to find two omissions. One was the fact that – like Watson – the price for the steel itself was too low because they had not quoted for low-sulphur steel. Another omission was the wooden balustrade on the Grand Staircase. Like Watson, they had been nonplussed by the problems of dealing with wood in a steel contract. Eventually, rectifying the omissions brought Hare into the same range as Watson and Rowen, rather than being the outright winner on price.

When the group looked at Watson's bid they discovered that they too had not quoted for low-sulphur steel. So while they were lower than Rowen at the moment, if Rowen had quoted for the correct type of steel, and if Watson's price had to be adjusted upwards, Rowen's price would be more favourable.

Ian Blake picked up Rowen's bid documents and flicked through, looking to see what they had done about low-sulphur steel. 'Ah!', he said, and read from the document: ' "We believe that scope exists for savings in the cost of raw material if the areas that require a low-sulphur content of steel can be identified, rather than a blanket requirement for the whole structure." So they've included for it. That could be a major turning point in the bid analysis.'

When the other bids were analysed in a similar way, all the original figures had to be adjusted, not always in an upward direction. Rowen's bottom line actually went down. At the end of the meeting, Blake looked back with some satisfaction at the preliminary results. 'It's been a very good day today. We've got a cost-plan figure of £7 million, and we've got a range that we're looking at at the moment between £5.49 million and £6.1. It's going to be somewhere between those two figures. In terms of Rowen's and Watson's price – well, particularly Rowen's price actually – it's going to come down by possibly £200,000, that sort of order. William Hare's price needs to be uplifted to take into account all the work they've missed. That could go up by as much as £300,000. I reckon both companies [Rowen and Hare] are going to meet in the middle.'

But price, although important, wasn't the sole consideration. There were a number of other factors that Schal needed to explore with each of the lowest bidders.

'There are all sorts of issues tied into the recommendation of the bid beyond the price. There's a big training commitment [on-the-job training for local people] that we're looking for; we're looking for adventurism, if you like, in terms of programme and sequencing beyond what we've actually identified ourselves. And we're looking for opportunities for time-saving, obviously, given our latest situation.' The day's discovery of asbestos was fresh in Blake's mind.

Although Watson's adjusted figure put them in the top three, Ian Blake wasn't hopeful about their prospects of getting any further. 'I feel that Watson in relation to William Hare and Rowen Structures will probably fall away within the next week or so. I think we'll find that William Hare and Rowen Structures will get quite close to each other in terms of value, and it'll be a case of getting the best from those two.' But Schal decided to include Watson among the companies called back for more detailed discussions, although it took some time for them to make that decision, and so Geoffrey Taylor, the person most likely to hear first if they were still in the contest, was on tenterhooks for a while.

'We reflected on the next action,' he said, looking back six weeks later. 'When to start pursuing it, when to start telephoning the client or even telephoning any other people who might hear what's going on. We did some of that, but the client wants to speak to you when he wants to speak to you, and therefore it's a fairly frustrating and long-winded job, and if he doesn't want to speak to you he's difficult to get hold of. So when eventually we did find him, the message was, "Come down and let's talk", so we were very reassured and comforted and, dare I say, confident. And the meeting was held, and we put on what we hoped was our best team and we answered an awful lot of technical questions. We also answered a lot of leading questions, some of which may have gone against us and some may not have done.'

Taylor explained that ignoring the client's desire for low-sulphur steel in the prices was deliberate. 'The low-sulphur steel was a contentious matter and we were not prepared to go along with that. Another one was the Grand Staircase, which we feel is a difficult job. It's easy to do it cheap and cheerful, but I think it would rebound, and we put in an awful lot of money in that side of the job, and we explained that to the client and we asked if we could have some kind of comfort [assurance of financial support] in that respect, but I feel that all these matters made us look as though we were being a little bit argumentative and negative. So we walked away from the meeting thinking that perhaps we hadn't been as positive as a client would want us to be.'

During these more detailed interviews, Schal had to be on guard for the possibility that someone might be so desperate for the work that they would deliberately leave themselves in a situation where, down the road as the project evolved, they would be unable to complete the work because they had underpriced it.

'One thing you don't want to get into is a horse deal,' Blake said. 'I'd like to think that with some comfort the figures are the price for the job, because at the end of the day what I'm looking for is a contractor who has got the right price in there, who's not going to be coming back looking for ways to get the money back in terms of claims against the Tate or anything of that nature, and I want the contractor to make money. I want the contractor to be happy, I want him to be productive. It's important to us, so at the end of the day we've got to make sure that the price they do put in is not something that they put in just to win the job and then try and get it back later on, as unscrupulous contractors try to.'

After two weeks of deliberations, and further discussions with the likeliest contenders, Schal decided who would get the Bankside steel contract. Meanwhile, Geoffrey Taylor and his colleagues heard nothing. 'In every job, there's a period when the phone doesn't ring, and for some two or three days the silence was deafening. I can't remember whether it was rumour or whether it was said at the meeting that there were three of us being interviewed. We believed that the three were going to be reduced to two or maybe one after these interviews and eventually I telephoned Ian Blake at Schal and he told me that we were not going to come down from three to two.'

On 1 July Ian Blake and his team were preparing themselves for a final decision meeting with representatives of William Hare and Rowen Structures.

'Tomorrow,' said Blake, 'it'll be a case of Hare's and Rowen's really putting their actual team who would build the job in front of us, giving a presentation of exactly how they going to build it: and we'll see how good they are. At the moment there's virtually no difference in cost, it's no longer really a cost issue, although that is important. What's perhaps most important now is that we finally select a company on the basis that they are the best contractor, who understand the job, can adopt a pragmatic approach to trying to regain some of the time we've lost – which is an important issue – and are in tune with the philosophy of this job.'

Rowen Structures were awarded the steel contract, for a price of less than £6 million. They had managed to keep the price low with a schedule change that was fed into one of the final meetings: that they could do the whole steel structure in fifteen weeks instead of twenty. Ian Blake was asked what he felt about the outcome of the steel tendering process. 'Well, ecstatic, I guess,' he said. 'We're now looking to let this package under £6 million. We've got a million pounds now that's going to pay for a lot of the problems we're currently experiencing.'

Watson's were of course disappointed. They really thought they were in with a chance – as indeed they were. Fortunately for Geoffrey Taylor, whose livelihood depended on bringing in projects to the company, about the time they heard that they'd failed to get the Tate contract they had a better piece of news about another project. 'We were very fortunate in that at about the same time we were bidding for a multi-storey office block down in Canary Wharf, and the phone *did* ring and we were awarded a job of similar proportion. At the risk of being disloyal, though it was certainly not as high-profile or as exciting perhaps, but a job working for Sir Norman Foster as architect is always quite a stimulating experience, so we shall look forward to that.'

There is little or no feedback in the construction business for companies whose bids fail. Asked if he would have done the same thing again, Taylor said, 'Yes, I think we probably would, dammit.'

Peter Emerson, managing director of Rowen Structures, was delighted that his company had got the Tate contract. It was a tricky job to carry out successfully – working inside old structures is always more difficult than erecting steel on a virgin site – but he thought he and his colleagues had set a realistic price and a tight but achievable schedule. And certainly Ian Blake was heartened by the fact that five weeks could be shaved off his overall construction schedule, already running several weeks behind.

And the potential delay was to get worse. Yet more asbestos was discovered on 1 July and no one was quite sure where it came from.

'We can only pin-point it to the central zone of the Turbine Hall,' Blake explained. 'We believe it's come from some material that's been trapped behind the steelwork and the blasting operations have somehow dislodged that, it's gone into the atmosphere, and hence we find it on the scaffold. We've also found it at the base of the chimney in the areas that we've got to sandblast, which means that we really ought to be checking out the whole of the chimney – in fact the whole steel structure right the way up to the top. We're going to get an abseiler in there to examine quite how bad that is. If it is [bad] we'll have to seal off the whole chimney and clean it whilst we're progressing with the works inside the main building.'

It took weeks more to get rid of the asbestos, which had settled over a much wider area of the building than people realized. The blasting work on the steel had blown the toxic fibres in a fine dust, and caused it to settle on the Turbine Hall floor and the scaffolding that had been erected for the paint-blasters to work on. Now the floor and the scaffolding had to be cleaned and Ian Blake suspected that the hundreds of wooden boards that formed the scaffolding platforms at each level would have to be destroyed. And added to Blake's scheduling worries were concerns about the extra cost.

'We've currently got about twenty asbestos strippers inside the building,' said Blake on 1 July, 'and we're working double shifts, so there's two teams to try and clear this up. They're also working weekends. The material itself is contaminated waste; it has to be bagged in a special way and has to go to licensed tips. To get that material to those tips is very expensive. Allied to which, because elements of asbestos have found their way on to deposits already in the building, for example the lead that was blasted off the steel, all the debris inside the building is deemed to be contaminated, and that's one of the major expenses. Added to which there's the delay to the project, which when you [add up the extra] designers' fees and the knock-on effects to other trades, it's significant. In order to try and mitigate those sorts of delays, one has to take extraordinary measures, and those measures tend to be expensive: extra screening; resequencing of works, all those sorts of things.'

Eventually, the effects of the failure to decontaminate Bankside before it was handed over were to cost about one and a half million pounds, money which came out of the Tate's contingency budget while they argued for the next three years over who would pay the final bill.

By the time the asbestos problem was dealt with, the work schedule had effectively been delayed by two months. Ironically for an event that came to a head on the day the steel tenders were being opened, it was Rowen's offer of an accelerated steel erection schedule which offered a saving of five weeks over what Schal had predicted, that the Tate team saw as a possible way to mitigate the effects of the asbestos problem on the overall programme. How wrong they were was to become apparent very soon after Rowen started work on-site.

14

A Narrow Escape

By the middle of 1997, the architects had spent more than two years working with the Tate team, moving from preliminary designs to more detailed drawings that paid respectful attention to the suggestions of the Tate. There were quite important differences between the competition design, used as a starting point, and the building that was being locked into place during 1997 by the imperatives of construction. One floor had gone, for example, as a result of the need for plant rooms. The Grand Staircase had emerged from a one-day meeting in Basel. The Turbine Hall wall had become solid rather than glazed. And there were many more minor changes in floor layout, escalators, and external buildings.

There was a rhythm about the process. As a result of Nick Serota's early concerns about Herzog and de Meuron's ability to control the project from Basel, they had agreed to establish a base in London. Harry Gugger spent more time on-site than Herzog, but Herzog still came to London for important meetings or events, monitoring day-to-day progress from his base in Basel. 'Harry holds everything in his hands,' Herzog said, describing the working method they had evolved. 'He deals with the local architects, and with [the Tate], on a daily basis, and I don't work on a daily basis on the project. I don't have to remember everything, and to keep everything in my head. We have regular meetings in the office [in Basel], led by Harry, and we talk about everything, every week – about every design issue – so that's like a common design approach. And if there's something where I feel there is a lack somewhere, or we have to design something new, I start doing drawings or sketches, so that's a new step. So the project doesn't always have the same intensity for myself. It's like in different stages, and Harry and myself come together and say, "Well, we have to make a step in terms of the landscaping", for example. Then we try to figure out what we can do. We show it to Pierre. We discuss it, and if I'm not happy with it I keep it and try to find out solutions myself.'

Sheppard Robson, the firm of English architects appointed on the insistence of Serota to ensure that Herzog and de Meuron's lack of experience of British construction wouldn't penalize the project, had appointed John Hendry, a young, slightly anxious-looking architect, as their main point of contact during the first two years of the project. He took a rather jaundiced – if admiring – view of Herzog's working methods. 'Jacques is involved in almost a superficial way on the project. It's quite strange: he tends to put very concentrated time into the project, not over a long period of time – he jumps in and out of projects. And Harry's there very much to make sure that Jacques has the influence on the project because the view in our office is that Jacques is very much the ideas man, and that he comes in sometimes disrupting everybody for a period of time.' It was this process of disrupting everybody, whether carried out by Jacques or by the other Basel architects, that had led to some of the early angst Schal and the Tate had experienced over continual changes in design when the drawings were meant to have been completed.

'One of the reasons that the problems went away,' Hendry said in mid 1997, 'is that Jacques realized that he couldn't keep coming and trying to influence things, so Harry was given the remit to carry forward the design as it stood.'

Herzog's working methods as seen close up by Hendry in the early days of the project had something of the painter or sculptor about them. 'I wouldn't say he does things in a kind of rational way. He very much comes up with inspirational ideas almost instantaneously. It is very interesting to watch him. He was coming into the studio [in London] maybe one day a week for maybe a couple of hours in the morning, a couple of hours in the afternoon, and he would attack specific areas of the building; and it was more a question of him saying, "I don't like the way you've done this, I think we should have a look at it again and make it better," than necessarily him coming in and saying, "This is the way I think we should do this". He uses the team to actually develop ideas. And then we'll stop when he thinks the idea has developed sufficiently.'

For Harry Gugger, Sheppard Robson were the most suitable of the companies Herzog and de Meuron had interviewed when they were told by the Tate they had to have a British associate, but still for the Swiss firm they lacked something. Gugger summed this up by saying, 'They are not really willing to break their heart for architecture' – by which he meant that in the search for solutions to problems they sometimes stopped too soon and ended up with a solution that was maybe not the best architecturally.

The Tate had always liked Herzog and de Meuron's passion for art and artists, and Herzog himself would often be drawing as he thought about a problem. But these were not the neat figurative sketches of some architects, where a recognizable architectural shape or feature was tried out in several different ways on paper, rubbed out here or there, changed and refined until it looked like a piece of a building. Herzog's sketches, some of which were exhibited in New York, are along different lines and seem to spring from a different source. 'Drawing suspends thinking,' he wrote on one, above a charcoal drawing of woven slats like a garden fence panel. Many of Herzog's buildings have the forced simplicity of a sketch. If you only use a thick stick of charcoal and rough paper you are compelled to think in broad blocks and wide curves, coarse-grained textures and simple shapes. And even as the architectural plans evolve, a sketch of a corner, a surface or an aperture can lead to a new and better idea.

Even the construction management team, the people for whom the apparent indecisiveness and mind-changing produced the most problems and anxieties, sometimes found themselves carried along by the sheer energy of the architects' working methods. There were times when Ian Blake actually enjoyed the working relationship with the two architects. 'I've been at a meeting when all of a sudden Harry stood on his head,' Blake suddenly said one day. 'Apparently that's yoga or something, I don't know. He just decided he needed to stretch his legs. I was also at a meeting where – I'll never forget it – where Jacques decided that it was time for him to go for a run along the Embankment and so he did. You know you're dealing with some strange people, but it makes it fun. Building should be fun after all.'

Peter Wilson witnessed Herzog's break for freedom as well. 'None of us will forget it,' he said. 'Jacques needed a break and we sat around for over thirty minutes waiting. Eventually he was spotted sitting in the gardens getting over his run.'

During 1997 a series of events occurred that could have seriously soured the relationship between the Tate and the architects. Herzog and de Meuron was one of ten architecture firms invited to submit designs for a new extension to the Museum of Modern Art in New York. (Rem Koolhaas was the only other one of the ten who had been in the Tate's final thirteen.) It was an invitation that, for them, marked an important stage in the increasingly high profile they were acquiring in the world of modern architects. To the Tate people the height of the profile was partly due to them, to the fact that Herzog and de Meuron were designing the largest new modern art gallery in the world. Peter Wilson was not surprised that they had been invited and he felt – or at least hoped – that the Tate Gallery of Modern Art project would not suffer if they eventually won the competition. 'You wouldn't need to be a fortune teller to know that they would be asked, given the profile of our project. My personal view is that we got them first; ours is much the most interesting and high-profile project; and that however much interest and involvement they would have in doing a project in New York, ours would be more interesting to them and so we need not worry if they were appointed to do that project. Bankside wouldn't suffer.'

Like any prudent client, the Tate had looked carefully at the situation early on in the project, when it became clear that, as with any architect, they could not insist on the exclusive services of Herzog and de Meuron. 'We've taken a very responsible approach to managing risk,' Wilson said. 'And we've always looked at what the risks are, from people leaving the project, to things that could go wrong. And since Herzog and de Meuron getting another project has to be a risk to us, whatever major project it was, we have to consider it seriously and make sure that the understanding that we have with the practice is kept, once there are distractions around. But first of all our project has got to the point where we're in detailed design. The opportunity for Jacques to come to the UK and change something that makes a substantial difference to the project is past, I think, or nearly past, anyway, and certainly would be by the time they were doing any work on the Museum of Modern Art in New York if they got the project. And I can't see that the resource at that level is going to be lacking, or a threat.'

Harry Gugger was giving what sounded very much like the party line: 'The chance is very little, first of all, and it depends very much on what happens on this competition. I don't think that MoMA will announce just one architect as their architect. I think it will be in collaboration with another or maybe even three architects, and then again I think it depends very much on the design approach. I don't think it will be a huge problem. I mean Jacques and Pierre are in America already now two days a week, because of Harvard – they are teaching there and this could be incorporated in these trips. But we are far from being the architects of MoMA, so we even don't discuss this issue at the moment.'

But Nick Serota was not amused, and there was what one observer described as 'a lot of toing and froing between Nick and Jacques'. Serota felt that Herzog and de Meuron should devote all their attention to the Tate at this crucial stage. He also felt a bit miffed that they were going after another modern art gallery, one that was a rival to the Tate for publicity and, more importantly, for funds. There were only a certain number of rich donors in the world; the Tate was still short of its target; and Serota was good at squeezing dollars out of US benefactors and didn't want their funds to be diverted nearer to their home.

John Hendry at Sheppard Robson felt that if Herzog and de Meuron thought that the MoMA project would benefit from what they had learnt working on the Tate, they might be in for an unpleasant surprise. 'If they win it, they'll find life a lot tougher doing something in New York than they are in London. The project management and the systems that exist here are a lot more lenient on the designer than they will be [in the US]. There's been a very sympathetic approach to the way that Herzog and de Meuron do things, and I think the Tate wouldn't have taken them on as an architect if they weren't prepared to allow that to happen.'

After the ten architects had submitted outline schemes for the

MoMA project, the field was narrowed to three in April – a Japanese architect, Yoshio Taniguchi, and two Swiss architects: Bernard Tschumi, who is a US resident, and Herzog and de Meuron. The concern among the Tate Trustees and Serota rose, but there were also signs that Herzog and de Meuron were aware of this and tried to allay their fears.

Speaking in July 1997, Serota said, 'We have managed to develop a way of working with them on our project which has meant that our project and the MoMA project have been kept discrete from one another. Jacques has been even more assiduous in attending meetings here during the past two-and-a-half to three months than he might have been otherwise, and from our point of view I don't think that the MoMA competition has in any way affected progress on our scheme. There was a very difficult moment in January and February, at a moment when it appeared that the design work on our project was beginning to run behind schedule, and I was undoubtedly concerned that if their attention was taken on to the MoMA project we would suffer even more. But I think Jacques has managed to cope with it very well and I think it's been very profitable, the way in which we've been able to work together over the past two or three months.'

Behind the scenes, however, the picture wasn't quite as rosy as Serota painted it. Before one Tate Trustees' meeting, shortly after the news that Herzog and de Meuron were on the MoMA shortlist, Serota got together with a small group in a side room for a crisis discussion. He was late for the main meeting and, according to one observer, 'was tight-lipped throughout'. By objecting to Herzog and de Meuron trying for the MoMA project, it seemed as if Serota had got himself into a no-win situation. If Herzog and de Meuron were to get it, his fears would be realized; if they didn't get it, it would seem as if MoMA had rejected the Tate's architect and therefore the Tate. If it had been any other museum or project, Serota would probably not have been so worked up about it, but MoMA was different.

One of the Trustees, Michael Craig-Martin, an artist, was ambivalent about the whole business. 'I have to say that I thought, as an artist, if you're offered another wonderful project, it's very difficult to say no to it, and in that sense that part of me says, "I'm not surprised". On the other hand, as the client, the whole situation was very unfortunately timed because it couldn't have occurred at a more sensitive moment in terms of the planning. If it had happened six months later it wouldn't have seemed like such an important matter. The fact is that it came absolutely at the central point of the design problems. This is a vastly greater project than anything that Herzog and de Meuron had done before. They'd had some experience of exhibition space design, but on a terribly modest level. Now they have learned a fantastic amount from the Tate by doing this project, and I think this has been true of everything about this project: the people involved have tended to be young. I mean, Harry is a young man.'

Not all the Trustees were concerned about the issue. Janet de Botton said, 'There were some Trustees that were very worried about it, but I wasn't.'

Peter Wilson was close to Serota throughout the project and had worked with him for some years, so he was a pretty reliable interpreter of Serota's motives and preoccupations. 'Nick's point of view was that it was a distraction for Jacques when he ought to be treating our project as the one and only great museum project that he was involved with, and that he shouldn't be distracted by going to one of our major competitors, because that's what they are. Nick also worried that because Herzog and de Meuron represent a particular strand in modern architecture and that we had had the vision and foresight to choose an up-and-coming – Jacques would probably say "established" – practitioner in that particular genre, that if MoMA chose Herzog and de Meuron, we would be in some way slightly diminished in some respects by the fact that we weren't the only ones who'd done it. And that wasn't just a PR thing or a "we-did-it-first" kind of thing, but Nick thought might actually reflect upon some kinds of fund-raising in the United States. I didn't have the same view of it. I felt that, if you choose an up-and-coming practice you must expect them to get attracted by other people. I felt wholly flattered that MoMA put our choice on their list. I didn't see it negatively. But I don't have Nick's insight into these kinds of issues. I felt we could have done more to help Herzog and de Meuron rather than spend our entire time being concerned that they might point in another direction. I also thought that since it was clear that Harry wasn't going to disappear from sight to do the MoMA project, that actually having Harry focused on it and Jacques concerned about other things might make life slightly easier on occasions for us, because Jacques has this tendency to parachute in and have big ideas.'

While Herzog and his colleagues back in Basel somehow found the time to jet back and forth to New York for meetings and other competition activities, and the Tate waited to see if their fears would be realized, other members of the wider project team got on with their jobs.

For most of the week of 21 July 1997, community relations officer George Cochrane was busy with the final preparations for the Tate Fête, a summer fair organized by the Tate to reinforce community spirit in the Bankside area and enhance the process of consultation. The fête was one indication of the care the Tate took to be seen to get on with their neighbours. But Cochrane also had his hands full with a range of community activities, designed to keep the local residents on the side of the new Tate rather than against it. Newsletters, regular meetings and exhibitions, tours of the changing building, hotlines, careful attention to working hours, window-cleaning – there was almost nothing the Tate wouldn't do to allay or forestall residents' anxieties.

At the end of the week, after several days of baking sunshine, the area around Bankside was under grey clouds and drizzle. But undeterred, local artists like Belinda Sosinwicz set to work. Her task was to clothe the plane trees on the edge of the site in giant knitted cardigans. The Tate had allocated £15,000 to the fête, and Sosinwicz was one of dozens of locals who were setting up stalls and displays as the grey clouds gathered overhead. The fête was held around a sunken grass area on the south side of the power station, and small children ran up and down the paved sloping sides.

The Bankside team had been encouraged to turn out in strength for the fête and to bring their families. Even the project manager Dawn Austwick was here, a few weeks from giving birth. In spite of the worsening weather, they were determined to soldier on. Nick Serota, in black mac, strode around the stands under a dripping umbrella and did his best to look happy. Then, before it was time for him to open the fête officially, Austwick and Serota conferred about the speech he was to deliver and decided to switch the opening to inside the visitor centre.

As the rain got worse, everything moved indoors, and dripping people crowded into the already crowded visitor centre, where the traditional middle-class activity of face-painting took up a modern art theme.

Cochrane's spirits were undampened by the downpour and the disappointing turnout. He was an old enough hand to know that power and influence don't always depend on numbers, and that someone in his job had to rely on a different kind of drip-drip-drip effect from a rained-out summer fête. 'Every Thursday in the last ten weeks, the local residents have been involved in designing the space for the fête, in looking at the amount of stalls we'll have, sorting out who's going to be performing, the whole of the planning and the organization. So it's about bringing people together. And that's quite a new experience for them, as it is for us. But there were still people, fewer than when I started, who said, "Oh, it's all PR – you're a PR person." And, to be honest, if I was here to do PR, I wouldn't be here, because I'm not interested in that. One of the things about working with communities is that it is a bit like a jack-in-the-box, I always think. Once you've got the lid off, it's really difficult to get it back on. And that's why I think that Bankside will always be a different gallery to Millbank, in a sense. I think Millbank's obviously going to change. But the fact that I'll have been working with the local community for four years; that we've now got an education worker who'll be working with the community for two-and-a-half years – that will inform the whole way the gallery operates and the whole sort of approach that the gallery has to the area around it.'

During the summer and autumn of 1997, there remained a suspicion in the Tate that the architects' minds were not always fully focused on their needs, if only because Jacques Herzog actually appeared more often than before, in an attempt to persuade the Tate that MoMA was not a distraction. On 8 December, in a unanimous decision, the Museum of Modern Art in New York announced that it had awarded the commission for its new extension to the Japanese architect, Yoshio Taniguchi. Jacques Herzog was not amused. He didn't like the winning scheme – which was not surprising. What *was* surprising was that Herzog felt deceived by the friendliness and interest that the assessors had shown in the final interviews, and he obviously misinterpreted that as an indication that Herzog and de Meuron had won, rather than as the normal tactics of anyone interviewing someone for a job or a contract, who tries not to give away his feelings at the time.

Looking back when the MoMA competition had been decided, de Botton summed up her feelings about the events. 'I thought that MoMA would have been probably ill-advised to take them,' she said, 'because it would have meant that their scheme would have been compared and judged by ours. Bankside is a building that we can do – more or less – what we want with, and the project at the Museum of Modern Art is nothing like that. But I didn't think that they'd get it, and I was completely convinced that if they did get it, that Bankside would come out better, so I didn't find it bothersome. Nick was worried about a different aspect of it, which was the involvement and concentration and logistical possibilities of running both jobs, for a group of architects who are based in Switzerland.'

Serota gave his interpretation of how the MoMA assessors had come to decide against Herzog and de Meuron. 'From what I know of the final decision-making process at MoMA, Herzog and de Meuron were in there as a very serious contender at the final stage. The fact that they were working for the Tate was not held against them in any respect. And I don't think the final decision was taken, as one or two people have suggested, on the grounds that, "Well, Herzog and de Meuron are working for the Tate and, therefore, MoMA New York needed to take another architect to have a unique position in the world as a museum of fine arts, architecture and design." I think it was on the merits of the schemes that were put forward by Taniguchi, by Tschumi and by Herzog and de Meuron that Taniguchi finally emerged as the chosen architect. I wasn't entirely surprised by that because I think that the Americans and those people commissioning an extension to that particular building were always likely to go for a solution that was a form of refined modernism rather than one which was working slightly counter to some of the precepts of modernism. I mean, there is something quite frequently awkward or, if not jarring, at least unexpected about the solutions that Herzog and de Meuron provide. And it's one of the things that attracted us to them as architects. In the circumstances of New York, that kind of disjunction could appear more jarring against the background of a very smooth, lean building of the kind that the Museum of Modern Art currently has. And so there was always going to be an inclination to go for, as it were, a velvet glove, which is what I think Taniguchi is a master at.'

One thing the whole affair highlighted was the way in which – in spite of just failing to get the MoMA contract – Herzog and de Meuron were being catapulted into the ranks of world architects. And some of this was Serota's doing.

'I was relieved,' Serota said, 'in that I think that our Trustees have made an enormous investment in these relatively untried, untested architects. And one of the benefits of that investment will be the fact that we have a unique and singular building, and had the museum chosen them it would have been less so. I think I'm also relieved for Jacques and Harry, because I have a great regard for them as architects and I think for the long-term development of their practice, it's going to be much more healthy for them that they're not doing two great museums of modern art, rather than a museum of modern art and as they're now doing, a cinema complex in Basel, the Laban Centre in Deptford, and a whole range of other projects that will broaden their vocabulary and experience. It will leave them in 2002 and 2003 in a much stronger position as a practice than if they'd taken on the Modern and then had to strain to complete our project and also dig deep into themselves to create a museum in New York. They would have had to say no to all kinds of other projects and I think, in the long term, they'll benefit.'

15

Grey and Red

In late September 1997 the east end of the building was ready for concrete to be poured. This was really the last stage in a complex series of activities to prepare the floor for the massive steel superstructure that would have to be assembled to hold the six floors of the main building. Although the original power station had a foundation slab, this was riddled with voids and tunnels and nobody really knew enough about them to calculate the strength of the floor at the places where columns would have to sit, so the engineers had decided to lay a new concrete 'raft' on top.

A network of steel reinforcing bars was being assembled across the floor, forming a mesh of horizontal and vertical bars through which the concrete would flow. The solid, reinforced slab would have to contain ducts and pipes and cables that would be embedded in the floor in perpetuity to carry building services such as water, drainage, power and so on. Before the concrete was poured those pipes and ducts had to be positioned in space, suspended on wires from the reinforcing mesh, until the concrete was poured around them and held them tight. Because there would be no further access to those facilities, it was important to make sure that they were not blocked and that they were connected in the right way. If something were to go wrong once the gallery was up and running, there would be some extremely expensive digging up to be done, and it might even be that there would be no way to correct it.

The company that got the contract for the concrete was called Birse, and its site agent was Paul Hewlett. In the early days of the project he was a young man with a spring in his step, looking forward to a really interesting project. 'Like most people, when I first came to the site and actually viewed the building, I was pretty gob-smacked.' Hewlett was sitting in his Portakabin at the east end of the site. It was 23 September 1997, and he and his team had spent six or seven weeks preparing the ground for the concrete-pouring. 'When you stand on the outside on the viewing galleries looking through, it's such a huge space, and you take a step back and say, "How are we going to do that?" I'm pleased to be here. I really like the building, I think it's fantastic; well built by our forefathers.' Only the fact that he lived in Dover – 'it's a bloody long way to travel' – took the edge off his excitement; that plus the fact that a complex job like this presented a lot of opportunities for error. 'Numerous things can go wrong,' he said, 'things that cost us amounts of money, and would be vast problems. If we're halfway through the concrete pour and the pump breaks down, or the concrete plant breaks down, that's when we have to really kick in. We can't just leave one of these things half done. There's £15,000 worth of concrete in a bay.'

Concrete behaves in a very unforgiving way and has to be handled carefully. It arrived on-site in a non-stop stream of trucks, about fifty a day, each containing about five cubic metres. These were backed up to a pump, which had to push this thick mixture of stones, cement and water through a pipe a hundred feet long. At the other end, the mixture was poured where it was needed, to surround the steel bars that give it strength. As well as solidifying, the concrete undergoes chemical changes after it's been sitting around for a while. If this happens halfway through a pour it could affect the strength of the whole slab.

Graham Bennett was in charge of quality control for that day's concrete-pouring. He is a man with unexpected depths. With a dead-pan expression, and choosing his words carefully, he explained what he thought of the job. 'It's a firm foundation on which to base my life, I believe,' he said. 'In the short time I've been with the company I've already had two pay rises and that compares very favourably with the dole, or working part-time for three pounds an hour as a telesales assistant for a double glazing company. Extremely favourable to either of those options.'

Birse is a company that has attracted a lot of attention in the construction industry through what could be described as a 'born again' approach to the business. Peter Birse is a very rich Christian and apparently said recently in public what one industry insider summarized as, 'We've been bastards'. Among the sins laid at their door by others was the fact that they took ages to pay their bills; but one sin that Mr Birse wanted to atone for was the fact that the company wasn't feminine enough. This was partly a reflection of the fact that, like most other construction companies, they employed a very low proportion of women, and partly a laudable desire to get more feminine values into relationships between client and contractor, employer and employees, foremen and workers.

Paul Hewlett explained how this worked in his job. 'Rather than us guys just banging the desk and thinking we know best, women are far more perceptive on a lot of things. This policy affects almost everything I do, in my working life and in my personal life as well. Relationships with my colleagues in this office; the building of the team environment, for example, here with Schal and Ove Arup. The way that we approach that these days, it's so different from how things used to be. We're not confrontational at all. We look to be proactive on things. We try to be open and honest with each other. We try to work with integrity, and it's a good way of being.'

But Peter Wilson at the Tate was cynical about Birse's new 'feminine values'. 'I think that it was clear that they'd done *something* to themselves that meant that they felt that they were now embodying these principles, but it seemed to me that the only time that I saw the principles at work was when they were asking me to throw away good business sense and be fair and reasonable and pay them whatever they asked me. And from what I've read in the construction press, there are a lot of other people that don't think they've changed either.'

On Wednesday 24 September, the day after Hewlett had been so upbeat about the project at Bankside, his ability to be non-confrontational was to be sorely tested when Schal and the Tate were infuriated by two silly – and avoidable – mistakes that occurred during concrete pouring.

The concrete is poured in separate rectangular areas, enclosed by wooden 'shutters'. These are like a fence over a metre high around the network of reinforcing rods. When the concrete is poured it is the shutters that hold it back and form the sides of the slab. On this particular day, as the poured concrete pushed against one part of the shuttering, it gave way. Someone in Birse had failed to put in the short vertical rods that were meant to support that part of the shuttering against the pressure of the concrete. As the concrete hardened there was a sad little tongue of it encroaching on the adjacent area that still had to be poured.

As if that wasn't bad enough, when they came to pour the next section of slab, the concrete pump (subcontracted from another company) broke halfway through the pour. Graham Bennett knew that these pumps were temperamental anyway. 'We've used this company several times, and several times there was a problem with the pour, usually caused by the machinery. And at one time I thought, "Well, we may have to try and struggle on with the pump that we had originally," and so I thought if we've got to live with it, I'll personally name it the *African Queen*, after the river steamer Humphrey Bogart managed to nurse all the way up the Zambesi or whatever river it was. Some of our operatives were not dissimilar to him, in that they knew the pump inside out, and could sometimes make it continue to pour, but not always.'

Birse had an arrangement with another contractor to supply a replacement pump within half an hour, but this arrangement broke down too and as the concrete slowly hardened over several hours, Birse and Schal looked on with horror. Because of the halt in concrete-pouring the area on the bottom of the building was looking like a concrete chamber of horrors. First, the displaced shutters and extra tongue of concrete. Now a whole portion of the slab, half-poured so that at one end it was at the correct height and then, some way along, the height dropped in a gradient that left a wedge of concrete like a piece of Cheddar cheese.

As the concrete solidified and the pump failed to arrive it was clear that it would not be possible to pour more concrete on top of the existing material. The slab was part of a very thick base for the steel skeleton that would carry the galleries. It had been designed to take the weight of seven floors of building and its strength depended on its integrity. The individual particles of concrete lock together very firmly as they cool and dry out, and they are further strengthened by the embedded network of steel bars. But once the concrete has hardened, that binding effect no longer applies to any concrete that is poured on top of it. Effectively there would be the equivalent of a geological fault at the interface between the old hardened concrete and the newly poured material.

There were two possible solutions. One, favoured by Ian Blake in his darkest moment of the week, was to insist that Birse chip out all the hardened concrete. This would have meant chipping between and around the network of steel reinforcement bars, just like trying to remove all the honey from a honeycomb without damaging any of the wax cell walls. It was fortunate for the blood pressure of the Birse executives, and Paul Hewlett, that this suggestion was never put to the company. Instead, the engineers devised a scheme to embed vertical steel reinforcing rods in the hardened concrete before pouring the new stuff, so as to anchor the two lots together. They were only happy to allow this once they had worked out that it would support enough transverse shear force, so that any sideways forces would not cause the slab to crack along the fault.

Paul Hewlett no longer had his usual cheery smile when he spoke about Black Wednesday. He had learnt a lesson: 'Always have more than one pump on-site. It's a hard lesson to learn, in that we were bit, and bit very hard. It's cost us a lot of money. What lesson *can* you learn? If we have two pumps and the two break down, if you had three pumps and three break down . . . I thought that we'd covered every angle that we needed to. Obviously we hadn't.'

What everyone in Schal was trying to avoid as they wrestled with the concrete problems was that in years to come, when the concrete slab was embedded under seven floors of rooms, public spaces and galleries, some weakness might become apparent which had to be dealt with at huge expense. 'If anything does go wrong with this slab,' said Graham Bennett, 'it's going to be more than a million pounds to put it right. You can put a million on a million. And the final amount will be a lot.' Then, in a fine example of Birse management-speak he said, 'But hopefully, due to our particular attitude to work that exists within the organizational culture first, we're going to hand this product over with zero defects, which is the attitude of our company, actually, that's what we promote: "Right first time, every time", which is why this was a particular blow.'

'I travel five hours by train to work here every day,' Paul Hewlett said, 'and this sort of thing just makes me sick.' In his wallet, Hewlett had a small printed card that had been issued to Birse's employees. It carried a series of mottoes and he described how at times, if things became stressful in a meeting, he would take it out and read through it before reacting. It read:

> Birse:
> We are:
> In integrity
> Brave and learning
> In open and honest communications
> Profitable on all our jobs
> Paid for what we do when we do it
> Dealing with issues at the speed of light

'By referring to that card,' Hewlett explained, 'as I did the other day, the standards on it are quite clear. "Being integral." "Open and honest communication." That's OK. "To be brave and learning." Well, I'm certainly learning, with what happened with the pump and the subsequent dealings on it. "Deal with issues faster than the speed of light." We did, we dealt with it. You know, it was a challenge, it was there, and we dealt with it. And one of my favourite ones is, "To be paid for what we do, on time." Many a time you carry out work and it's months down the line before you even see the recompense. So, yeah, they really did help me through those couple of days.'

One small delay to the concrete that was not Birse's fault was caused by a Tate party to introduce the great and the good to the interior of the building now that construction was under way.

On the afternoon of 7 October 1997, a group of party organizers had put up a plastic roof over the east end of the Turbine Hall. When it sagged with the water from a passing rain shower, men with brooms pushed the water off the plastic from underneath. Strange electronic music emanated from speakers and echoed around the walls and roof.

At about six-thirty the guests began to arrive and were issued with hard hats and reflective vests before being shown down to the basement level and given a glass of champagne. There was no knowing who was there, from a distance. The view from the bridge that crossed

from the south entrance to the Boiler House was of about 300 identical
hard hats milling around, and only by going down to the floor and
walking right up to someone was it possible to tell Peter Mandelson
from Dawn Austwick.

Ian Blake was there, quietly proud of the fact that his team had
reached this point in the construction without too many major problems. And the party itself had added a little pressure that had helped
to get the building to its current state. 'The milestone has been the
fact that in the last week we've taken the Turbine Hall roof off, and
literally days ago the far end of the Turbine Hall was full of tons and
tons of rubble which was contaminated. You'd never have thought
that a situation like we're standing in today could ever take place. So,
a tremendous effort by everybody to get to this stage: remarkable.'
But he wasn't complacent. 'The most critical thing we must do, we
must start the main steelwork erection in the Boiler House on the first
of December. That is a critical, psychological milestone to achieve.
We must get to that point, and we're struggling.'

Blake's optimism and enthusiasm were a good sign, considering the
troughs he had occasionally been through in the previous two years,
from fears that the architects would never stop designing, through
the asbestos problems, to the problems with concrete. He and his
colleagues knew that the steel erection, due to start in under two
months, would have to go smoothly. He also knew that this work
had not got off to a good start as Rowen's had already begun to get
behind with the detailed drawings that were essential to fabricate the
steel. This was something that in the normal course of events would
be expected to sound a warning note in Blake's head. But there was
one other thing Blake knew on this night of the celebrations, something
few others knew and something that made him less worried about
the steel than he should have been. Blake himself would not have to
worry about the project for much longer. He was about to leave the
Tate Gallery of Modern Art at Bankside.

In January 1997, when the design parameters of the Turbine Hall
wall were solidifying, even if the colour was still undecided, the Tate's
Head of Gallery Services, Peter Wilson, had realized that, having
worked with the architects for two years, he still didn't understand
their overall vision for the building. 'It sounds obvious if you go back

and look at the plans, that the galleries are smooth and white and simple and box-like, as we always anticipated they would be; as Herzog and de Meuron's earlier studio and gallery designs show. And it's also clear that the public spaces, the public circulation – inspired by the fact that the Turbine Hall itself is a rougher kind of space – are more intricate, less highly finished, darker, and the texture of them is kind of rougher. And that's a bit like the Ricola factory that we visited of theirs. But I only recently came to an understanding of how that's actually meant to be a language for the building. The black, darker, rougher spaces are the roots, the blood vessels, if you like, and then the organs are the galleries, the display spaces, and other more finished and coloured spaces – the restaurant or the seminar rooms. And I actually realized for myself how important that is to them, and realized that I'd had a particular concern about how light and airy the Turbine Hall should feel, but that that's actually not what they're aiming for. And I've also complained bitterly about only lighting the Turbine Hall from the new objects that Herzog and de Meuron have designed into the Boiler House façade. I'm probably guilty of not having understood – or they're guilty of not having articulated to us clearly enough – how important that is to them in the overall scheme of things.'

Wilson's 'blood and organs' analogy was to be reflected in a design review meeting that took place in December 1997, when the 'heart' of the building, in Herzog and de Meuron's view, was on the agenda and when another controversial colour was discussed. The main design issue was to do with the decor of the auditorium, a large lecture theatre on Level 2, next to the café, and visible through a glass wall from the Turbine Hall. There were three Trustees at the meeting, two of them artists and men – Bill Woodrow and Michael Craig-Martin – and the art-collector Janet de Botton, accepting cheerfully the role of Trustees' representative of womankind. Both Herzog and Gugger were there, along with Nick Serota.

Harry Gugger kicked off the meeting by showing two sample auditorium seats covered with orange fabric, in the colour the architects proposed for carpets and seats. They had all seen an earlier version at a previous design review, and the architects had been sent off to try again.

'We like this strong colour, and we also have strong colours for the shop, for the café, for other public areas – but different colours. So, the colours should play a key role there, and they should be very meaningful, very thoughtful. We can discuss today, especially because we have two artists among us, that maybe one alternative is to leave the orange for the chairs and the carpet, because we always wanted to have this common colour of something that you sit on and walk on, because this helps you be seated. However, what we could discuss is whether the walls and the ceiling could have another colour, also a strong colour ... We want to have something very warm, very warm. We don't want necessarily to shock. This is not the idea.'

Gugger pointed to various fabric samples in different shades of orange, pinned to the wall.

Serota got up and went and sat in one of the seats.

'We've widened it a little bit so it's quite comfortable if someone sits next to you,' Gugger said.

'You mean Peter?' Serota said. The bulky Peter Wilson had not yet arrived. 'I think if Janet were here [she was also late] she would immediately say the fabric is too hairy, much too hairy, because when we saw it before she said it's just very uncomfortable for someone who has tights, or whatever, to sit on.

'Stockings,' said Bill Woodrow, one of the artist-Trustees.

'Stockings or tights or whatever. She just said it's much too rough.'

After some discussion of the cost of the seats, Serota said, 'We've always said right the way through this project that we want to have enough money to be able to have real quality in the parts of the building that people touch. And this is a paramount example of a part of the building that people touch. In fact, I can't think of another part of the building that people will touch more with their bodies than this bit, unless they all lie down on the floor.'

At this point Janet de Botton came in and was ushered to one of the chairs. 'It's better than some of the samples that we were shown last time. It's not as uncomfortable. The thing is, I think it's different, isn't it, for women, than for men, sitting on these chairs. When women sit on these chairs, they're itchy and unpleasant.'

After more discussion of the colour of the seat fabric, Serota dealt with broader issues of colour. 'There is the question of the colour palette throughout the whole museum.' He turned to Herzog. 'You yourself said a few moments ago that you wanted to make these more social areas within the building feel very welcoming and in quite strong contrast to the rest of the building. And therefore, we want colours that are "contemporary" colours, but I think it's quite important that they shouldn't be too sharp and harsh or too acid. That doesn't mean to say that they have to be chocolate and beige and turquoise – as it were, seventies colours. But I think that they do need to be welcoming and soft. And at the moment, my feeling is that if you see this against the black steelwork and the dark grey, and you will see this orange glowing at you from the Turbine Hall, you will get this feeling of – not yellow and black, but it's tending in that direction.'

At this point, Bill Woodrow came up with an observation that was to shift the discussion towards the red end of the spectrum. 'The analogy of the heart of the building is quite interesting, in terms of colour, and to actually use that to go much more towards blood colour. Because this colour' – he indicated the orange samples – 'is – well it's not seventies for me, it's sixties, and . . .'

'No, *I* think this is sixties too –' said Serota, 'I said I don't want to have a seventies feel either.'

'I'll put my beads away,' said Woodrow. 'It's got too much white in it. Also, it's sort of harsh and . . .'

'I was just going to say I have exactly the same feeling,' said Michael Craig-Martin, the other artist-Trustee. 'I think that the general direction of the orange seems to be OK, but it should go more towards red. You don't want to go towards a maroon, that kind of deep red. But real red, real blood red.'

'I would be very happy with more red,' said Herzog.

'I also think we should get it darker than this orange,' said Serota. 'I actually think that will become dirty very quickly and you'll get hand marks along the top of the seats.'

'The problem with the orange colour –' Bill Woodrow said, 'I don't know if this is just a cultural thing, but in this country it has connotations of school – primary school and secondary school.'

'Really?' said Gugger.

'This particular colour, yes.'

The group discussed whether the walls of the auditorium should be the same colour as the carpet and seats, and what strong colours should be used for some of the other 'social' spaces, like the shop and the education area.

At this point, Serota made one of the broad summaries he is very good at producing at certain points in meetings. 'At the moment,' he said, 'we have the grey concrete floor in the Turbine Hall. We have a very dark steel skeleton structure, and a lighter grey on the walls. We have glass, and we have areas of wooden floor visible as you come in. So, that's all a fairly neutral palette, although some warmth will come from the wooden floor. Then it's a question about how you play with the colour beyond that. I know, for instance, the staircase has always been described as black but, actually, the staircase is a very important signal of communication through the building. If you make it black, you're actually taking blackness right the way through the building, in a certain way. There could be an argument for making that a colour.'

'But it is a steel structure, and painting steel with a strong colour is very problematic . . .' said Herzog.

'Very seventies,' said Serota.

'That is something I would really have a problem with,' Herzog continued. 'The nice steel colours are always dark, like ships.'

'There's also a big difference between a kind of luminous grey that has a lustre to it, and a black, in terms of what you touch and what you feel.'

'Perhaps with the grey that's on the structure of the Turbine Hall,' said Craig-Martin.

'No, we always intended to have a warm not a cool black,' said Gugger, 'and I think it's very important that the colour we use on the stairs should reflect that it's a steel piece.'

Jacques Herzog added, 'And also, I personally would like to stay with the dark, because I think the dark is more powerful, but then go for colour, real colour, in other areas. So, we have the advantage of the steel, which is dark, but it's also less powerful when it's painted, it's less obtrusive, visually, something which is black, is less obstructive, when it's not a big area. But then, within this grid, to have places of strong colours, which also gives you information where you are.

And I think we should be driven by these ideas of what the areas mean and what people are doing. And if we have almost like a pool, you look down and you see this blue colour in the videotech, maybe even in the shop. The orange or red in the auditorium, and maybe a third colour in the education area. That could change the character of the building without, necessarily, making everything brighter.'

It was a valiant attempt by the architects to cling to the darker colours they seemed to love so much in the steel and walls of the Turbine Hall, but it hadn't yet won Serota over. He explained why. '*We're* all very familiar with this building,' he said to the group, 'and one of the things that happens when people come in, especially when they come into the Turbine Hall for the first time, there is this incredible sense of a "wow" factor. But it's quite clear from the reaction to the images that we've been showing people, that there's also a feeling that people are beginning to have, that this is a very bombastic building and that it's a very masculine building, and it's very powerful. And I think that for a lot of people, it's actually becoming an intimidating building and that, furthermore, it's becoming a building where the art is very remote from them, that it's somewhere up there, and they come into this building and there's a danger – it's only a danger – that this will be seen as having almost a fascistic sort of feel to it. And I'm picking that up from quite a lot of people and it worries me, deeply, actually, at the moment. And we have to find a way of making this building welcoming in a different sense. It isn't an airport, it isn't a shopping mall.'

'I agree totally,' said Herzog, not agreeing totally, 'but it has never been our intention to enhance this masculine side of the building: on the contrary, we tried everything to disturb or destroy this symmetry. And I think colours are very important, but I don't think the overall colour of the structure should be questioned. I rather insist on having strong colours, as I said, for the auditorium, for the other areas, and also have artists do work in this area, when you come in.'

It was now Harry Gugger's turn to summarize the position and move the meeting on to other topics. He felt that the architects had made their case, and heard the Tate's, and there wasn't much more to say at this point. 'I feel the conflict, and I think the duty we get from this meeting is pretty clear. We have to come back with a clear proposal and a look at the overall building and where we would like to have colours. But my personal feeling is that working with colours in a museum, we're getting very close to art, and that's why we are so timid in using these colours, and why we are looking for support. And who is really developing this? Is it an architect? Because it's then going to be an artistic concept, in a way. And that's a very delicate task.'

Michael Craig-Martin had one last thing he wanted to say before they moved on, perhaps to provide the support that Gugger sought. 'The thing that strikes me that's been most successful about your proposals about colour – which are actually, really, very strong, because they involve very large areas, for instance, the flooring in places, the whole of the auditorium – is that they can work precisely because they're not details. The use of colour that I think would not work is if we start to paint all the steelwork and the handrails and so on – that's not what we want. But I think that in the boldness of the whole building, to have very significant blocks of colour that are almost neutral but very strong – I think you can place that through the building, and – and I think there's room for really quite a bit of play with that.'

The colour discussion was finally rounded off by Serota. 'I'm very conscious,' he said, 'that this is the first time that you're really getting serious feedback from us on the issue of colour, other than to say, "In principle, we think the idea of strong colour is a good one." And we can only take it forward from this kind of a dialogue. We're all searching to try and make something which is different from what we've seen, and different from what we know, and that's always difficult.'

'And we, really, now more than before, would want this building to be the best museum in the world,' said Jacques Herzog (it was only a few days after he had learned that Herzog and de Meuron would not be designing the new MoMA).

A mischievous smile came on to Serota's face as he said, 'I can only tell you that yesterday afternoon with the Trustees, I repeated to them that you had said something of this kind, and there were peals of laughter.'

Looking back at the discussion a month later, Peter Wilson cast some light on the origin of Serota's worries about the orange colour in the auditorium, and on the value of having several Tate Trustees attending meetings about design decisions. 'I thought what was motivating Nick to question the colour was that at least one person he talked to on the fund-raising front had hated it, and that had made him realize that it was possible for people to really dislike it, whether they were giving us money or not, and I think he just thought it was a bit extreme. Then, I think, when he thought about it a bit more he thought that, for the auditorium's function as a space in which images of works of art are going to be projected, to have that extreme a colour might be bit over the top. I've always been quite relaxed about it because I remember that we had the same debate with Jim Stirling over the lecture theatre in the Clore Gallery, which isn't quite as bright colours, but was not neutral drab grey, and there've been many criticisms of that space of one sort or another, but colour hasn't been one of them. But you know, if anyone's taste is going to be involved in it, then it ought to be Nick's as well as Jacques and Harry's, and I thought in that respect they had a reasonably intelligent debate about it.'

16

A Poisoned Chalice

Rowen Structures' proposal in their tender bid to cut the time it would take to erect the steel had been a godsend to Schal, already faced with slippage from the asbestos and roof problems. Now Rowen had to deliver, and almost straight away it turned out to be more difficult than they had anticipated.

They had pored over the drawings in some detail when preparing their bid. But, like Watson Steel, they had had only a few weeks to assess and cost a very large structure. The structure – the building within a building – consisted largely of vertical steel columns and horizontal beams. These were usually connected at right angles to each other, although there were also diagonal pieces of steel to brace the structure. In estimating how much time it would take to produce detailed drawings for the steel fabrication Rowen got it badly wrong, as managing director Peter Emerson explained. 'The difficulty is, when you look at the drawings for the Tate project there appears to be on the face of it a lot of repetition. There looks to be a number of beams that repeat through the job. When you actually get down to the detail that you never can do at tender stage, there are subtle differences that really mean that the designers, instead of detailing one beam that repeats a dozen times, in fact have got a dozen different variants. So that's caught us slightly off guard, but we've increased resources both in design and drafting to compensate for that.'

Emerson's apparently relaxed response – being 'caught slightly off guard' – was not shared by Ian Blake. 'It's a hell of an effort that needs to go in now,' he said in late October, 'but it's critical, absolutely critical.' Rowen had to send about a thousand detailed drawings of steel connections to London, to Schal and Ove Arup, who had to check and approve them before Rowen could start on the fabrication work. Two weeks before fabrication was due to start, Arup had still not received any drawings, and ideally Rowen needed four weeks between having the drawings approved and starting work.

And while the midnight oil was burning in Rowen's drawing offices near Nottingham, their on-site engineers were discovering another problem down at Bankside. To be fair, it concerned a part of the job that was less to do with steel than with concrete, but Rowen were required to do it because it was an essential precursor to steel erection – and the job didn't really fit into anyone else's category of work. Schal had built into the steel package the task of preparing the retaining wall that ran around three sides of the Boiler House (those that coincided with the exterior walls of the power station) between ground level and basement level like a dam, with a wide base narrowing towards the top. This wall would now have to take the 4,700 tonne weight carried by the steel columns supporting three sides of the steel framework. Each of the columns would rest on the flat top of the wall, a concrete structure built fifty years beforehand and therefore of suspect stability. The wall would have to be strengthened at each point where the foot of a column rested above it.

Peter Emerson described the task. 'The works that are being carried out by us to the retaining wall represent a fair amount of risk. The fact that we're cutting pockets on to the top of a fifty-year-old concrete wall and drilling through that wall to provide restraint to prevent the wall "squelching" when the load comes on is definitely something that's out the ordinary, and I suspect not too many people, particularly steel fabricators, have been involved in that line of work.'

Rowen's engineers on-site, Gary Hatton and Steve Gibson, had the unenviable job of seeing this through. With a team of about sixteen men they had to drill through the old walls of the power station basement, thread long cables through attached to clamps on either side, and then tighten the cables so that the old concrete wouldn't shatter under the weight of the steel frame.

'The wall was about six foot thick,' Gibson said, 'and drilling through with a special tool with a diamond bit, we encountered all sorts of obstructions in the walls, and it's took a bit longer than what we expected.'

It wasn't only the obstructions that made it take longer. The men had to put grouting – sealant – between the plates and the wall, and some of this seeped into the hole for the tension cables. When they tried to tighten them, the grout stuck the cables firmly to the sides of the holes. It was the tension in these cables that was to give the wall under each column the compression that would support the weight, and when they discovered what had happened Rowen had to chip out the grout, remove the cables and start again.

'It's caused us quite a lot of grief,' said Hatton. It also caused Schal, the Tate and Stanhope a lot of grief as they saw their schedule slipping inexorably in the face of these problems. But these works were not part of the fifteen weeks' erection time Rowen had promised – they were part of the preparatory work, some of which could continue in one part of the building after steel erection started in another.

And steel erection did start on time. On 3 December 1997 Ian Blake's milestone was achieved (almost) as the first steel column was erected on the concrete floor at the west end of the building. But Blake was no longer on the project to see it. He had been increasingly unhappy with the way the small-company atmosphere of Schal was changing, as the company that owned them, Tarmac, expanded and brought in large-company ideas, to the detriment, Blake thought, of the clients he worked for. 'It's becoming more and more difficult to work in that environment, under the current situation. Maybe I'm looking for something that won't exist but I want to be in a position where I can perhaps control my own destiny rather than the other way round.'

Two days after the first steel erection, his replacement, affable New Zealander Mike O'Rorke, described himself as 'a bit like a swan at the moment, all calm and serenity above and paddling like hell underneath'. O'Rorke had been rushed in by Schal to take over from Ian Blake and he'd spent the previous month or so with Blake trying to grasp the size and complexity of the task he had taken on. 'I love construction,' he said. 'There are two reasons. One is because we're very much a people-orientated business – there'll never be robots climbing round scaffolds laying bricks, so we'll never be automated to the extent that industry is. And the second thing is, you start with a concept and a big hole in the ground, and one day you walk away and you've actually built something. I still get a buzz out of walking round London, Saudi Arabia, Burma, wherever I've built buildings, and you look there, and there's something left, not so much a monument to yourself but just that you've built something and you can see something for it. That's a big buzz, it really is.'

O'Rorke had a lot on his plate in his first week on the job. 'We're in for a very difficult period over January to March. Getting the steel frame up and the concrete floor slabs down efficiently and safely is the first of our big hurdles.'

After the first column went up, a steady stream of steel arrived at the site from Rowen's fabrication plant, choreographed according to a sequence prepared by Gary Hatton and supervised by Steve Gibson. Gibson was aware that from the earliest signs of problems – the late drawings and the retaining wall delays – the Tate and Schal would be watching them very carefully.

'We've got a very nervous client that seems to worry about everything,' Gibson said. 'They tend to be in and out all the time. Plenty of communication.'

Quite a lot of that communication came from one of Schal's on-site construction managers, a voluble man called Peter Barnicoat, who wasn't too worried about how popular he was with the contractors. 'It's a tough old game, building, and you have to stand your ground. My role is to serve the client, and to ensure that the client gets everything that we've bought from the package, and that the job is first class and that the quality and everything is in accordance with specification requirements because my role, to sort of flower it up a bit, is a "guardian of the specification". And it's not very pleasant, it's not very nice, but I'm afraid I'm not going to turn a blind eye and bodge a job of this nature. I will expect all the bolts to be tightened up in the correct manner, and all the lines and levels to be in the correct manner. And I expect it to be erected in a safe, professional manner as well. And logistics and management pre-planning aspects Rowen's didn't carry out, I was insistent on asking for. And, yes, it is a bit painful and bloody at times, but I'm afraid I have to serve the client's end.'

At regular intervals in the weeks following the start of steel erection, Barnicoat was given cause for concern, as he walked the site every day, poking his nose into every aspect of the job, as he was paid to do. On a morning in late January 1998, Adey Lower, the steel foreman, was gloomy about the day's target. 'I've got about eight blokes sitting around doing nothing at the moment because a crane isn't working.' Rowen lost three days as a result of this breakdown. And once all the cranes were up and working again, they faced another snag. Lifting each piece of steel from the back of a lorry and lowering it into position so that the erectors could bolt it on to the structure was much trickier than anyone had expected because of the presence of the existing steel structure left over from the power station.

On the day of the crane breakdown, Mike O'Rorke was attending a project review meeting in the visitor centre a hundred yards or so from the scene of the problems. There had been little or no 'easing in' time for him, and he now had to convey some bad news to the project team. After explaining that Birse were still on-site, O'Rorke went on, 'The steelwork is even more disappointing: Rowen's are three weeks behind schedule. There are three reasons why. One, they are steel erectors not concrete workers. Since they won the package they have consistently failed to recognize the complexity of the retaining plates, and failed to react fast enough, and recent grouting has exacerbated the problems. Second, problems with threading the steelwork through the existing roof structure. It's not our problem, it's Rowen's – they always knew it was there. And third, an over-optimistic view of a fifteen-week programme. With hindsight, we shouldn't have agreed to it – it's unachievable.'

O'Rorke was in an unusual situation, and the way he handled it may have seemed tactless. New on the job and faced with the results of decisions that were not of his own making, he laid out clearly and succinctly what had gone wrong. In a sense, that wasn't doing anyone any good, but he probably saw it as clearing the ground for a discussion of what to do about it. But for the Tate team, Mike O'Rorke wasn't just Mike O'Rorke, he was Schal, and it was Schal who had discussed Rowen's bid at great length and been seduced by their promise of a shorter schedule.

Peter Wilson was very worried. 'The question you're going to be asked is: the first two contractors you have on site are behind – is your programme real?'

'– and did we buy it properly?' Andy Butler from Stanhope, who had recently joined the team, chipped in. 'That's the question I would ask.'

'We bought a fifteen-week programme that was unachievable,' O'Rorke said succinctly.

'There's a hundred per cent failure rate at the moment,' Butler said. 'Is this going to stop?'

O'Rorke tried to dig himself out of the hole he was in with a neat about-turn. 'Two months ago we were saying, "We are not going to hit the first of December, because we don't have any drawings." Two months down the line we're sitting here with steel coming out of our ears and it's just a matter of erecting it.'

Andy Butler had replaced Ron German as Stanhope's project manager, so it was his job to attack O'Rorke when things that were Schal's responsibilities went wrong. They were both northerners, but where German was firm but polite, Butler was blunt and direct. It was an appropriate change of approach, for two reasons. First, in the early days of the project, Ron German was an invaluable ally in setting up the working relationships for the Tate between the various companies who would help to build the project, and these relationships were often at a senior level where German's detailed knowledge could be applied to setting the right deal and conditions, in meetings at Millbank or Stanhope's, or in the visitor centre at Bankside. By the time Andy Butler came along, many of the issues that he had to deal with cropped up on-site and every day, and had to be addressed in a more immediate way by face-to-face – sometimes 'in your face' – discussions. Both men could give out the same message, but German would only *imply*, 'Don't give me any bullshit'. Butler would say it.

But Butler would also give credit – or blame – where it was due. With the steel fiasco, he knew that at the time of the tenders Stanhope and the Tate were kept closely informed about progress, and everyone was delighted to be offered the chance to save a million pounds. And Rowen's arguments had been plausible. 'On the face of it,' Butler said, 'the job looks very simple. You've got a large box out there and you're filling it, from a steel point of view, with a steel frame. What everybody underestimated was the difficulty of threading steel within an existing roof structure, working within existing elevations, and the tolerance issue, and the complexity of the steel. They were just over-optimistic, overeager to win the project. Unfortunately they're paying the price for it now. The project's paying the price.'

Rowen Structures were paying the price too. 'There's not a job like this at the moment in London, to my knowledge,' Peter Emerson said. 'Four thousand tonne of steel in a black hole, confined all round by an existing nineteen-forties indeterminate structure, with several thousand individual components in there. It would be stretching the bounds of probability too far to assume that every one of those was going to fit like a hand in a glove.' And Emerson was beginning to feel it personally. When he was asked later if there was a low point in the steel erection saga, he said, 'I guess there was. Probably after Christmas, when the realization really came home that we were in the shit, basically, and we needed to find a way out of it, and we went away and focused on that. For a while, I suppose, it was almost there twenty-four hours a day. But in that situation, we, as a team, looked to be positive.'

One positive step Rowen took, at their own expense, was to bring in larger cranes, called luffing cranes, capable of lifting steel from outside the building. As if to punish them for believing they could overcome their run of bad luck, March brought in high winds which prevented them using the new cranes. 'Sod's Law conspired against us,' Emerson said. 'Anything that could go wrong, went wrong. We encountered probably one of the wettest, windiest periods of time in this country in the last few years, and we got two luffing cranes out there that simply aren't tolerant to that weather. So everything that could possibly happen, give or take a tidal wave up the Thames, has come along to mess us up.'

Gary Hatton and his Rowen colleagues were run off their feet. 'We're actually working on around about four fronts,' he said. 'We've boosted the labour on the site and we're working on every angle we can to try and pull back any time. Unfortunately we're stuck with hours and the constraints of the residents, so what we're trying to do is to actually throw as many men at the available hours we can, to try and mitigate any circumstances.'

Rowen went to Mike O'Rorke and asked for permission to work at weekends, but O'Rorke said 'no'. 'I've ruled out seven-day working on two grounds. One's on safety – you can't work for a long period of time in the field without having casualties. So from a safety point of view, I'm against extended periods of seven-day working. And at the end of the day, we have residents in the area, and they have lives to live as well, and the problems that Rowen's are incurring are not of *their* doing, so why should they be made to suffer?'

Through March and April, Rowen pressed on, and the Boiler House gradually filled with columns and beams, followed by steel decking. It was possible now to see the multi-storey layout of the building from down on the floor of the Turbine Hall. One effect of the rising steel structure was that it gave support to the brick walls and their cathedral windows. Up to now these had been held stable by the rusting steel roof trusses that spanned the roof of the Boiler House, along with two steel towers that were built outside the north walls to hold them steady. With support now being provided by the interior steel structure, it was time to remove the roof trusses, so that work could begin on raising a new steel structure above the parapets – a structure that would frame the Light Beam. Rowen even found a way to speed up the truss removal. Instead of cutting them up in sections, they brought in a 400-ton crane to lift them out in one piece, saving a lot of time.

Workers with oxyacetylene cutters freed the first roof beam from the structure while the crane supported the load. Soon it was tethered by just one connection and as the hot flame melted through that the truss swung gently upwards a few inches.

Mike O'Rorke at last had something to be pleased about. 'We're actually at a gala point at the moment, with removal of the roof trusses,' he said. 'Getting the big twenty- and thirty-ton trusses out is a big boon for the job, and if we have any potential for speeding up the erection of the steelwork at high level, it's with those trusses out.'

But there was still an undercurrent of criticism of O'Rorke among the senior members of the client team for the continuing schedule slippage, and he resented it. 'I would say that I'm not out there erecting steel; I'm not fabricating it; I'm not designing it; I'm not drawing it. If anybody could come along now and show me some clever solution to claw back the lost time or even to speed up the remaining erection, then I'd love them to come forward. But the reality of it is that there is no magic solution. It's very much in the hands of Rowen's, and whatever Rowen's do will be the end result.'

In fact, as different members of the team reflected on how matters could have got so out of hand, it was clear that no single factor was to blame.

For Peter Wilson, 'No one could say that any party to this process who knew about building got the period of the contract right. We had twenty weeks, it's taken thirty weeks. It's not that Rowen's resourced it badly throughout, they didn't.'

'But, at the time,' O'Rorke said, 'we were struggling to get over the issue of the asbestos and the Turbine Hall roof was starting to rear its ugly head. So it would have been pretty foolish of anyone to stand up and say, "Well, OK, we know the trade contractors offered us fifteen weeks for this sum of money, but let's let them do it in twenty anyway." '

O'Rorke was a construction man, not a diplomat. Andy Butler was sometimes dismayed by how O'Rorke presented information to the client. 'If Mike had a problem,' he said, 'it was the fact that perhaps sometimes he sensationalized matters and it sets tremors of fear through the whole Tate hierarchy. He's – perhaps volatile's the best word. He can be abrasive, and he did rub one or two people up the wrong way.'

O'Rorke saw things differently. 'I've always found that honesty is the best policy and that if there's bad news, it should be told. But there's been several high-profile jobs, the Jubilee Line extension is one of them, where people have stood up and said, "No, look, this is what's really going on". And they don't stay in that position very long.'

After pressure on Schal from the Tate and Stanhope, a more senior member of Schal was brought in, ostensibly to help out at a difficult time. Dale Sager, a smooth and relaxed American, joined the Schal Bankside team. He was someone who could be guaranteed not to upset the client. He had been an architect in the US, more in management than design, and had decided to move across to construction management. The result was that people like Andy Butler dealt directly with Sager. It didn't take O'Rorke long to realize that it was time to move on, and with the completion of the structure at Bankside he left the project.

Amidst the prevailing gloom, dominated by the Rowen crisis, Sager took over the reins and argued for a sense of proportion. It sometimes seemed as if three out of four problems with the construction of the project were being blamed on Rowen's. This was probably not fair, but it was becoming a standard excuse. 'Rowen are not a hundred per cent guilty for the problems, now or earlier,' said Sager.

There was a small consolation for Rowen in that, in the face of the financial loss they knew they would have to bear, at the end of the day they were seen to have behaved honourably by the client. Peter Wilson described a trade contractors' meeting attended by one of Rowen's executives, who got up and said, 'Doing this project is like scaling a wall thirty metres high'.

Wilson commented, 'That was something we hadn't appreciated, and we hadn't appreciated how difficult it was going to be building a new frame inside an old frame. So, they contracted to do the work; they were bullish about how quickly it could be done; and they were wrong. They've paid a huge cost penalty in that. But they behaved absolutely honourably throughout over money.'

'I don't think I've ever seen a contractor fail to the degree they've failed here,' Andy Butler said. 'And they underestimated everything in terms of its complexity, in terms of the volume of the work, working within an existing envelope. And, I think, to be honest, the whole team did. And it was only, probably, six or ten weeks into the process, that people started realizing what we really had here. And I think the whole team have got sympathy with Rowen. And I think they deserve some credit for sticking to the task.'

But that credit was unlikely to be in their bank account. By the final reckoning, the fifteen weeks promised for steel erection turned out to be nearer thirty. The cost of the delays was a complex figure to work out. It wasn't just that Rowen had to pay their own people for twice as much work, as well as the hire of equipment over a longer period, and extra cranes to try to speed up the work. There were also the costs the Tate had to bear as a result of keeping other contractors waiting to do work which had been scheduled to start at the original completion date for the steel. And the project as a whole couldn't be allowed to drift on for fifteen weeks beyond its targeted completion date.

There followed complex negotiations between Schal and Rowen, taking several months. Rowen had won the contract for a price of £6.1 million. Schal reckoned that their failure had cost the project hundreds of thousands of pounds and so were holding back on Rowen's final payment. Eventually a figure was agreed which meant that Rowen were paid £5,950,000 – £100,000 less than the contract price. They had spent a lot more. One estimate put Rowen's costs at well over £6.5 million.

In all the final calculations, as Andy Butler pointed out, the settlement didn't cover 'the full costs that the client [the Tate] incurred, but the client has taken a very pragmatic and moral view, I believe, inasmuch as, contractually, we had Rowen's bang to rights.'

In July 1997, as the concrete pourers worked their way up the building and Bankside acquired the look of a floored building, Peter Emerson looked back over the last year. 'We won the job for better or for worse, and we've delivered the job, almost. We're not going to make any money at it, which is disappointing. It's a project that we dearly wanted to win, it's a project that we were pleased at the time to have won, and we felt, perhaps with hindsight rather too optimistically, that we could improve upon the programme that had been set. What prevents this happening in future? Well, once bitten, twice shy. We've been around as a business now for fifty years, and this is the first and only time we've been in this type of situation, and we sure as hell don't intend being there again.'

17
Grand Stair

The Midlands village of Kegworth's main claim to fame is as the site of an air crash in 1989, when a plane trying to land at a nearby airport crashed short of the runway and was the scene of a highly publicized rescue operation. But for the new Tate, Kegworth was the site of the construction of one of the most important architectural elements in the building – the Grand Stair. Peter Emerson knew a challenge when he saw one, and since Rowen were a steel fabricator and erector, with no experience of complex staircases, they looked for a specialized company to make it.

The company that was given the subcontract, True Brothers of Kegworth, known to everyone as Trubros, is based in an old light industrial workshop built probably a hundred years ago, and employs eighteen or so metalworkers led by the foreman, Ivor Lovesey.

Lovesey is a jovial, well-rounded man, who has worked in light engineering all his life. He started in the business at seventeen and is now in his early fifties. In early December 1997, he was supervising the work on a number of the landings and stairs that were in various stages of fabrication, lying about the floor of the cavernous workshop. Behind the anonymous modern doors were two large areas separated by a brick wall with arched doorways. There was a din of bashing and clashing and fizzing as men with masks cut and welded pieces of steel together, while others trundled completed elements from one area to another.

Although work had begun on the treads and risers that formed the stairs, as the men assembled them into individual flights there was a nervousness in the company about the quality they were required to produce in the balustrades. These were solid sheets of 3 mm thick steel plate, which would encase the stairs all the way up the building, boxing in each flight down the sides. Herzog and de Meuron had specified that they wanted a smooth, continuous surface, even though it would have to be made up of separated sheets, butt-joined.

'This is quite an interesting staircase,' said Lovesey, with a degree of understatement. 'It's the first time I've had such a massive flight – I think it's twenty-eight flights, or twenty-eight levels altogether going up, and it's been quite a challenge for us. The big problem is the architect didn't want any signs of any welding down any back joints. That's not easy with stairs. We're not allowed to use body filler. So it's got to be as good as we can get it.'

Adrian Waters is managing director of Trubros. Once his company had got the job, and the workers at the plant had understood the design and the nature of the work that was required, he noticed a different attitude to this particular contract. 'In many instances, we do contracts time without number and they really go through the workshop just as a drawing with a piece of steel shown on it and it comes out the other end and we take it to site. They don't really know what they're making – they know it's a part of a building, a part of a staircase, a part of a landing or something like that, and they don't really get involved with it. I think from fairly early days they've caught the atmosphere of this project. They're rolling along with it now, they want to make it right. It's different to most of the balustrading that we do, and they want to be part of it.'

This difference of atmosphere in the factory didn't have much to do with an appreciation of the design of the staircase. It was more to do with the eventual location of the stair, in a prestigious new art gallery rather than just another shopping mall or office block. In fact, Waters barely concealed his own lack of enthusiasm for the staircase design. 'I feel inevitably that it won't suit everyone's taste. I like to think I'll be pleasantly surprised by it all. I think a lot of people going into this type of gallery will appreciate it rather more than myself.'

In the early stages of the project Waters shared a general nervousness about being able to achieve with steel plate the smoothness the architect wanted – or rather the smoothness he thought the architect wanted. A meeting was arranged for the architects to look at a mock-up of the steel sides of the stairs, showing Trubros' best attempts to produce a smooth surface with no signs of the joins between the plates or the spot-welding that had been carried out on the back of the sheets, which sometimes produced barely visible indentations on the front.

'It is quite clear, and plainly shown on the drawings, that the steel balustrading will be fabricated from three-millimetre steel,' Waters said. 'Having spoken to the architect, I felt that he would have probably achieved the result he was after in a very, very smooth finish using an MDF boarding all painted to his specification. Very much easier to join, and they do come in very much straighter sections. We would supply the supporting steel on the balustrade and it would have ended up a lot truer section. The problem being that with three-millimetre plate, or any other thin steel plate, when the process of welding takes place, and indeed grinding [to finish the joints after welding], the plate will deform. And this is a problem that we've had to encounter in the works by putting a lot of supporting steel in there, purely to stop it deflecting as much as we are able. So we provided possible alternatives – glass reinforced plastic or some form of timber.'

You don't have to know much about the approach of Herzog and de Meuron to know what their reaction would be to the suggestion that they clad their staircase in MDF – a synthetic, dense, smooth, wood-fibre-based boarding. And Adrian Waters soon found out.

'I attended a meeting on-site with the architect, who I feel appreciated the efforts that we'd gone to, but he made it quite plain that he had his ideas on how the stair was to look, and a very useful meeting it was. I think it possibly only lasted about an hour and a half, but I felt more than ever we knew which direction he wanted it to go. He was not expecting it to be a hundred per cent smooth, and wanted it to appear monolithic.'

It was all part of the overall aim of reflecting the industrial origins of Bankside rather than fighting them. The monolithic steel staircase was in keeping with the concrete floors in some of the galleries, the unfinished wood floors in others, and the cast-iron ventilation grilles in the gallery floors. Gugger knew that people's expectations of a refined design for the gallery might sometimes get in the way of achieving the finish they wanted. 'We've had a set of drawings, and they read something completely different from what our expectations are. We are looking for a *shipbuilders'* piece of work on this Grand

Staircase, and we are not looking for nicely lined up steel. It has to have the expression of steel and of being a heavy piece. And therefore, I was always confident that they would build it. And I was very surprised that the first comments coming back were, "Well, this is impossible, we'll never achieve it". And I just said, "Why don't you do a mock-up, and we'll look at it?" And that's how it turned out to be, so that we are happy with the mock-up and they are now confident that they can build it on budget and maybe even below cost-plan.'

Herzog himself was in no doubt what he wanted. 'It should have been done in concrete originally, and it would have been the most simple thing, but concrete is too heavy, and we don't want to overload this building with structure. So it was suggested that we do the stair in iron and steel, which is fine, which is very good, but this is now a technical problem, to do it as heavy and monolithic as we want it to be, because we want it to be a Grand Stair which doesn't cause noise when you step on it, which is not one these trendy stairs you have in every boutique, in every shop and even in some museums where you have steel stairs and when you step on them you hear the steel. We want it to be a heavy piece where you just walk up, and when you do that, you need to use thick pieces of metal that need to be welded and to do that properly is a technical challenge. Of course I don't build the pieces myself, but we are in contact with everything which is being mock-upped. We certainly don't say, "Do whatever you like," because we will never get what we want.

Trubros were also worried by the use of wood for the handrails and treads.

'We're not carpenters,' said Lovesey. 'Excellent engineers but not very good at wood.'

Adrian Waters was rather dubious about the whole idea of combining wooden elements with the steel, particularly after hearing about the shipbuilding style Herzog and de Meuron wanted. 'I found it to be a very strange combination on this particular type of stair,' Waters said.

But after he said seen a detailed mock-up, including the wood element, he said, 'I'll apologize. I think it looks very good. And I feel that he has created something different to what is in most buildings. Something that people will look at, which is obviously the aim of a Grand Staircase.'

But which wood would it be? The architects initially specified a little-known and somewhat rare wood called 'wenge'. This is apparently pronounced 'wengy' with a hard 'g', but Waters understandably pronounced it to rhyme with Penge when he described his first reaction. 'We could have done it in wenge,' he said, 'if we could have waited a few hundred years for the rest of the timber to grow. There really is not sufficient quantities of the timber available in the world today to say that we could do the Grand Staircase at the Tate Gallery of Modern Art in that particular timber.' Wenge was, he continued, 'very hard, very dark and very unobtainable'. Fortunately, before the forests of the world were scoured for wenge trees, the architects were shown a sample and said they didn't like it after all. They chose stained oak instead. Waters and his colleagues breathed a sigh of relief.

Once the major design decisions had been made, Trubros were handed the drawings and set to work, and the metal flights and landings began to pile up in the workshop. But on 8 December 1997, Ivor Lovesey stood despondently in front of one of the Grand Stair landings, propped up in a yard in front of the factory, where it had been taken after the work on it was finished. He was facing the possibility that six pieces like the two-metre-long section in front of him would have to be thrown away and replacement pieces fabricated.

Some time in November 1997, one of the architects working on the details of how the staircase was to be connected to the steel structure discovered that at Level 2 the east side of the staircase as drawn got in the way of a lift-machine room. This turned out to be a serious error and one that was very difficult to correct. The best option was to move the whole staircase several centimetres to the west, and this meant repositioning the steel columns that it was to be connected to. Such a course would be expensive and delay the schedule further.

Peter Emerson of Rowen Structures, who would have to do the work, was entirely willing to make the change – at a price. 'The architects have asked us, can we accommodate a shift in position of the staircase at this point in time? And the answer is, "Yes, we can." It's the architects' prerogative, the client's prerogative, if they want to change something. After all, the gallery's going to be there for decades to come. So we've been sympathetic insomuch that we've said yes, we can accommodate a change, but obviously it comes with a price tag which is quite a lot of money, and also a time tag. It would affect our ability to hold the original programme because it means reworking a lot of design, drawing, fabrication and methodology to bring it right up to speed.'

While work at Trubros in early December proceeded as if nothing was going to change, a decision had to be made, and soon. There was to be a regular design review meeting on 18 December and the issue of the staircase error was put high on the agenda. The meeting was, in any case, to be followed by a final review of a mock-up of one flight of the staircase to make sure that everyone on the team agreed with the final details of how the wood and steel were designed to fit together.

The worst mistakes are the ones we make ourselves. Other people's errors we can eventually live with, if only through the comfort that comes from blaming someone else. But when the error is our own – and we are unable to do anything about it – the consequences can fester. Harry Gugger believed that the interference of the lift-machine room with the staircase was a design mistake. Even though it wasn't he personally who had made the mistake, he was responsible for the team that drew up the plans and he felt he could and should have spotted it in time to correct it. So when he came to present his case to the Tate team at this meeting he was pretty worked up, and part of the stress of the moment was the belief that it was nobody's fault but Herzog and de Meuron's.

The meeting had originally been convened to discuss and approve elements of the stair design as shown in the mock-up. It had already been postponed once, and now decisions had to be made. So there were the three Trustees who sat in on these design reviews – Janet de Botton, Bill Woodrow and Michael Craig-Martin – plus Tate regulars Serota, Dawn Austwick, Peter Wilson and Andy Bramwell, a Tate architect on Peter Wilson's staff. Then there was Andy Butler from Stanhope. Harry was there to present his case, and Jacques was there to give moral support, or so it seemed.

For the lifetime of the building, Gugger thought, people would notice a small ledge – an unintended consequence of the design error – as they walked up the stairs, a ledge that would gather dust and that would seem out of place in the rugged, rectilinear contours of the building. Clearly not all visitors would notice, or if they noticed, care. But some would and they would think the worse of the architect for leaving it there if something could have been done about it. And even if none of the visitors noticed it, Gugger himself would know it was there and see it every time he visited that part of the building, and it would hurt.

Gugger had various solutions. The first was one that it was too late to put into operation. The error had been discovered four weeks ago. If at that time all the interested parties had come together, with a will to correct it as cheaply and efficiently as possible, he believed that something could have been done. It would have been four weeks earlier in stair manufacture; four weeks earlier in steel fabrication; four weeks earlier in the programme; with a little more leeway for reprogramming. But this was not done. This was the UK, not Switzerland, and there were hierarchies, and lines of communication, and relationships, and construction managers, which meant that the issue had to be dealt with along the lines of formal procedures. So the issue was handed over to Schal, and Schal thought about it and talked about it with Rowen, and Rowen talked to Trubros, and Trubros and Rowen both looked at their very tight schedules and made two observations to themselves. (1) Any changes we make to solve this problem will make the pressure on us even harder than it is, and (2) if Schal did want us make changes in what we are fabricating we would be entitled to relax our schedule by at least a week if not two, which would give us a bit of a breathing space for all the other deadlines we are trying to meet. And Stanhope, in the person of Andy Butler, knew that those thought processes if not checked could lead to a delay of weeks in the entire programme.

As at most of these meetings, the absence of a plan – fifteen minutes to discuss this, another fifteen for that, and so on – meant that the first items always got the lion's share of the time, and that sometimes quite significant items got left till last when there wasn't much time for discussion. Peter Wilson saw this as part of Herzog and de Meuron's tactics to try to get new ideas through, since it could happen that if a contentious issue was raised too early, or even in informal discussions beforehand, it could be rejected by Wilson and Schal before it even got on to the agenda. By suddenly bringing up an issue for the first time in a larger meeting, where an ally or two might be lurking or where there just wasn't time to discuss it fully, there was a chance it might get through.

By the time the meeting was ready to turn to Gugger's concerns, it was nearly 11.30. They had been discussing other topics for two hours, and Serota had to get away at 12 o'clock. Gugger had a diminishing amount of time to set out the issue and the arguments. He started his pitch by describing the problem, not concealing that it was Herzog and de Meuron's fault. He did, however, remind the meeting that in the early days of the design, he and Jacques had argued strongly with the engineers for a lift-machine room in the basement or at the top of the building, and been overruled. (In fact this was a red herring, since at the time this suggestion had nothing to do with any interference with the position of the stair.) The current 'solution' in his view was no solution because it had the effect of distorting the Grand Staircase around the corner of the lift-machine room. The most drastic solution, and the most elegant, was to move the whole staircase 70 mm to the west, keeping the relationship of risers and landings all the way up. This is the solution that would have involved rejecting six of the landings that had already been manufactured at Trubros.

After describing the mistake, Harry turned to the cheap and nasty solution that had been proposed, standing in front of plans on the wall that showed the offending design from front and side like the police photo of a criminal.

'This is the agreed solution at the moment,' Gugger said. 'We could make it work technically, but it leads to a little balcony here where there will be dust sitting on, and this will tell everybody for fifty years that the architect made a major mistake, since this stair will be there a long, long time. And I really don't like this edge. A proposal to overcome this is a pure realignment of the whole stair, all the way up, sitting symmetrical into this slot, creating a larger slot here, on the banister, which I think is very nice, so, if you wait in front of the lift-motor room . . .'

Gugger was interrupted. 'How much is it costing?' Serota asked.

'This costs £25,000 and it costs two weeks' delay on Core 2.'

Serota exploded, in a sort of controlled way. 'It's not on, Harry,' he said. 'It's not on, forget it. It's just not on. We cannot possibly start rebuilding the steelwork and redesigning the steelwork. They're on-site: we've said from the outset, we cannot do it.' He was particularly concerned about the fact that Rowen's had been pressured to work overtime to catch up on the steel programme. 'We cannot have these people working over weekends and Christmas, at huge cost, and then say we're going to have a two-week delay.'

After trying to explain to an unconvinced meeting that the change he wanted was not as drastic as people believed, Gugger changed tack and offered some alternatives. This again was what Peter Wilson saw as a Gugger tactic. As he put it afterwards, 'These fallback positions, often clearly pre-rehearsed, meant that we didn't listen to the first idea with quite the same receptiveness as we might otherwise have.'

'I developed a further option,' said Gugger, 'which certainly would not cause a delay. We have lined up the stair here in the centre, and we create a special landing, one landing of the stair, which can be built in the factory. It doesn't have an impact on-site, and this landing would be built as a larger landing. And would then be inserted and we would have a change of this landing here, and the landing on top there, so it's not a structural change to the core, it's a change to the stair landing.'

Jacques Herzog chipped in at this point, explaining that he would be happy with this change, but would still have preferred the more expensive one, because it enabled them to make a small design change which would improve the join of the stair and the wall by the lifts. And, said Herzog, it would only add two weeks to the schedule.

'Two weeks' delay is a quarter of a million pounds,' Serota said. 'It must be. It must be. We really can't. We have to spend the money on the things that will really make a difference to the building.'

'The trouble is,' said Peter Wilson to Gugger, 'you just do not have money for those kinds of delays. Every time you cause a delay, even if it's only a day, we open ourselves up to negotiations about claims with the contractors, in ways that we simply don't want to do. And there are just other things to do with the money. Every time we find a problem like this – and no doubt there will be others along the way – we're going to have to solve it in the most practical, pragmatic, quick way, and it's not going to be perfect. But I for one, I'm not going to spend money like that. It's just money thrown down the drain. You spend months buying packages seriously competitively, and the moment you give the contractor an opportunity to make a claim back at you, you lose all the effort you've put into competitive bidding. And we just can't do it. We have to find the quickest, easiest way out of every one of these solutions. And it isn't going to be perfect. No building is ever perfect and you're going to have to live with the imperfections. It's just wasting time and money sitting here talking about it.'

'This stair is going to be here for how many years?' Harry asked.

'It doesn't matter, Harry,' said Wilson. 'It won't be there at all if we don't do it to budget.

At this point, Jacques Herzog made a surprising intervention, almost as if Harry and he were doing a 'good cop/bad cop' routine. 'But Harry,' he said, turning to Gugger, 'maybe there will be other fights where we would be happy when the client would rather accept our proposal. In this case, we can very well live with it.'

'But what Peter's saying, he's even not accepting this option,' said Gugger. 'This option asks for a different landing here, a landing is not produced here on-site, [it is] produced in factories, and can't have an impact on the programme. I'm sure that if you go and consult these contractors, they will tell you it has an impact, but it can't, and it's just a matter of talking to them and convincing them that they can do this.'

By now the meeting was beginning to take on the characteristics of a witch hunt. No one, even his own partner, seemed willing to take Gugger's concerns seriously. In fact, before the meeting, aware that the problem had arisen, the senior Schal and Stanhope managers had had some discussion among themselves, and Peter Wilson had also alerted Serota to the situation. Out of that came a determination to put up a united front. Andy Butler now explained why. 'Only Monday past, we had the MD of Rowen's down here. They're on an exacting programme, which they're struggling to keep up with, working long hours, et cetera. If we do this: one, it sends the wrong message; secondly, it does open the doors, there's no doubt about it. I'm very conscious of the message that we're sending to these people. There's a direct cost, which is whatever it will be, £10,000, or something of that order, but it's very difficult to disprove the consequential delays. I do feel for Harry,' Butler wound up, unconvincingly.

'But we're only talking about one landing,' Serota pointed out.

Butler knew that the amount of refabrication time wasn't really the issue. He knew, as Gugger did, that giving an inch to a contractor in difficulties can lead to the theft of a mile. But that didn't make it defensible and Gugger broke in with a bitter complaint. 'See, if I hadn't been a toolmaker myself, and if I hadn't done things like that with my own hands, and if I didn't know how this works, I wouldn't be pissed off, but I am pissed off because I know about these things, and I just don't believe them.'

Ever the pragmatist, Wilson intervened and said 'The whole reason for going down the construction management route in the first place is to get ourselves out of the position where an initial low bid is followed by a series of claims and a settlement at the end of the job so that the job costs much more than it did in the first place. If you leave them an opportunity to do this, they could well do it to us.'

What had been intended as the tag-end of a meeting turned into a detailed analysis of the subtleties of the construction programme and a rehashing of how much time it would really take to put into operation one or other of the options for correcting the design mistake.

Serota, in spite of his initial severe reaction, actually came in on Gugger's side at times, trying to get to the bottom of what the true cost might be of the changes Gugger wanted to make.

Behind Gugger's impassioned plea was the knowledge that design mistakes can sometimes affect the client as well as the architect, something he had learned on a previous project in Basel. 'Trust me, I learnt a lesson,' he said, 'when I did the engine depot a few years ago. There was one corner which I knew was not good. And I pointed it out to the client. They said, "No way!" We built it, and we suffered a lot, the client, and myself, later on. Then we changed it with diamond saws and whatever. You have to believe me if I tell you now, this is wrong, doing it like that, it will be also wrong for you, for the users. That's why I'm here and that's why I'm doing my job.'

Once again, Herzog came in on the side of the Tate. 'But on the other hand, Harry,' he said, 'we cannot ask our client to accept a delay of a week, if the people who are building the gallery say this is certainly what it will take. That's why we also have to weigh the risk, because we will be faced with other things, which will probably be even more crucial. And I don't want to be on the other side, but it's just something we have to accept. More and more building today means that we are under such a pressure of time and money that very few changes can be done.'

It was time for Peter Wilson to spell out some home truths. He had sat through enough of this artistic hand-wringing and had something he wanted to get off his chest. 'It is in the nature of this meeting to be about visual things, so we're very concerned about it. But can I tell you that over the course of trying to get the engineering on budget, I made ten, twelve, fifteen compromises that affect the engineering performance of the building, in ways that are as significant as visual compromises here. And just to talk about spending ten, twenty thousand pounds, when we struggled and agonized for weeks to get back into budget on the engineering, it just doesn't seem credible to me that we can consider it.'

During a final flurry of discussion, when Dawn Austwick tried to make sure that Andy Butler had got a reliable estimate of the possible delay from Rowen, Jacques Herzog took Harry Gugger off to a corner of the room, where they had a *sotto voce* conversation. As Andy Butler paused for breath in his reiterated argument for the quick, cheap, ugly option, he felt a hand on his shoulder. Harry was standing over him. He had made up his mind. 'OK,' Gugger said. 'We tried hard. Let's go and see the mock-up.'

Gugger realized that the Tate was not going to pay to move the entire staircase, and had decided to accept the unsightly ledge. The whole event had a pleasingly dramatic quality to it, with all the satisfaction of a neat, complex and – for the Tate – happy ending. And like all good dramas, it had been preceded by rehearsals.

An hour later, Gugger sat on the steps of the mock-up of his beloved staircase, constructed in a draughty corner of the Switch House, and looked back at the way the meeting had gone. He claimed to have taken the decision to bring things to a quick conclusion on his own, rather than as a result of being pressured by Herzog. But he also knew that Herzog didn't take the mistake to heart in the way that he himself did. 'He gave signals that he is more relaxed about this odd corner. It's not his mistake. I mean, it's not my personal mistake but I feel more directly involved and more responsible. So maybe he gave me in the meeting signals that I could go this way. But I decided without consulting him.'

Gugger felt that no one in the meeting really visualized the problem in the way that he did. 'I think that's really our duty, that's why there are still architects in the world, so that we can imagine and have a sensitivity towards things which other people can't imagine just looking at the plan: they don't have this imagination. So that I can translate in my brain things into reality at the stage when others can't. And taking their sensitivity towards things as my responsibility, that's what I see very much as my duty. I have had many experiences in my career where I gave in, I was not tough enough, I didn't fight enough for a solution, and I had to find out later on that people were very unhappy and in fact shared my opinion, but at the time just didn't worry because it was not visual to them, it wasn't present for them. It's only there when it's built – you know.'

The discussion of the Grand Stair design mistake was a rare example of where disagreement and differences of practice between Herzog and Gugger came out in the open. And as the senior partner and co-founder of the firm, perhaps Herzog realized that there were bigger issues at stake. 'I hope that the future proves me to be wrong,' said Gugger, speaking of Herzog's attitude at the meeting, 'but I think he's a very strategic man. But I made this such an issue because I think if we lose this one we will lose many others. And Jacques just doesn't have that feeling. And this is also for me a new experience. In Switzerland this would not happen. We would realign the stair, I swear to you. I would know these contractors, I would have talked them personally, I would have convinced them. It's a job with a certain reputation, it's a job of a certain size, they make a lot of money out of this, they are under pressure, they are doing a good job, but they could give a little bit more. There is still something to give, you know, there, and I would have gone that far with them, I'm quite sure. And the problem is here I have to discuss this through the construction manager, who might not be as convinced as I am that it has to be removed.'

One small mystery about the meeting was why Serota, usually so sympathetic to the architects' point of view, was so hard on them, at least at the beginning of the meeting. It turned out that there were several reasons, as he explained three months later. 'First of all, I was hard on Harry on that occasion because it was the first I'd heard about it. And I felt that he should have been able to anticipate that there was going to be a problem and not tell me that we had to spend another two hundred, two hundred and fifty thousand at two hours' notice. I also felt that he was trying to use me to overrule the decision that Peter Wilson had already made; and, as it happens, I agreed with Harry's view about that particular construction detail, but I felt that I couldn't possibly undermine Peter's authority, and if I had done so I would have been in a position where Peter would have almost no place in the chain of authority over Harry. I also felt that Harry is an incredibly inventive architect and that he would probably find a way out of the problem for himself. I think he has actually managed to do that and eliminated some of the awkwardness of that conjunction of staircase and steelwork which he was worried about. The question is whether I will wince each time I see it. And I'm sure that I'll more often take the stair than the escalator, and therefore I hope I won't wince every time I look at that detail.'

Part Four

1998–9

Art
and
Artifice

18
Thinking about Art

With so much attention focused on the design and construction of Bankside, it was easy to forget the purpose for which the building was being constructed. Week after week with the Bankside team, Nick Serota and Peter Wilson worried over walls and floors and colours and light; costs and schedules and staffing and access – creating a large container for empty boxes which would one day display art. Very rarely did a particular piece of art or a particular artist come into the discussions, even with such an art-focused firm as Herzog and de Meuron.

But of course, this was a geographical illusion. Back at Millbank, Serota and his colleagues were carrying out parallel discussions with a team which grew as the gallery design evolved and the opening date got nearer. In deciding to split the London Tate into two, there were some tricky decisions to be made about what went where. The Millbank site would be a gallery dedicated to British art up to and including the twentieth century, while Bankside would be international modern and contemporary art (including British). But there would be overlaps, since some modern British art would have to remain at Millbank. From the beginning the Tate team had decided to use the new gallery as an opportunity to think in new ways about the display of modern and contemporary art. Of course, for many people there is no obvious *old* way to think about these topics. The avant-garde – almost by definition – breaks any previous set of rules and there is no known art historical process by which, sooner or later, they can be fitted into any very meaningful scheme of categorization, although they usually *are* arranged in categories by chronology or nationality or even just by consensus. Probably most people who work at the

Tate get confronted continually by people they meet in pubs (or wine bars) with layman's questions about modern and contemporary art. Nick Serota says that the most common question he is asked is, 'Do you like everything that's in the gallery?'

'The answer has to be "no",' he said back in 1994, shortly after the Tate had announced that it was acquiring Bankside. 'However broad my interests and sympathies and taste and so on, people seem to assume that a work of art is something which you have to like and if you don't like it then it can't be good. If I go to the theatre, to a play, people ask "do you like it?" But almost immediately they move on to questions that are much more interesting than that very direct question of like or dislike, and I think the same should be true for the visual arts.'

The word some modern art experts use is 'engage' – a work of art has to *engage* the person looking at it. Jeremy Lewison, one of the Tate curators, seemed to use this as a shield against almost any reaction to a work of modern or contemporary art, including hostile ones. 'People actually enjoy being negative about things,' he said. 'And you can only be negative about it if you've actually engaged with it in one way or another.' And for Lewison you don't have to understand a work of art to engage with it. He's not even sure whether anyone truly understands works of art. 'I think it would be impossible to say that anybody understood any work of art, full stop. Because as art history shows, the interpretations of works of art change. So you can only understand it as far as you're able to understand it in any given moment. And what you bring to that work of art in your interpretation of it will shift all the time. So it is all right not to understand. What you're looking for is a response. And a response indicates an understanding of a kind, but it's not necessarily *the* understanding, because I don't think there is such a thing.'

Talk of 'engaging' and 'responding' can infuriate critics of contemporary art, and it certainly has a feeling of unfalsifiability about it. If you run a gallery on those lines, you can point to any reaction – unthinking delight, hostility, curiosity, ridicule, withdrawal of funding – as evidence that the audience is 'engaging' with the art and that therefore you are doing your job. Any reaction, that is, apart from apathy. A gallery that no one visited would soon be forced to close its doors, and the Tate is clearly not that sort of gallery, with its 'football crowds' at the weekends.

In 1995, Jeremy Lewison was deputy keeper of the modern collection, responsible with the help of eleven other curators for foreign art from Impressionism to the present day, and British art produced by artists born after 1880. Already he and his colleagues had started trying to imagine what they would do with display space that was equal to the entire space at Millbank. They were working on the basis that there are many histories of art. 'The idea of modern art going from Cubism through all the other isms to the present day in a single line is completely discredited, and if you want to see that kind of thing you only have to go to the Museum of Modern Art in New York, and until recently you used to be able to follow that line. Cubism, Futurism, Surrealism and this ism and that ism. We work on the basis that there are many histories of art and histories within histories, and that all these things are going on together. It isn't just the history of the avant-garde. At the same time as the so-called avant-garde there were people working in very traditional forms of art who have equally valid and important things to say. And you need to show them alongside each other, and sometimes you need to show them in the same room.'

In beginning to decide on the Bankside displays, Lewison and his colleagues were constrained by what the Tate actually had in its collection, and what it could borrow from other collections around the world. 'We have no American art before 1940,' he said. 'And this is a huge gap, and it would suggest to anybody coming to the Tate Gallery there wasn't American art before 1940. But of course there was, and it was highly distinctive and very important. It's unfortunate that it's now beyond our reach financially to get the major protagonists in that area. So we would hope to be able to go to somewhere like the Whitney Museum of American Art and say, "Please could we borrow four or five works by Hopper, or a collection of works by a number of different artists and show them for six months or nine months or a year alongside works of that period by other artists?" '

The discussions that went on at Millbank in 1995 and 1996 involved a large number of curators and ranged widely without coming to any clear focus. Meanwhile, Serota and his colleagues were designing and building the new gallery in a way that seemed to leave out some of the Millbank staff. Whether or not there was a deliberate downplaying of the role of the Millbank curators, Serota decided in 1997 that time had come for the decision-making about what would be exhibited at Bankside to be put in the hands of a much smaller group of people. In 1997 Frances Morris and Iwona Blazwick were appointed to two new curatorial posts specifically concerned with Bankside.

Blazwick was an exhibition organizer and a former director of exhibitions at the ICA in London, and Morris had worked with Lewison as one of the curators of modern art at Millbank and had curated several recent successful exhibitions. She was also known for spending a lot of time in artists' studios and coming up with ideas for new kinds of displays. She is a small, short-haired, active woman in her mid thirties, and her questioning, exploring way of speaking conceals firm opinions and a comprehensive knowledge of swathes of twentieth-century European art. Serota describes her as 'an effective and in some ways understated operator, who has real convictions which are based on deep thought, which she then enunciates in a set of principles and sees are carried through.'

In October 1997, on the day of the party for the great and the good at Bankside, Morris stood in the double-height gallery, dwarfed by its huge volume, and talked about the task she and her new colleague faced, after years of somewhat inconclusive internal discussions at Millbank. 'We have to now review all those thoughts, and our own thoughts, and begin to look at the kind of hard realities of how those ambitions actually marry with what we've got in the permanent collection here. One of the reasons we have to do that is that how we arrange the collection will impact on where the walls are going to go, so the architects are chasing us for those sorts of decisions. We also have to start ring-fencing some of our works, because other collections call on us to lend works to their exhibitions, and I think there's going to be a particular call on important works for the Millennium, because museums and galleries in this country and throughout the world want to do spectacular, celebratory, critical, forward-looking, backward-looking exhibitions, and we need to be able to tell those institutions over the next year or so that we can't lend them certain categories of works or certain iconic pieces from the collection.'

The overall philosophy of Bankside would be the same as that pursued at Millbank. 'It's the interwoven story of art in the twentieth century. So that art from America and Europe, largely speaking, has been seen in conjunction and juxtaposition and in comparison with British art. And that's something that we can do here for a British gallery of modern art that cannot be done in New York and cannot be done in Paris, and that's the unique opportunity of why we need our own Tate Gallery of Modern Art.'

Iwona Blazwick, who shared the display-planning with Morris, is a thoughtful, unfrivolous person, with a passion for contemporary art and a strong academic background. While Morris took responsibility for displays, Blazwick was thinking about future exhibitions, but they both spent a lot of time on both topics. In the administration building behind the Tate at Millbank, Morris and Blazwick jealously guarded a small room whose walls were plastered with yellow Post-it notes, with names of artists, isms, political terms, twentieth-century events, social movements, and other reference points around which the new gallery arrangements might cluster. The plan was that they would have a series of informal brainstorming sessions between themselves and with invited guests from among the Tate staff, working up to a presentation to Nick Serota at a point where some clear structures were beginning to emerge. On the basis of his reactions they would go away and refine their ideas for a more formal presentation to a wider group.

One important aspect of the process was to be aware of other modern art galleries and how they dealt with the same issues. In 1997 a new modern art museum opened in Bilbao. The building was designed by the American architect Frank Gehry, and the museum was an outpost of the Guggenheim Museum in New York. Morris and Blazwick together with Caro Howell, an early appointment to the Bankside team in the education field, decided to visit Bilbao.

As the three women set off from their hotel in the centre of Bilbao, Howell kept her eyes peeled for the first sight of the museum they had come to see. The buildings that lined the street were ornate, rectangular nineteenth-century apartments, and there was the occasional fountain or central plaza at the junctions with other roads. They were almost upon the museum before she realized that it had been staring them in the face, brightly sunlit, for most of the last stretch of their walk. The museum is so unexpected, so out of character with the canyon-like road that leads towards it, that your perceptual apparatus shuts it out, disqualifies it from the category 'building', until you are forced to admit that, yes, here it is.

The Guggenheim in Bilbao had been through the same process that the Tate were to experience over the next two years: taking a brand-new set of galleries and stocking them with a mixture of modern and contemporary art. How had they made their decisions? What criteria had they used to decide on how to arrange the collection? What was their policy on exhibitions? Had they any works of art that were specially created with the specifics of the building in mind?

It was a beautiful day in Bilbao – only early February, but a pale blue sky and bright sun shone at a low angle on the shimmering titanium scales that clad large areas of the building's surface. Gehry has a thing about fish. He designed a Japanese fish restaurant in the shape of a fish – not just an outline on the ground but the whole fish rearing its head to attract the eaters. And the Guggenheim in Bilbao had one huge, long gallery with gently curved sides and a high curved roof, that people spoke of as 'the fish gallery'.

There is something about the experience of seeing the Guggenheim Museum in Bilbao for the first time that makes you want to laugh. Not laugh at it, but laugh with pleasure at its existence. If humour comes from unexpected juxtapositions, as some po-faced theorists believe, Gehry's Guggenheim is a gallimaufry of such juxtapositions – curved walls meeting straight at crazy angles; fluttering titanium scales meeting creamy, orthogonal limestone slices; slanting glass windows meeting curved ultramarine walls.

The Tate group were to be shown round by the museum's curator Cristina Portell, and the head of education, Martha Arzak, and they were all due to meet up in the reception area of the administration wing. As they stood around waiting, they noticed an intriguing detail about the design of the reception area, something they assumed Gehry and his team had failed to realize in time to do something about it. There was a staircase rising out of the reception area and the end of one of the I-beams that supported the staircase stuck out exactly at head height, and projected into the area where the Guggenheim's security guard sat. Clearly, it wouldn't have taken long after the opening of the building for the first occupant of the desk to stand up and give himself a nasty knock on the skull as he collided with the sharp corner of the beam. This turned out to be the case, and the beam end was now clad inelegantly in several layers of bubble wrap to soften the blow when, as was bound to happen, the same collision took place.

The group set off round the museum, empty of visitors because it was closed on Mondays. The huge atrium soared above their heads, revealing several layers of the museum, as galleries, balconies and walkways all appeared and disappeared at different heights. Over one of these balconies, giant white canvas leaves drooped, their stalks emanating from a large spherical shuttlecock. Through the many areas of glass, the old city kept showing itself, brightly lit and baroque.

Frances Morris is ceaselessly inquisitive. She carried her responsibilities lightly, as a key decision-maker for Bankside's collection. As she went around Bilbao, she asked question after question. Did this artist visit the gallery to see his work in place? Who decided to use this room in this way? How much did the Guggenheim tell the Spaniards what to do? Did they ever think of putting Brancusi next to Giacometti, instead of separating them by several rooms? If the museum was meant to reflect Basque and Spanish art, why was there so much American contemporary art?

Iwona Blazwick was thinking about Bankside's exhibitions policy. The Guggenheim curators weren't giving much away about *their* exhibitions policy, although they did reveal that they were planning an exhibition of traditional Chinese art, an odd choice for such a startlingly modern collection. Blazwick is tall, blonde and glamorous. Sunglasses pushed up into her hair, she strode the marble floors and made the occasional cutting remark, which may well have passed the curators by. When Señora Portell mentioned that Anselm Kiefer was considered a great artist, Blazwick muttered, 'Considered by some'.

The Kiefer room puzzled them all. In a huge space, maybe thirty metres long, were seven Kiefers, mainly flat artwork, collage and paint, with a lead, glass and paper sculpture on the floor. Quite a large proportion of the museum's whole stock of display space, but why? The Tate group seemed worried that, in spite of the good intentions of the Guggenheim organization to make this an autonomous Spanish museum, it appeared all the strings were being pulled from New York, and that a chance was being missed to make this something more than an outhouse for some of the Guggenheim's existing collection that they would otherwise keep in store.

In the 'fish gallery', the group saw a dozen or so huge works of art, some created specially for the space. As they wove their way through a sinuous Richard Serra corridor created by two heavy wavy sheets of steel, Blazwick reminded the others that art can sometimes be fatal, as demonstrated by another Serra sculpture that fell on someone and killed him. At the entrance to the gallery is a tall cylindrical maze, *Labyrinth* by Robert Morris, which admits only two or three people at a time, since its passages are too narrow for people to pass.

Every space in the gallery is different, and many rooms have curved walls, something which can make it difficult to display flat art. Gehry's extravagant building is actually about as different as you can get from Herzog and de Meuron's austere, rectilinear design for Bankside. It is also a much more intrusive building, distracting the visitor from looking at the art because the building itself is so compelling.

As Morris, Blazwick and Howell relaxed in the bar of their hotel in the evening it was clear they had mixed feelings about their experience.

'I think Bankside will be just as stunning in its own way,' Morris said, somewhat defensively. 'I really do, actually. That's the response I've got when I've taken artists about the site: they are completely knocked sideways by its scale and its height and the number of bricks.'

Caro Howell was more impressed. 'When we got lost trying to get there – which is very odd considering we were about two streets away, flailing around with our map – and a woman standing next door to us just pointed, it was at the bottom of the street like a spaceship had landed. Now, that is completely extraordinary. And Bankside is going to be wonderful and beautiful but it doesn't have that kind of quality.'

'You're fired,' joked Morris. 'I think it's extraordinary and wonderful and amazing, but it's a great folly as well, and Bankside has this incredible rootedness on its site. And once you strip away all the rubbish around it, it will be an absolutely stunning building.'

'I think the Guggenheim building is very performative,' Iwona Blazwick said. 'It's very much about the body, somehow. It surprises you and it choreographs space, and it's transparent, it's Gothic, it makes your spirit rise, in a sense, and it's very organic. And the works that seemed most successful there were works which responded to the architecture, so that it was a spatial experience really, even more than a retinal one, in a funny kind of way, just the way you moved around the space was tremendously exhilarating, I thought. But I wondered whether . . . what would happen if you had a very tiny, exquisite watercolour: my sense is that it would just vanish. And, in a way, works which dealt with the architecture were the most successful. What did you think?'

'It's an interesting parallel to what we're trying to do in London,' Morris replied. 'To a degree, in London the collection is the given. We've got a collection of twentieth-century works of art from Britain and abroad, and we've got to house them and we've got to create a series of events around them and we've got to communicate them and we've got to interpret them. And I get the feeling here that the building is at the centre, and that, over there in New York, there's a resource, which is the Guggenheim collection, which can be sort of picked off and pulled over, and installed in various different ways. But the building is the bedrock. And I absolutely endorse what Iwona says: the really exciting artistic experiences today, for us, or for me, were the Sol LeWitts wall drawings in the leaf-shaped room, and a Jenny Holzer, the digital piece – works that had been made by artists who'd visited the building, seen it unfolding as a structure, and responded to it.'

Blazwick was worried about the fact that a Spanish museum had such a strong American influence over its collection – not surprising, really, since the whole museum was a branch of the Guggenheim. Nevertheless, the museum had been built in a politically significant part of Spain, the Basque country, and its collection might have been expected to reflect more of the culture around it.

'I think the thing is that it reinforces the canon,' Blazwick said, 'which is that art is encompassed by this one city called New York, that's the problem with it. Also that it's so partial, and yet it presents itself as being a survey of some sort, so you're not aware of the nationality of the artist, you didn't think, well, hang on a minute, why is it we're in a Spanish museum and we just see there's a lot of

German artists, there's a huge amount of American artists, and a couple of Spanish artists, and maybe a smattering of French, and one British: where are the Latin Americans, and China, and where's Africa? Those questions don't get foregrounded, because it's just given as natural – "This is it, folks, this is how history is".'

In helping them think about how to display art at Bankside, it turned out that Bilbao couldn't really provide any models that the Tate could use. Frances Morris explained why. 'The building is complicated, it's complex, but there is this block of more classical galleries that house the core collection, which is, largely speaking, chronologically hung. And that probably is relatively coherent and it draws on masterpieces from the Guggenheim collection. That's one strand of the way they've displayed art. Another strand is that they have acquired groups of works by single artists, and they are being funded to provide a collection for Bilbao. And those works may have been selected by New York, working with Bilbao, but they represent artists like Schnabel, Basquiat, Clemente and Kiefer. So, they are resources housed at Bilbao to draw people locally and internationally, because it's what gives the museum its special character. And then a third strand is site-specific works that they've commissioned for the opening, and possibly will continue to commission. So I don't think those particular organizing principles are ones that we can adopt at the Tate, because we have a much broader collection, and the difference is we have a kind of responsibility because it's a national collection, and it's taxpayers' money, and every British visitor has a right to see what is "our Tate Gallery". And I think, gathering from what the curators have been saying today, there is a feeling in Bilbao that "it's our gallery, it's our building". But I wonder whether they feel that it's their collection. It's a Basque building in a Basque capital, but the collection has been brought in from abroad, and most of it's here temporarily, and I think that makes a fundamental difference.'

The following day, the three Tate staff had an opportunity to see the Guggenheim when it was full of visitors. Robert Morris's *Labyrinth* now had a queue of schoolchildren waiting to enter it, and there was a full-time attendant outside to control the traffic flow.

As they explored some of the galleries they hadn't seen yesterday, they were pleased at the absence of doors, an issue that was a constant

topic of discussion at Bankside. But they also had some caustic comments to make about labelling and about the way the museum tried
to keep visitors at a distance from the artworks.

As they sat on a cylindrical bench in the sunny entrance hall they
discussed what they had seen, against a deafening background of
excited Spanish schoolchildren.

'The signage is appalling,' Morris said. 'The signage relating to
works of art just doesn't work. In a well-meaning way they've tried
to separate signs from works of art, but it's very difficult to interpret
them or find out information about the particular works you're seeing.'

'And in some instances impossible,' Caro Howell chipped in. 'We
actually couldn't work out what one sign related to at all. So we were
standing there trying to piece it together, and even with the name of
the artist, we couldn't see the work it referred to. Also if you have to
search for your signs and then when you get there the information
you're given is absolutely minimal, all it does for the visitors is irritate
them because they've had to go seek it out and then it's not helpful
when they get there.'

Morris then said, 'It's one thing spending more time reading a sign
and getting information from it than looking at the work at art, which
is a problem we have at the Tate; but it's another thing spending more
time trying to work out what the label is meant to be telling you and
which work it's referring to. That I found frustrating. The other thing
I noticed in passing is that there are a number of warders, or invigilation
staff, who are really shepherding people, keeping numbers down,
preventing people from going into the labyrinth piece, for example,
and also preventing more than six people going into the Boltanski,
and that is very labour intensive. It's a massive add-on in terms of
cost to have to have people to do the job of signs, and therefore I
think that's maybe something we have to think about for the way we
display work at Bankside.'

On their tour that morning the group had stopped to observe
visitors looking at a collection of Joseph Beuys vitrines standing
against a wall, and were amused at the way some of them stood on
tiptoe a metre or so from one vitrine and tried to peer into the top of
the tiny structure inside. The natural approach would have been to
get nearer to the glass case but there was a thin black line along the

floor to keep visitors back and they were paying slavish respect to this minimalist barrier. The Tate team were in two minds about this method of crowd control.

'People really rigidly stick to it,' said Howell, 'but the problem is that they've placed it very uniformly and not actually considered in some instances the work it's applied to. So there are some Beuys vitrines and for one, the line is in front of it at the statutory distance and that's fine, but for the other, if you're not particularly tall, if you're in a wheelchair, if you're a child, the line is way too far away. Everybody was sticking to that, and then couldn't see far enough in to actually see what the exhibit is. And so there is some fine-tuning needed there.'

Caro Howell had a sharp eye for aspects of the museum that would help or hinder the task of educating the visitors. She had been involved in the early discussions with the Tate Bankside team about the education spaces and she could see evidence in Bilbao that, in her view, they didn't take their educational spaces very seriously, particularly in the light of the extraordinary nature of the rest of the building. 'We started this morning having a look at the auditorium and the education workshop space. It made me realize how lucky we are that we've been brought on board when we have, when a lot of the architectural plans are still open for negotiation. For instance, at Bankside not only is there wheelchair access into the auditorium, but there's actually wheelchair access on to the stage. And we went to the auditorium here and negotiating the stage is very difficult and when I asked, "How would you get a wheelchair on to the stage?" [the answer was] you can't except with great difficulty. And with the education spaces at Bankside, there's a number of things that are issues which I have come across and have been able to negotiate with the architects and have sorted out. One contrast with the rest of the building here which is so free-flowing and soft and open, is that in the rooms that we saw today the chairs and tables for children were really adult provisions for children. It was quite hard-edged, it was quite institutional.'

Frances Morris added, 'They seem to be an add-on, and they're very much behind the scenes. One of the ideas behind our thinking about educational resources at Bankside is that they should have a close physical relationship to the galleries, and therefore the education rooms are separated merely by thin wall, a glazed wall, from gallery space, circulation space; but here it very much feels down a long corridor and away from the presentation of art.'

As the group left Bilbao, Frances Morris summed up what she saw as the basis for the next major task they faced: pinning down the organizing principles for the Bankside displays. 'We're clear about one thing,' she said, 'and that is that we will break the collection down in terms of display into discrete and relatively self-contained units, so that it is possible to visit a section of the gallery and have a coherent experience of the art on display there. Each section should also have a clear relationship to every other section. And what we're debating at the moment is whether those relationships should be chronological, whether they should be formal, or whether they should be aesthetic.'

In the next six months, the Millbank room full of Post-its was going to come into its own as Morris, Blazwick and their colleagues began to present to Serota and the curators their pioneering new way of presenting modern and contemporary art to the public.

19

New Directions

Michael Craig-Martin lives in a house in North London whose interior he designed himself, as an open space with three different levels and a flight of vertiginous steps with no rails, down which small children could easily tumble. In March 1998, as he sat in an artistic chair in front of an artistic lamp, one of his more abstract paintings covered most of a wall behind him. He was talking about the search the Tate was carrying out for a director for the Tate Gallery at Bankside. As one of the Trustees, Craig-Martin was closely involved in that process.

'I would say in the world of museums, this has to be the most wonderful job in the world. And I think it's important that it should go to somebody who is of a younger generation. Nick is over fifty and I think it should be somebody in their forties. One of the brilliant things about the appointment of Nick was that he himself was then in his early forties. What that meant is that at the period of his life when he had the most energy, when he had a lot of time, when he was not under pressure of retirement or any of these things, he'd been able to give the full weight of the central part of his career to the Tate, and the Tate has benefited fantastically from that. Now I think the Tate can repeat this in this appointment, and that seems to me to be entirely the right thing to do.'

By pointing out that the Trustees preferred someone younger than Serota he was referring to the fact that it had occurred to Craig-Martin and a couple of other Trustees some time ago that Serota might be able to be director of Bankside as well as director of Millbank, at least for the first couple of years of the new gallery. But this idea had been firmly sat on by the majority of Trustees, and Serota himself had not really thought it could work. While Craig-Martin agreed with the decision not to appoint Serota, he gave up the idea reluctantly.

'This whole project would never have happened without Nick, and he has been the inspiration for a lot of people. It is very difficult therefore for those of us who've been involved since the beginning not to think of Nick as the director of it, because there's almost been a feeling that it was an inevitability. On the other hand, when looking at the total responsibilities of this new institution, where there are four museums – Bankside, Millbank, St Ives and Liverpool – it is a single institution and it will need an overall director, and each one of these places will need to have a form of directorship. In that situation it was decided that it was not possible for Nick. First of all, the Tate needed him to be at the top, and to be looking at the total picture in order to establish this new complex institution, and if he was at the same time as doing that trying also to be the director of Bankside, that that would be too much of a burden and impossible. I can't help feeling in my heart a little sorry for Nick that he can't be this person, but I don't think he's going to be entirely separate from it and I'm sure he would work very closely with the new director, but he will not be the director.'

Back in December 1996, Serota had said only that he was 'unlikely' to be director of Bankside. The Trustees' final decision was made in the summer of 1997, and by early 1998 Serota was explaining that the search was on for someone to fill 'the most exciting job in the contemporary and modern world'.

'There was, of course, a long discussion with the Trustees as to whether we needed such a person,' Serota said. 'There were members of the board who felt quite strongly that this was a project which I had guided from the beginning and that, for a number of reasons, I ought to be the person who was the director when it opened, and indeed for the foreseeable future afterwards. But in the end wiser counsels prevailed, and we advertised the post and we've had a range of very strong applicants.'

Asked whether he was on the side of the 'wiser counsels', Serota just said, 'I'm on the side of the greater good for the Tate Gallery. And I thought the best solution for the Tate Gallery was to have a director of the Tate Gallery of Modern Art who was distinct from the Tate Gallery of British Art, and distinct from the whole organiz-ation. And had I been ten years younger I would have wanted to apply for the post. But I thought that for the institution as a whole, the right thing at this stage was actually to try and find someone who could be the director of the Tate Gallery of Modern Art.'

One reason Serota gave for encouraging the Trustees' decision was a shared belief that whoever was director of Bankside would have to stay around long enough to see it grow. 'One has seen too many major projects that have opened and then fallen flat on their face – not that I think that this one will, but I just think that it's important to think about the future as well as the present. And one needs to build in succession and one needs to build in a new generation of thinking.'

The question now was: what sort of person could bring this new generation of thinking, and do it in the shadow of Serota? Craig-Martin hinted that the Trustees had set their sights on someone from outside the United Kingdom – shades of the Tate's choice of architect for Bankside. 'This a museum of international modern art, and I think it is proper that [the post] has been advertised internationally and that there have been applicants from Europe and from North America and that there will be a shortlist which will include people from different countries, and the possibility is certainly there that the director of Bankside could be a foreigner, which would be a very unusual thing for a British museum, if not unique.'

The shortlist actually contained two Americans, two British and two continental Europeans. It was the job of the decade, if not the century, for modern art curators and directors around the world, and it was said that if everyone who had said he was on the shortlist really had been it would have been a very long list indeed.

While Serota and the Trustees were whittling down the list and interviewing candidates, Frances Morris and Iwona Blazwick were pushing towards a deadline for presenting their views on the organization of the displays to Serota. The Post-its had evolved to flip charts, and the two curators plus Dawn Austwick gathered one morning in March 1998. Serota was late; he apologized and said that he had been having lunch with someone he described as 'unemployed royalty'.

On the table was a cardboard model of some of the existing wall layouts for one of the levels, which the group referred to from time to time during their discussions. Every profession has its shorthand, and as the three experts exchanged ideas over the next hour, names, movements and art historical terms were bandied around in a whirl-wind tour of the twentieth century. The thirty or so books piled up on the floor of the room showed that the group had read widely over history and philosophy as well as art. There was clearly a predetermined order to what Morris and Blazwick had decided to present, working up near the end to their preferred arrangement, but on the way to that endpoint, they threw up a number of other ideas that Serota liked and felt could also provoke some new ways of thinking about the arrangement of the collection.

Iwona Blazwick was the presenter of the ideas, moving around the room from sheet to sheet of flip-chart paper stuck to the walls. It would be easy for an outside observer of the meeting to get the impression that the three art experts – Blazwick, Morris and Serota – were conducting a seminar on the more abstruse aspects of art theory, unconnected with the fact that they were planning a gallery for a very general public audience. One of the first ideas to be presented to Serota, for example, was called 'Strategies of Making'.

'We were just brainstorming around strategies of production, pro-cess, intention, concept,' Blazwick said to Serota, 'and we came up with four broad areas, one of which for example was about automatism and the automatic, about trying to bypass the making of a work of art to make some very intuitive, non-controlled relation between inner thought or expression and gesture, and the work of art. And we're thinking about chance, relinquishing control, flux, primordial impulses, the irrational, the unconscious, and so forth. Another broad sphere that we looked at was the representational, to do with mimesis, observation, the copying, equivalence, printing, the ready-made and so forth. Another cluster was around construction, modelling, fabrica-tion, sculpting. And another cluster was about linguistics, text, epis-temology, knowledge, concepts. What do you think of this one?'

This framework, which wasn't the one eventually used, was never-theless a good template to test whether it would be possible to place any modern artwork somewhere in galleries organized along those lines.

Serota thought for a moment. 'Well,' he said, 'it's overtly didactic to the point at which most of the works of art on view would have to be seen as illustrations of a set of principles.'

'It has one interesting thing,' said Morris, 'which comes up again in a number of other options, and that is that artists could be situated in a number of different zones, and therefore as a framework it would allow a possibility of change over time within a broad framework that would remain fixed, and certainly when we begin to think about how we would circulate and redistribute the collection over time, the structure that can remain with internal variants will be quite important, and therefore though I don't think Iwona and I would advocate this as a model, it demonstrates something that might be quite positive in a model. But I agree, it's didactic, and it's maybe very difficult to extrapolate from it to your average visitor.' Then she quickly added, 'I know we don't have an average visitor.'

In fact, although this was one of the more academic frameworks the group came up with, their discussion was actually no more divorced from the needs of their public than an Ove Arup discussion about bending moments of steel I-beams was divorced from the need to stop the roof falling on gallery visitors. All professions have their jargon, technical terms and shorthand.

Blazwick and Morris took the group at a canter through eight other ideas, from 'Geographies' to 'The Zeitgeist of Ideas', 'Decades and Defining Moments' to 'Tendencies and Characteristics'. There was one constraint the group kept coming up against – the fact that most of the art displayed would have to come from the Tate's own collection. In describing 'Geographies', for example, Frances Morris said: ' "Geographies" came out of looking at the way the Pompidou Centre had done their shows, choreographed around geographical centres, and we wondered whether we couldn't overlay, broadly speaking, a chronology with a sense of geography and movement between centres, and so moving through time, we identified Paris, Berlin, New York, Milan and London as possible focal points for clusters of displays, and by the time we got to New York we . . .'

'Decided you didn't like it,' Serota interjected.

'. . . decided we didn't like it,' Morris continued. 'But, nevertheless, the idea that you might do something within a broad framework of geographies that might take on board fluidity and exile and borders and geography in a wider sense, remains a possibility for individual displays, which is why it has remained there.'

Serota liked the idea but was dubious about doing it justice from works the Tate owned. 'There's no way that the Tate's collection could give that map at present, even if we add in certain things that we would like to add in over the next two or three years. But I don't think that the ideas contained within it should be entirely ruled out. In fact, they have more potential than some of the things we've already been talking about in the sense that one of the messages that I think we need to convey is that without having a simple "Paris, New York, Rest of the World" sort of story, which is effectively what the Museum of Modern Art in New York did, I think what it does help to explain is that art is a social activity and that it comes about in part, and that works are made in part, in response to what other artists are doing and in response to social groupings of different sorts. And those groupings may well have been physical in the nineteen-thirties in Paris or again in New York in the nineteen-forties as people moved into exile in New York and grouped together. And now they're based on communication of different kinds, most commonly through magazine correspondents, but there's a much greater sense of people talking to one another across the world. So that principle might well inform some parts of the displays that we do otherwise.'

In spite of the high-powered nature of their exchanges, the two curators were occasionally on shaky ground when they stepped outside their immediate interests – and admitted it. Frances Morris introduced a framework they'd called 'History and Society'. 'We really began with 1900 and worked through to the present day and tried to put down what we perceived as being . . .'

'What you could remember,' Serota chipped in with a grin.

'. . . what we could remember *of our O levels*,' Morris said, picking up the joke. 'Interesting really. We could remember very little about the first decade; we knew an awful lot about the nineties.'

Each of the ideas presented had been tried on other curators and art experts, and Blazwick and Morris had obviously begun to focus in on their own favourite, which they now presented to Serota.

'We began by thinking of the traditional nineteenth-century genres in art,' Morris said. 'We put down portraiture and the nude, landscape, still life, and narrative history painting. And how they have moved in the twentieth century to a multiplicity of subjects and themes arising from them. Then we made connections between the twentieth-century subject and the earlier genres, and extrapolated subjects around the body, subjects around the environment, subjects around the everyday and subjects around society, as broad areas of interest and activity which can be traced back to the earlier genres. So that there is an art historical thread behind all these four sections, and yet the sections themselves deal with subjects that exist in art and life, and engage with ideas from every area of human activity. And so the idea behind this model is that each suite – or four suites will each be, broadly speaking, organized around a chronological examination and chronological distribution of works from the collection along these themes and sub-themes within them. As an exercise we took the environment as a theme and tried to make a list of artists who would have a connection with the theme and we underlined the ones with monographic potential or the potential for becoming the centres of clusters of groups.'

'When we say environment,' Blazwick said, 'we mean either land or urban scape or the phenomenal world – it could be cityscape or it could be space, light, sound.'

'One interesting aspect of this,' said Morris, 'is that you could situate bodies of works in one particular suite of galleries for a year or two years, and then see them in another suite of galleries in a very different context, and therefore over a period of time one could readdress Abstract Expressionism for example, in terms of its place within society; or you could look at it within the body, and then you'd begin to see it pitched in relation to, you know, for example, Surrealism for two years; and then show it in relation to post-war Paris.'

Serota then said, 'But to make this effective in year one, you have to split some of these in year one, rather than being categorical, because otherwise people will misread it.'

'You mean split the isms?' said Morris.

'Yes, I think the same thing has to appear in more than one place in year one,' Serota said.

It was clear as the group explored the idea that was to become the organizing principle of the new gallery that it was very different from the public's current expectations of the layout of art galleries and that it might have to be shaped in some way to meet those expectations.

'What is the means by which we convey to the public two things? One is which are the most influential and important artists in the twentieth century, and which are the most important works in the collection?' Serota asked.

'I don't know whether the collection really is about that,' said Morris, sharply.

'It is about it for a lot of visitors,' Serota said.

But Morris added, 'I do feel strongly that any visitor needs to be able to come and say, "What are the most important works?" and to be given a map and then they go and find them. But I don't think they should necessarily be grouped together in one room.'

Serota tried to explain. 'I suppose what I mean is, how are we are going to indicate through this that in spite of our limited collection, and with the works that we have, Duchamp, Warhol, Beuys, Matisse, Picasso are towering giants in one sense of twentieth century?'

Using the idea as a starting point, there were many questions that would have to be answered over the next few months. How could the intellectual scheme be fitted into the hard structure of the gallery layout, with rooms of different sizes and lighting conditions? Would every work of art the Tate wanted to display actually find a comfortable place in one of the four areas? How would artists, curators and Trustees react? And the new director of the gallery who was yet to be appointed? All those discussions were still ahead.

Although this might have seemed like quite an amiable and informal meeting as it had unfolded over the previous hour, there was a lot at stake. The Tate team was determined to have a well thought out, logical and coherent system for organizing the collection in the new gallery, one that would help visitors in a new way to understand some of the underlying currents that have conditioned the art of the twentieth century. They believed they could do it, and so confident was Serota that what they would come up with would be pioneering in the art world that he warned everybody to keep the results of their deliberations confined to a small circle of Tate staff and advisers. 'We're beginning to get to an area of difficulty in terms of how we start speaking about all this, both within and outside the gallery, because we're beginning now to get into an area of intellectual property, in terms of the fact that there are quite a lot of other museums that are thinking about this question at the moment, and we want to make sure that the first place it happens is the Tate. We don't want to see it four months earlier at the Pompidou Centre.'

On the morning of 20 April 1998, a month after the curators' meeting with Serota, senior staff at the Tate were gathered together to hear the name of the new director of Bankside, who was to be presented to the press in the next room later that morning.

All the hints about looking abroad for a new director, and the general atmosphere of Europeanism that had been initiated with the selection of Herzog and de Meuron, were confirmed when a chubby, smiling Swede walked into the boardroom after an introductory build-up by Serota to a dozen or so journalists. He was Lars Nittve, currently director of the rather confusingly named Louisiana Museum of Modern Art, near Copenhagen.

In May 1998, the following item was published in a British fortnightly periodical: 'A Swede has been appointed to run the prestigious £4 billion new Museum of Modern Garbage in an old power station in the heart of London's no-man's-land. It is believed to be the first time a root vegetable has been given a major role in the arts in Britain . . .' The periodical was *Private Eye*. Lars Nittve had made it in British society . . .

Lars (pronounced 'Larsh', although Serota always stuck to the English version) Nittve was like the cat that got the cream in the days after he learnt that he was to be the first director of the new Tate. He heard on Good Friday ('It was a very good Friday for me'), and a week later his appointment was announced to the world. He had only been in his previous job for three years and in fact had coveted the Tate job for longer than that. When he became director of the Louisiana, a journalist had asked him, 'what next?'

'Well, basically,' Nittve had replied, 'I actually have a contract until I'm seventy here at the Louisiana, and it's my intention to stay here. This is a fantastic museum. It has a great potential, and I want to develop that.' The journalist pushed him harder and then Nittve said, 'I can only think of one museum that could be so attractive that I could think about it, and that is the museum that will be the Tate Gallery of Modern Art. That sounds to be like as close as you can get to the ideal.'

Nittve seemed to have everything the Trustees and Serota had been looking for, starting with youth – he was forty-four years old. For example, he shared Serota's enthusiasm for converted industrial buildings as art galleries.

'I think that converted industrial buildings, at this time in history, seem to be the absolutely best museum buildings for modern and contemporary art, and I think there are many reasons for this. One thing may be that you don't put the same pressure on the audience in terms of high culture; you don't have so many symbols and signals, as you do when you have major staircases and colonnades and long sequences of galleries. It's also the fact that most artists' studios look – even though it's a smaller scale – basically like Bankside, and they have done that for a long time. Brancusi's studio was an old workshop, a kind of industrial space, and in a sense the works feel at home in that type of space. Usually, the museum architecture gets better in these cases partly because buildings like these tend to control the architects' egos, and also because I have this feeling that the architects start at the most important end. Normally architects spend a lot of time thinking about the façade, the exterior shape of the building, and then finally, you come to the galleries and light and things like that. Here you actually start with the galleries and with light, and the most important things for the display of art. And I think that is very good for the museum. More energy is put into the most important parts of the museum.'

By the time Nittve arrived, it might seem as if the architects' energy had already gone into the gallery to such an extent that Nittve would be presiding over a building over whose design he had little influence. But in fact, the Tate team had been aware of the timetable for appointing a director and, as Peter Wilson explained to Nittve when they first met, things were less fixed than they seemed. 'I thought the thing I needed to do first was to explain to him that no matter how it's drawn and built, it's got lots of flexibilities for the future built into it, which he need not worry about right now, and compromise the project completion, because the building is very flexible.' He was clearly aware of the possibility that Nittve might want to change things. 'Of course, he might think that that was just exactly the thing he ought to do at this stage, to imprint his authority on the scheme.

And I think we've left lots of opportunities for him to do that. It's very much a blank slate at the moment. If I were him – and I would be telling him this – I wouldn't do that in a kind of "head-to-head with the architects" manner: I'd wait. I'd wait a year or two before doing anything different. And there are lots and lots of opportunities for doing it differently from how it's conceived and drawn. You don't have to have fat walls, you don't have to have straight walls, you don't have to keep the light boxes that we've got on the ceilings – you could take those down and put in different lighting schemes relatively cheaply, almost within a temporary exhibition budget.'

Another view of the gallery that Nittve shared with Serota and the Tate Trustees was the need to pay attention to the surrounding community. 'It has to be a museum that's not only a tourist attraction, but a museum that's really rooted in the area where it exists in the local community, and I think it's very important that we don't repeat the mistake, for example, when the Centre Pompidou opened, when actually a part of the city was torn down where some poor people lived and the Centre Pompidou landed like from the moon, this big machine, and there was no connection to the community around it. And it's very clear that the Tate Gallery of Modern Art is going to be something totally different.'

Nittve seems an easy-going sort of person, polite, unassertive, unopinionated. He gave an interesting account of how he developed a relaxed attitude to modern and contemporary art as a result of disillusionment with an earlier dogmatism in his youth. 'When I was a teenager and into the early twenties, I was a very firm, solid Marxist and I really thought that I could basically explain everything in the world with the system that Marxism provided. And of course at some point the system started to show that it broke down, it didn't hold together, you couldn't explain anything; and if you followed an explanatory system to its end it always broke. And I think this experience – for me it led to a relationship to the world and what's happening in the world where I rather say "yes" than "no" to uncertainty and to change and to flux, and to things that are in between that can't be defined. And I think this is a lot what art is about, trying to formulate things that can't be formulated, for example, and to me I think that art partly encourages me to continue to be affirmative about the uncertain, the undefinable and also in relationship to change.'

Like Serota, Nittve was going to be confronted time and time again with the public incomprehension of some contemporary art. The more the new Tate aimed at a wide public, the clearer it was going to have to be about the question of uncertainty versus understanding. Somehow, people had to be given 'permission' for the two to coexist in one observer. 'Most people are curious about why does [a work of art] look the way it does. But I also think about the collection and the relationship between the collection and the audience as a process of learning and unlearning. On the one hand you want to give the audience tools to understanding and coming to grips with the art, and to be able to use it for their own purposes, for their own self-understanding and so on. On the other hand, I think it's also important to indicate in a sense that there is no one way to understand a work of art, or to see an artist or to see an artwork.

'I remember a person in the galleries of the Louisiana who had walked through the museum, had seen the Giacomettis and seen the Henry Moores and the most contemporary works, and he said, "I just don't get this. And I'm walking and wondering, 'Is it me, or is it the art?'" And of course he was leaning towards the thought that it might be the art, because he didn't think he was a stupid man. And then I told him a story about something I had experienced when a friend of mine took me to a cricket game in England. We never see cricket in Scandinavia, we don't know anything about it, and I sat beside this man that had brought me, and he was excited and everybody else was excited and they reacted to things, and to me it was a totally enigmatic thing going on, and of course at some point I had to think, "OK". First I thought, "This is a stupid game. I mean, this is ridiculous." But then I thought, "There are thousands of people here who think this is great, so maybe it's me." And of course, I didn't know the rules, I didn't know the place, I didn't know the teams, I had no history with it, and it became meaningless. And in that sense you can learn something without coming to a final conclusion also about an artwork. The more you know, the more you see.'

20

The Trouble with Harry

In February 1998, the first elements of the Grand Stair were driven to London from Kegworth, and the long process of installation began. As each floor of steel rose in the west half of the Boiler House, new landings and sections of steps were installed, in an operation made tricky due to two factors. First, there were very tight constraints on fitting the required number of levels into the height available for the staircase. Second, the void that had been left for the staircase in the steel was a complex shape which was slightly different at each floor, the result of factors like the lift-machine room, variations in the layout of rooms on each floor, interactions with the plant rooms, and so on.

As Trubros and Rowen battled to erect the staircase in the midst of delays in the main steel framework, Stanhope and Schal staff began to dread what would happen next, as a series of problems arose. One day in July 1998, Andy Butler of Stanhope Properties described just a couple of them.

'Basically,' he said, 'the staircase has been installed to the wrong levels.' It has to be admitted that this did seem pretty basic. But what had happened was that the floor finishes at the point where the stair landing met the floor of the building were a different thickness from the finishes on the landings, so there was a small step where the stairs met the floors.'

'We're now breaking off connections, and jacking the staircase up,' Butler said later. 'It's quite an awesome task.' He quickly added – lest Harry Gugger should be in earshot – that this didn't mean it would now be possible to move the whole staircase sideways, to correct the architects' error of last December.

And just to add to the confusion, as flights of steps were delivered to be installed above each landing, it turned out that some of them had extra steps. A world-weary Butler seemed to think this was a small cross to bear by this stage. 'To be honest, the cure is worse than the disease. So, we'll live with those, and the architect's reasonably relaxed about that. You've got to view it in the context of the volume of information that even an element like this will produce in terms of design information. And a draughtsman makes a mistake. Unless both the architect and the engineer specifically focus on it – and they're not looking at this in isolation, they're looking at this in the context of three hundred other drawings – it happens.'

When the progress in steelwork allowed the staircase to rise from Level 2 to Level 3, someone walking up the newly installed flight of steps noticed an ominous lack of headroom at a certain point on the stairs. The underside of the flight above formed a sloping ceiling for the flight below, and at one point on the flight of steps, the vertical distance between step and ceiling was below the statutory minimum. This could not, by law, be allowed to remain.

'If you're six foot plus and walk down there with a hard hat on, you'll hit your head,' said Andy Butler. 'We were trying to shoehorn a very contrived design, and we were struggling with head height in several places, and we had it right on the minimum. Now, arguably, we should have picked it up, but there was nowhere to go – we just couldn't get it to work – and they were just hoping that when they got to the top they would get the minimum. Well, that never happens.'

In designing the staircase, the architects had drawn each flight so that there was enough headroom – sometimes only just enough. But there are always tolerances that have to be allowed in construction. The level of the concrete raft in the basement could end up slightly higher or lower than it should be; each floor of steel may vary a little; and the dimensions of the elements of the staircase itself may vary slightly.

Harry Gugger explained how it was so easy for such things to happen. 'Building is in centimetres, you know, so you lose very easily two centimetres. First of all the structural slab might not be in its exact position; then you have a build-up on the floor – so two mistakes can easily add up to two centimetres just like that. And this has been the case there. It would have been nice if it would be perfect, but they're just going to have to cut this piece out and set it back.'

In Gugger's view, there was a pleasing quality to the variations the visitors would experience as they climbed the staircase, and the different head heights at different levels was part of this experience. 'We liked this compression – the stair on your way up has different sensations at each level – so it was never the idea that it should be the same all the way through. The stair reacts to different conditions on the different floors, looking out on to the concourses and so on, and so we liked it that in one instance you would be really compressed. But I think certain people think that's just a bit over the top, and they would like it to be more generous, and this can be achieved easily by relocating this one flight.'

'Easily' was not the word the Tate team would have used. 'What we've got to do,' said Butler, 'is we're going to gain an extra hundred and fifty mil [fifteen centimetres] by cutting the staircase and setting it back horizontally. It'll cost about sixty thousand pounds and take about three weeks.'

Like many of the people on the construction side, Butler had never really warmed to the Grand Staircase. 'I think it's a poor element,' he said. 'I think anything that costs the amount of money it costs, it tells you that you've got it wrong. That staircase cost thirteen thousand pounds a tonne to fabricate. I've never known a staircase cost anything like that in my life. If the market doesn't want to price it and nobody wants to build it, you know you've got the design wrong. I'm no architect, and I'm not here to slag it off, it's just that I look for good value in any element, and that isn't good value to me. And we're still spending money on it, and we'll continue to spend money on it until we finish it.'

The finish date was surprisingly late in coming. Once the structure was in place – with its levels adjusted and Level 2 moved backwards to create more headroom – there was a large amount of work to be done on fitting wooden treads, wooden handrails, and lighting above the handrails. The design details of these extra elements, and how they were to be fixed in place, had to be approved by the team on a series of mock-ups, and that process dragged on and on through 1998 and into 1999. Colin Berry, a Schal site construction manager, was not pleased. 'We're still struggling with the Grand Stair, in that the designers are still tinkering with the design sixteen months after the first mock-up was completed. We still don't know exactly how we're going to build it, in terms of the timber handrail. We're still doing modifications to the base structure, over a year after it was first installed.'

It was no secret that Herzog and de Meuron were frustrated by many aspects of the fact that they were a Basel firm working on a London project. One of their concerns was that by splitting their team between two places they would lose control of the design. Their Basel operation, with its dedicated team and its unusual work habits – coffee at ten, football matches together, compulsory lunch – promoted constant informal contact between the partners and the other young architects on the team. As the work on-site moved from broad, large-scale construction towards the more detailed work on windows, stairs, floors and glasswork, Herzog and de Meuron tried to maintain the same sort of control that they had been used to in Basel. And this involved controlling construction as well as design, since every contractor's attempt to translate Herzog and de Meuron's designs into shop drawings for their own processes involved design decisions. Often in the UK this process was supervised more by the client than the architect, who had done his bit by providing the plans. But Gugger and his colleagues wanted to see the process through till the finished articles were on-site, something which the Tate hadn't expected. 'We've never designed something and handed it over and didn't care any more,' said Gugger. 'We are very keen on talking to the contractors and to make sure that they understand what has been put on the drawings, and they don't always.'

But the British contractors were not used to being talked to directly by the architect, and Schal were not used to allowing or encouraging that process to happen. Part of this was because they didn't want to open the door to changes that would affect the cost and schedule as a result of the architect having a better idea.

'Everybody is scared to death [at project meetings] if you come up with a better proposal,' Gugger said. 'And, of course, it's a disruption. But obviously, because we have these lump-sum contracts these contractors are really out there and just wait for the designer to change some things, so that they can get their feet into the door and say,

"Well, you disrupted our process of construction – we will have programme delays and discuss certain debts". So you are basically forced to accept what you designed two, three years ago, but your ideas might have changed. Or a contractor might just prove not to be able to achieve what you've designed – that's very often the case. They just propose what they've always done, and they haven't even looked at our drawings. And then, if you find out after a while that it's really not possible for this contractor to come up with what you would like to see, you may be much better off re-thinking your own idea.'

The British method – all communication mediated by the construction manager – had several drawbacks, according to Gugger. 'I come up with this proposal, then I have to communicate this to the construction manager, and he's going to communicate this – without me – to the contractor. And, already, in this step, something gets missed out. How can a construction manager who has to come up with a building on time, be enthusiastic in talking to the contractors about the architect's idea? He will say: "See, it is the architect who came up with this idea to realign these toilets. I see there are lots of problems for you – do you think you can deal with that?" And if you approach these guys this way, it certainly doesn't work out, this is pretty clear. But how else should he approach it? Because he's aiming not to change it, because he's much happier and much better off if we don't change it now.'

Gugger was surprised – naively perhaps – at how the good atmosphere there had been in the Tate team when Herzog and de Meuron won the Tate competition seemed to have evaporated once they were involved in designing and constructing the building. 'You come up with this international competition and have this very nice time developing a project with the client, and then, when it shifts to the construction, there is another atmosphere. It starts with people being replaced. There are project managers who are stronger and more skilful in the concept phase of the design, and there are project managers who are more used to dealing with sites. I think that's wrong. You gain qualities, of course, by replacing this person, but you lose qualities, important qualities, because the project manager who was working with you through the whole concept phase has an understanding of your ideas, and you have to start and to convince someone else again, and to talk him into your ideas. So I think there should be more people around who are willing to go through the whole process, who are more generalists, as we architects are forced to be.'

Gugger had these concerns in July 1998, as the steel was – finally – nearly complete and the concrete floors were solidifying all over the building. He could see that for another year at least he would have to be vigilant about the major phase that was about to begin, as the building was enclosed, the heating and ventilation switched on and the temperature and humidity controlled. The companies that were contracted to carry out the finishes were about to set to work, and Gugger wouldn't believe that they could produce the kind of quality Herzog and de Meuron required until he could see and touch it for himself.

Andy Butler, who observed Gugger's frustrations with the construction management system, put it down to a fundamental difference in timescale and cost between projects in Switzerland and Britain.

'They don't build at anything like the pace we build here. With their traditional forms of contract, by the time the contractor's on board, the job's fully designed, and they've had two years to go through the change process. And, also, [the architects are] managing it, anyway, and they're also managing all the funds, the whole process. I do have some sympathy with Harry. It's very difficult to come to terms with the rigours of construction management, but this is a very tight programme. In ten months' time, we hand this building over. If this was built in Switzerland, I guarantee it would be more expensive than it is here.'

By mid 1998, Dale Sager had taken over as Schal's senior on-site manager from Mike O'Rorke after his alleged abrasiveness led to him moving on. Abrasiveness was replaced by emollience, as the tall, laid-back American listened to the architect's complaints about the quality of the workmanship and used his considerable managerial skills to address the issues without alarming the Tate team.

At Sager's first project review meeting, on 2 June 1998, Harry Gugger expressed his unhappiness at the quality of work he was seeing on the site. 'I still can't cope with the situation over here. I think the general level of quality is terrible. They are now building shutters on the second floor and just the way they are putting them up is setting a level of quality which affects the other guy following on. He thinks, "If this guy didn't care, why should I?" In the middle of a row of five floor grilles, they just left one out.' What Gugger had seen was not just a grille missing from a hole: there was no hole either. 'And no one tells me and there's nobody I'm supposed to tell, so who knows about this? What I would like to see happening is that if there is an element of work executed for the first time we are invited to a quality check with Schal and this contractor.'

Sager tried to reply in a conciliatory way, although he was clearly still coming to grips himself with a site that was new to him. Gugger ploughed on. 'We would like to contribute to a culture on-site, to motivate these people. And if I find in a row of five grilles one missing, I'm freaking out and I think, "Who the hell cares?" and, "How can such an obvious thing happen?" and, "Is it under control?", and there might be larger elements that are more worrying than just cutting a hole in the slab again.'

On behalf of Schal, Sager accepted responsibility for the specific omission, but of course, what was required in Gugger's view was a new system, not just a new hole in the floor.

'You can approach this by telling the contractor that this is about the void you have to create in the floor and that's it. Or you can take him through all the trades – "After you is the screed; this guy has to work to this limit; then there has to be a metal angle on top", and so on – it's really just setting up a level of quality.'

'Dale, it's down to you,' said Peter Rogers of Stanhope Properties.

'We will put it in place,' said Sager.

Speaking about the situation later, Sager was less conciliatory. 'I don't agree with his criticisms. But I think that, coming from Switzerland, he has a different perspective on quality. They construct buildings differently. The architects have a much higher level of involvement. And I think that he's making judgements, and perhaps he's basing it on performance that is already out there, but there's a different level of quality desired in the UK, and a different level of quality purchased.

If there is a problem on-site, it will be made right. There are always problems on-site, and that's not anything new to construction.'

So it seemed that the British way included making mistakes first and correcting them, rather than not making them in the first place.

After the project review, the participants, joined by Nick Serota and Jacques Herzog, had gone to an outpost of the Tate, in Southwark, where they stored many of the works that they didn't have room to display. Here, in an empty warehouse space, the team inspected a mock-up of a gallery wall with a door in place. One point of interest was to see how the small gap between the bottom of the wall and the floorboards was going to be dealt with, since the architects had banned skirting boards.

Ten minutes after the group gathered around the mock-up and started to discuss it, Nick Serota arrived. Word of Gugger's concerns had already reached him. 'I've been told the workmanship's no good,' he said. As they inspected a sample of a gallery door and how it would fit into the wall opening, Serota was horrified. 'It's going to depend on such exquisite craftsmanship that we're not going to get it in every door. Isn't there anything we can do to improve the tolerances? At the moment it looks like something I might have knocked up at home.'

'It's pretty good, for you,' said Bill Woodrow, one of the Tate's artist-Trustees, who sat in on a number of the design discussions.

'Everything looks really cheap,' said Herzog.

One ingenious feature of the design of some doors was that they folded right back across the thickness of the fatter walls, so that they were not really obvious as doors. Today's meeting provided a chance to see if that idea could be made to work, but the task was made more difficult by the fact that the door provided today had a curve in it and bowed outwards.

'The question is, is the concept wrong?' said Gugger. 'This whole idea of hiding the door – is this the wrong approach? We're going to spend a lot of money trying to create this effect, and if it doesn't work it'll be far worse than just admitting that there are doors. We could even afford to have better quality doors. It's only worth spending the money if you get the effect that you're looking for. Part of the problem here is that we are looking at something that is not well enough made to register what it is that you're aiming for, because every time I look at this I see this bowing door.'

Next they turned their attention to the gap between the bottom of the wall and the floor. As Gugger introduced the topic, Herzog said, 'I wish to have no gap.'

'Technically, it's not possible,' said Gugger.

Herzog shook his head.

'We can't find any mastic that won't bleed into the floor,' said Ron German.

'It's very difficult to get mastic into a five-mil gap,' said Andy Butler.

'If we could have something and we fill it in and then we paint over?' suggested Herzog.

'If they bring in heavy art, the whole floor deflects to twenty-five millimetres, and no mastic does this,' Gugger said.

'If you have a gap you always have a gap,' Herzog said in a resigned way.

'It's a weird situation to argue with,' Gugger said. 'I am not in favour of mastic. I am not in favour of gaps either, but somehow I understand how this bloody building works.'

Dale Sager explained why the mock-up seemed in such a poor state, and why, for example, the door was bowed. 'The doors were difficult because they were in a situation that was not environmentally sound, so they absorbed water. And so it was impossible to see how it would ever come together. And it was clear the quality wasn't acceptable, so we will go back and put in a mock-up adjacent to the building. It will be dehumidified space, so that it is environmentally sound.'

He also explained the difficulties presented by the architects' insistence on little or no gaps at the bottom of the wall, and something else they insisted on – very smooth walls. 'It is very difficult to create a consistent gap between the wall and the floor; it is difficult to create that same gap at the ceiling; and it's extremely difficult to create a flat surface on a wall – and these are very tall, long walls, and they're untextured. And texture adds a level of cushion to the quality, so that the more texture on the wall, the less you need to make it flat. Little ripples disappear in the texture, and that isn't the case when they're super-flat walls, which are what these are.'

As these dramas were unfolding, and the architects' frustration increasing, Harry Gugger was gratified to find some moral support from another architect, David Chipperfield, the only British finalist in the Tate competition. 'This is an enormous struggle,' Gugger said. 'You might find, here or there, a little corner or a detail which you would like to improve, but you don't do it any more, because you know you will hit your head hard. There is this very interesting article I recently read about David Chipperfield, who, like many British architects, does most of his work abroad. And, in his case, he has hardly had any big commissions in the UK, and has a lot of work abroad.' He held up a trade journal containing the article, and read out a Chipperfield quote: '"In Britain, far too many architects are forced to work not with clients direct but with project managers and other intermediaries. These guys want to talk exclusively about budgets, timetables, and value for money. They are the kiss of death. How the hell can you measure the value of a gallery or a museum, much less a cemetery?" I think that's a valid point,' said Gugger, and he read on: '"In Britain, architects are digging their own graves by allowing themselves to give up their art, their history, their culture, to satisfy a new wave of managers who don't care that much for architecture itself. We are lucky we've ended up working with clients who do care and who want to be an active part of the whole process of creating buildings and shaping cities."'

'And I think this last paragraph is very important,' Gugger said, 'because, I should say, *we* are lucky, as well, that we have ended up working with a client who cares. Otherwise, I think it would be impossible. So, there is still this support from the client, and they are still somewhat motivating us in being an active part of the process.'

Gugger was to make his own contribution to knocking British construction practices when he was interviewed for an article in the British magazine *Building* in March 1999:

'I don't enjoy the site,' Gugger says bluntly. 'Things are carelessly put together and there are problems with how the site looks. Switzerland is paradise in comparison – the quality of craftsmanship is far better. In Britain I meet workers who were employed yesterday and will be gone tomorrow. How do the contractors know how good they are? In Switzerland workers go through an apprenticeship and work for companies continuously.' Gugger also has problems with how the site is managed. 'I am used to talking directly to trade contractors,' he says. 'Here you have to go through the construction manager. Some of my instructions have been compromised.' Working for Schal has been another problem for Gugger. Schal has used three different project managers in the twenty months the project has been on-site. 'Each time you lose key staff you lose knowledge from the project,' says Gugger.

Peter Wilson took a surprisingly tolerant view of Gugger's remarks, which had greatly annoyed Schal and its team. 'I think they were entirely understandable,' he said, 'given his background and what he sees in other places. We just do things slightly differently from how he's used to them. I think no one from Herzog and de Meuron actually gives themselves credit for how tolerant a building they've designed in terms of quality. Quality is not dependent upon absolutely straight lines at every point, but actually I think they've built a building that is pretty tolerant of the kind of construction you get in a big building. They make factories, and their factories are just as beautiful pieces of design as the houses that they make for private individuals, but they have different tolerances built into them, and I think instinctively they've built kind of factory tolerances into this building because that's what it requires.'

But this didn't mean that the Tate would look like a factory. 'It's somewhere between a factory and a private house,' Wilson said. 'It was a big industrial building; it's full of spaces that house objects that are created during an industrial age, and it doesn't have to be absolutely pure in every line. It's got a kind of tolerance and a roughness about all of it.'

Andy Bramwell, on Wilson's staff at the Tate, said of the *Building* article, 'A story which says that the architect doesn't approve of quality on-site is a bit like "Dog bites Man" really, and it didn't seem to bother anybody. The one thing I thought was slightly pointed about the article was the photographs, which had the feel of a "look at this mess – is it going to be finished?" agenda behind them; and there wasn't a single soul in sight in any of the photos, when we know there are five hundred and fifty people turning up here every morning to work.'

About the time of the publication of the *Building* article, and nine months after the peak of his concerns about quality, Gugger considered the issue again in the light of how things were now going on-site. 'It's difficult to talk about this, because I'm supposed to say that it's all great and it's wonderful. Someone has taught me to say, "Of course there are differences in quality, and some of it is wonderful" – that's the answer I'm supposed to give now. That's the English way to express it. There are also, of course, some things which are not a success, but it's best to try to be positive. Sometimes it just would be nice to come over and look at something and just feel good about it, and I must say very often this hasn't been the case – we have had to complain until it was adjusted. But we are getting there, and there are good results.'

For Peter Wilson, some of these issues, which Gugger complained about on many occasions during the finishing stages of the project, should have been anticipated. 'We warned Herzog and de Meuron from the outset that the kind of details they expected would be very hard to achieve. It was clear to us that standards of workmanship are higher in Switzerland. I'm afraid it's cultural, and reflects pride in the quality of what is done. Harry and Jacques, particularly, have always had a touching – and quite misguided – notion that if they had talked to the workforce rather than Schal, a different outcome would emerge. If it had been true we'd have fallen over ourselves to get them to do so.'

21
A Site for Sore Eyes

From the earliest days of the Bankside project, Peter Rogers of Stanhope Properties had been an active participant in the weekly – becoming daily – meetings that took place between the main groups responsible for getting the new gallery built on time and on budget. Stuart Lipton's company had been advising Nick Serota since the Tate first decided to seek a site for a new gallery, and although Lipton himself attended occasional meetings, it was really Rogers, Ron German, and later Andy Butler who supplied most of the expertise that Serota needed to help him be a good client. German was largely full time for the early phases of design and construction, with his own office at Millbank, while Rogers gave the impression of being a visiting fireman in a situation where fires kept breaking out all the time. He was a thin, short-haired man with a grin of steel. Peter Rogers blended the skills of civil engineer, developer, project manager and bad cop as he used his skill, his psychology and his contacts in the service of the new gallery.

He explained why the project needed someone like him at all, when the Tate already had a multi-talented team drawn from its own staff, plus a major British construction management company in Schal to ensure that the design was buildable, and that it was then built. 'We take a different approach to construction from many of the traditional people, partly because we've done the whole process and we actually understand how buildings are going to be used, why they're going to be used and, therefore, what sort of reaction there is to the way they're built and the way they're designed. Our input starts at the beginning and then we try and act as a catalyst all the way through the process. Clearly, there are project management functions that we also do. But our real skill is the base knowledge that we have.

'One of the most interesting things for me was that our start in arts projects came out of working with Nick on the Whitechapel Art Gallery, where we were asked to help him with the completion of a job that was running late, and had gone over budget. And we really used commercial office skills that we'd used on those types of buildings, to help an arts project. And the skills are transferable. And all of a sudden you realize, if you apply the same commercial judgements, the same pressures to a project, it doesn't matter whether it's a traditional office building or the Tate Gallery or the Royal Opera House, or Glyndebourne. And it's become a very interesting part of our business. It's different, it's fun, it's probably more challenging than the traditional construction, because the clients are more demanding, and the buildings themselves are more complex just because of what they're trying to do, and the architecture itself tends to be more interesting.'

To the outside observer, it could sometimes seem as if Rogers and his boss Stuart Lipton made a living by saying the blindingly obvious at times of crisis, but often it wasn't what they said but the forceful and sometimes brutal way in which they said it.

Peter Wilson, astute as ever, summed up the function the senior Stanhope figures performed for the Tate at the regular client project reviews. 'Those meetings do have people who parachute in and we ask them to be there and to do that sort of thing, and so inevitably they do produce a snap judgement, and in a sense, to borrow Stuart Lipton's turn of phrase, it's a piece of theatre, that meeting, where everyone gets a chance to have their actions tested against people who are not in day-to-day touch with them. I find those meetings challenging because Nick, and to a lesser extent Dawn, is not in touch with the day-to-day business and so they ask questions that you might have forgotten to ask yourself. We've actually been caught on the hop once or twice in the past year and the focus is now to make sure that we've prepared better for that. But I still expect things to come up that we haven't dealt with. And I don't mind if people do ask apparently quite fatuous – almost – questions because, at times, they're the sort of things that you might just have forgotten to ask yourself, and some-times they're right. And Peter Rogers is particularly good value in that kind of mode, and asks very searching questions.'

Rogers accepts quite readily the role of saying the obvious. 'We do it because the same things keep going wrong. The day-to-day problems of building projects tend to drive people to solving the day-to-day problems; they don't look ahead nearly well enough, with nearly enough forethought. So, a lot of it is repeating, "Why don't you do this?" Part of it, of course, is borrowing good ideas from other people. Like most industries, there's not that much real innovation. It's actually looking around, bringing in good ideas from other construction projects, even other industries, and slowly introducing them. Construction's terribly conservative. We hate change, and therefore even from that point of view, one's got to keep pressuring, just to try and make sure it gets done.'

Serota found Rogers' role a tremendous help to the Tate (not surprisingly since he had invited Stanhope on board). 'Peter's role is to be, at certain moments, the client's representative, and to argue on our behalf that certain things should happen. And he has enormous experience of the building industry. He has probably more experience than many of the people working in Schal, and therefore from time to time he can give them advice which we hope they'll take, and occasionally they have taken it; and it seems to have been to everyone's benefit, including Schal's.' Serota was speaking in early 1999, and he gave Stanhope credit for a lot that had gone right on the project. 'The role they've played, and their degree of success, may be seen by the fact that we're still on time and on budget, and that's not true of many other major building projects. And it's a pretty complicated building.'

Rogers was always a lively participant in the construction process and he was seen at his liveliest on the many site 'walkabouts' that he did, eyes peeled for problem areas, and indeed problem workers. Trailing Schal managers, architects and contractors behind him, like a monarch on some speeded-up royal progress, he would plunge into the bowels of Bankside and work his way to the top, firing questions, observations and recommendations into the air and relying on the individuals they were directed at to hear and act on them.

One such walkabout took place on 26 October 1998. Rogers, Dale Sager and John Carter, a bluff, immovable Schal construction manager, strode through the access passage that ran through the

Switch House and on to the bridge in the Turbine Hall. Barely pausing, they headed towards the back of the building on Level 1. As they passed the two escalators that would bring visitors up from the entrance level, Rogers asked how many were in. 'Just the two,' Sager said, and explained how they'd had some difficulty hoisting the huge pieces of equipment straight up, because of some projecting steel they'd had to work around. 'That was a mistake,' said Rogers and strode on.

Rogers had the habit of placing bets as he toured the building, bets which were probably never collected. 'You must owe me at least a fiver,' he said to Sager, referring to a bet on a previous walkabout. 'This steel hasn't been touched in two months.' Rogers was a keen advocate of the 'just in time' policy used in various industries from construction to aviation. Materials should be delivered to site as near as possible to the time they are needed. There are all sorts of reasons why this is a good idea, not least the fact that if something is in your possession two weeks or a month before you need it, you must have bought it too soon and therefore no longer have the use of the money that pays for it.

As the group waited to go up in one of the construction hoists, Rogers discussed when the hoist was going to be taken down so that the metal that was lying around could be used – the hoist was in the way of the construction it was meant for. When Sager told Rogers the hoist would go at the end of January, Rogers said, 'I'll take another fiver with you – the hoist *doesn't* go at the end of January.'

When they reached Level 6 and swept out of the lift, Rogers was halted in his tracks by an innocuous-looking skip full of rubbish. He peered closer. 'Christ,' he said, 'where are we using cork?' As they walked the floor, Rogers noticed odd puddles of water. 'Are we enclosed?' he asked John Carter.

'At this end we're having awful trouble with the wind. It's driving the water in.'

'It's fundamental to practical completion that we get the building watertight,' said Rogers firmly, in a statement whose tone was more important than its content, since any first year student of construction management would know that fact.

They stepped out on to the flat area between the base of the Light

Beam and the Turbine Hall roof, paused to watch some glaziers at work, and then stepped back into the building. Rogers' eyes lit up as he saw several large sections of ductwork lying around. 'I still ask why the hell do we allow so much material on the site,' he said to Sager.

In his calm, unflustered, lightly amused tone, Sager said, 'This stuff is new, being delivered right now.'

There was no way of knowing whether he was telling the truth, but it sounded good, although it didn't satisfy Rogers. 'How many days' work is it?' he asked.

'This week,' said Sager. Rogers turned to one of the people who was installing the ductwork, to get a sense of whether these pieces were really needed imminently, and the man explained the programme. 'I understand all of that,' said Rogers, 'but at the end of the day you make it much more difficult for people to work in here because you've got so much kit on these floors.'

'There's no one else working here,' said the man, doggedly.

'They go out there trying to put ductwork up,' Rogers ploughed on, 'and are trapped between pipes and other things.'

The man explained why this actually wasn't happening.

Rogers still had to make his point, in what was probably one of Stuart Lipton's 'pieces of theatre', to impress matters on the knot of courtiers. 'The whole principle of trying to get stuff in when you actually need it for a couple of days and no more is essential,' Rogers said. 'Look at the ductwork up here – there's got to be more than a few days' worth of work up here. And they're bringing more up.'

'I'm more than happy that we've got it here,' John Carter said. He would rather the security of knowing the stuff was around instead of risking losing a day's work while waiting for late deliveries.

'Yeah, but it's the wrong approach.'

Rogers should have saved his breath. The next hour was to be punctuated by the sight of heaps of ductwork, apparently on every floor.

It was an odd characteristic of such a complex site that it almost never seemed busy. Instead, there would be the occasional distant glimpse of a knot of men doing some wiring, or an individual workman inlaying wood into the steps of the Grand Staircase. Rogers obviously sensed this emptiness.

'How many guys have you got on-site?' he asked Carter.

'Three hundred and fifty to three hundred and sixty,' he replied.

'And they're all here, are they?'

Along one side of Level 6 there was evidence that the installation of Light Beam glass by a firm called Felix was not going well.

'Have Felix slowed up or is it just the wind?' Rogers asked.

'Wind and weather,' said Carter. 'It's been abysmal.'

'There's no wind today,' Rogers said, relentlessly.

'They're working down there,' Carter said, pointing to the next level down. Rogers peered through one of the empty frames overlooking the river a hundred feet below to check on whether Carter was telling the truth.

'Let's drop down,' he said, but he only meant to the next floor.

On the next level Rogers couldn't contain himself at the sight of more ductwork. 'You and your bloody ductwork,' he said to no one in particular. 'Look at it. There's fucking ductwork everywhere.'

Sager and his senior colleagues were obviously used to the Rogers technique and let his occasional theatrical outbursts pass over their heads while they studied nearby fixtures intently, but for those people exposed only occasionally to his strictures, it could be an uncomfortable business.

As the group walked through one of the plant areas on Level 6, a young site labourer was sweeping dust and debris into a small pile. He probably thought he was doing something useful, but he was soon disabused of that notion. When Rogers spotted the man, he said to Sager, 'Another man with a broom!' This was obviously another of Rogers' bugbears. 'I thought we'd scrapped those,' he said. Then, raising his voice, he shouted, 'Feller, stop doing that, it's a complete waste of time!'

The startled broom-wielder looked up at this enraged member of the middle classes and stopped in his tracks. 'Either get a vacuum cleaner or don't do it!' Rogers shouted. 'It actually fucks the plant up – all you're doing is putting dust up into the filters.' As they walked on, the young man probably didn't realize that he had had a narrow escape. On a similar walkabout recently, when Rogers had come across someone sweeping up the dust, he had seized his broom and snapped it in two.

Downstairs on the next level there was a pile of scaffolding poles lying on the ground. 'It's parked here waiting to go up to the sixth floor,' said someone quickly, anticipating Rogers' next question.

'I'm going to have a fine-system for all the kit. We'll have parking fines for all the stuff that's left around the site for more than forty-eight hours.'

'That'll come a little expensive,' said John Carter.

'I don't mind anything that comes in as long as it goes up,' Rogers replied. Two floors down and it was, 'Oh, look, more ductwork.' In the galleries on Level 4, Rogers noticed that one of the tall windows didn't open fully but seemed to be stopped by a blind fitting. 'Are they the right size?' he said to Sager. 'I'm 99.99 per cent sure they are,' Sager replied, with – for him – a worrying degree of uncertainty. (Actually, they weren't.)

As they walked through Level 4, Rogers inspected a room that was being prepared as a canteen to replace the Portakabin outside the east end of the building. Rogers suggested they add another canteen in the basement as soon as possible, to shorten the average distance a worker had to travel to the canteen.

When they got to the bottom of the building the Rogers party walked along the dark passages that ran along the north side of the basement, the old retaining wall that Rowen had had so much trouble with. There were pools of water on the floor and Rogers asked that somebody grout the gaps in the wall where the rainwater was coming in.

It seemed that Rogers treated every problem he came across as his to solve. Dirt or mould on a gallery wall? 'Find out where it's come from.' Walls damaged by people carrying things? 'Protect them with a bit of sacrificial board.'

Out on the floor of the Turbine Hall, Rogers asked about a huge area of rather scruffy boarding which seemed to be scattered haphazardly over the floor and up the ramp. It was there to protect the concrete from the daily traffic of men, cherry-pickers and forklift trucks.

'When you're looking at an area like this,' said John Carter, 'what can you do? We had an area at the British Library which we protected in a similar manner. We had it down for two years and took it up and the floor was perfect.'

'No, I understand that, but environmentally, the volume of timber that's going to be thrown away at the end of the job is frightening. Is there any reason why this isn't all pinned down?' He was concerned that the loose sheets of wood might be a safety hazard and trip someone up.

Finally, as they headed outside on the north side of the building to go round to the west entrance, Rogers spotted a trailer with several frames of broken glass, frames that should have been installed in the Light Beam. They were on their way back to Austria to be replaced.

'How long does it take to get them back?' Rogers asked the glazier in charge of the trailer.

'A very good question – six to eight weeks once you've ordered them.'

'Why does it take six to eight weeks to get a bit of glass?'

'They're a massive firm, they don't care,' said the man.

'We do have connections with the company,' Rogers said, '– if we need to push we can push it.'

'Is that the only thing that's holding you up?' he asked the man.

'The weather's not really done us any favours the last couple of days,' he replied.

'If you've got any connections there . . .' joked John Carter.

'This is England,' Rogers said. 'It always rains. I don't know what you expect.'

'There's the wind,' said the glazier. 'The wind on Saturday was just unbelievable, absolutely incredible.'

Rogers' obsessive interest in every aspect of the site, an informed interest backed up by a comprehensive knowledge of construction, showed how much there is that can go wrong and yet, in Dale Sager's view, how much there was that was going right, on a site as complicated as Bankside at a time of maximum construction activity.

'I think [the walkabout] was probably very trouble-free,' Sager said later in the day. 'I think that we will look at one or two things, but the majority of what we've gotten out of today's meeting was more along the lines of continuing along a vein that was started either two weeks ago or four weeks ago, on a previous visit.'

In Sager's view, Rogers hadn't pointed out anything that he didn't know already, but he still felt there was a point to the exercise.

'It's just so that we are on our toes, that we are one step ahead. I think that the value of such walks is that we do keep moving, that we are planning ahead, that we do know where we're headed, and that we anticipate the unexpected, and Peter is certainly the unexpected. He has a very good eye. I think that, in some ways, he sees [things] due to his experience, in other ways, it's due to a freshness of approach, and in others, he's looking for things that he's had troubles with recently on other projects. So, his eyes are different from ours.'

Later that day, Rogers gave his own summary of the things that had come out of the walkabout. 'The classic debate has been this question of closing the building and getting it watertight, which has to be done quickly. We've had no end of arguments here about getting temporary drainage and protection around the perimeter of the building so the building stays watertight. The big advantage of this building is that the walls were there originally. We had a shell, in a sense, and therefore I always thought, this is a big factory; get the roof and walls in as quickly as possible, and then get the people inside it working in a decent environment to build it. It's taken us longer than I would have liked to have seen it. We're nearly there. Persuading Felix, the glazing company, to get the glazing in around the building as quickly as possible is part of that debate. And there's always, "It's raining", or, "It's windy". We *know* it rains, we *know* the wind blows, and the nearer you get to Christmas, the more that is a problem; but it's still always told to you as if it was something new. Simple things – canteens, toilets, facilities for the men. Vertical movement. It's all to do with productivity. And the idea, you know, why do we need canteens outside the building? You should always try and get them inside the building if you can, because it puts the canteen nearer the workface. If it takes a guy ten minutes to walk to his break, his fifteen-minute break, all of a sudden, it's doubled, trebled in length, just in walking there. To and from toilets, similarly. Hoists – a big issue, moving materials, moving men around the project. We've been under-hoisted most of the time here, and it's one of my big worries that we simply do not look well enough at how you move materials around a building site. The excess of ductwork and pipework that we talked about, going round there, it's just too much on-site, it gets in people's way. It actually slows down the man installing it, because he can't move freely around the project to handle it. Slowly, those things are getting better organized. I mean, if you'd walked around the site a couple of months ago, you'd have found it much more cluttered. Today, there were distinct pathways you could actually cross and walk around the site. That's an improvement that's come through.'

And about the man with the broom, Rogers was unrepentant. 'It's a hobby-horse of mine. Sweeping with a broom is a completely futile exercise on a building of this size. It's like putting your finger in the breach in the dam.' (Except, of course, the point of *that* story was the huge effectiveness of a small gesture.) 'Worse than that, it's actually damaging, because all he does is sweep the dust up into the air, so, with all the plant that's in that area, what you're doing is filling the plant up with dust and dirt; or most of it goes up on the beams, which you've got to clean up anyway. There are lots of proprietary systems, industrial vacuum cleaners, which are much more useful. If you really do want to sweep an area down, because it's getting near finishing, then let's do it properly. That man's company is one I've actually worked with for years now to develop cleaning systems that work on building sites, so his people should know better, and the Schal people, the construction managers, should have known better as well.'

22

Down the Ramp

Six weeks after the Guggenheim Museum, designed by Frank Gehry, opened in Bilbao in October 1997, Nick Serota visited it, and swallowed hard as he thought about the implications for the new Tate of some of the things that seemed to have put pressure on visitor services at the museum. 'It made me terrified as to how we will deal with, in year one at least, not just two million visitors but the prospect of even three or four million visitors. No one's going to thank us if the cloakrooms don't function, if the café is overcrowded – and everyone says, "But surely they were expecting a success? They kept telling us it was going to be a success. How come they've managed to build something that doesn't have enough lavatories?"'

The visitor services at the new Tate were planned in detail quite late in the day, and perhaps the fear instilled in Serota by the Guggenheim came in time to prevent the Tate making the worst mistakes. Another significant visit to a new museum took place in November 1998, when Peter Wilson; Andy Butler of Stanhope Properties; Andy Bramwell, one of the Tate's architectural staff; and Tim Parsons, Schal's contract finance manager, visited the new Getty Museum in Los Angeles, designed by Richard Meier. It had opened with a lot of fanfare earlier in the year, and the huge numbers of visitors in the early weeks led to newspaper stories of the sort that Serota dreaded for the new Tate – shock-horror accounts in the *New York Times* of long queues for what seemed to be an inadequate number of lavatories.

The Getty is a very different sort of museum from the new Tate. For one thing it is isolated on its own site, away from any urban surroundings. To get there visitors have to get a special bus, or book spaces weeks ahead in a car park at the foot of a hill and then get a small train to the top of the hill. There they will find a series of elegant stone buildings designed by Richard Meier, containing a wide-ranging and somewhat unfocused collection of works of art and design. But as a day out it makes a stunning trip, with beautiful views over Los Angeles and out to the Pacific, pleasant walkways and gardens, a high-tech art information centre, and as much cappuccino as you can drink.

On a sunny Los Angeles day, perched above the pollution layer, the museum was a blinding vision of cream-coloured stone, rippling pools of water and green foliage. As Andy Bramwell looked around at the beautiful stonework, he said, 'They seem to have bought a quarry and cut it in half.' A close inspection of the stone – travertine from the same quarry as St Peter's in Rome – revealed small fossils scattered throughout the stone surface.

As the Tate group wandered around the museum grounds, they were looking at things that no one else gave a second glance to. Here was a shallow ramp down to a cafeteria. How did that compare with the Bankside ramp? What is this vehicle coming through the door, tyres covered in plastic? It turned out to be a special leaf-trimming vehicle for the dozens of potted trees and other foliage. It and the doors it came through had been designed for each other, so the vehicle moved smoothly through the aperture. Signs were a little modest and occasionally not very informative. The orientation map was good – an embossed brass model that was reasonably clear to understand.

As they walked through one of the galleries, the Getty curator showing them around said to Peter Wilson, 'Do you find yourself looking at the walls instead of the art?' Indeed he did, and only partly because some of the art was undistinguished. Having spent the last four years with architects who abhorred skirting boards, Wilson could see the effect on gallery design of the system that they had rejected. The floors were polished wood, elegant, luxurious and very different from the Tate's unfinished floorboards. In one gallery, as the curator explained, the floors were 'purposely distressed'. Wilson inspected a small cupboard in a doorway, with a solid stone door moving on chunky brass hinges. The hinges alone probably cost more than one of the Tate's entire doors.

Heating and ventilation; smoke detection and removal; security cameras; louvres that changed automatically to keep the light level even – everything that money could buy. It was a major contrast in almost every way from Bankside, apart from the fact that entry was free. And one reason for the difference, apart from the location, was the fact that the Getty people seem to have had an unlimited budget. Andy Butler had explored the museum's information system to work out the relative costs.

'It works out in excess of a thousand dollars a square foot of building, which is eight times what Bankside is. But they're meaningless comparisons, really. It is what it is, and it's fantastic.'

Part of the fantasy lay in the landscape, a series of open areas at different levels, ranging from formal pools, into which unobservant visitors could easily step, to a sunken garden with a winding path through exotic plants, and a cactus garden cantilevered out over the hillside. Everywhere was wheelchair-friendly – levels that couldn't be reached by ramps had lifts within easy reach. As the Tate group looked up at the stone façades, in the background Sister Wendy, the English nun who has made a name presenting television programmes on art, was proving the system while being wheeled around in a wheelchair by the producer of her next series.

By late afternoon, the team had visited the public galleries and the behind-the-scenes facilities such as workshops, loading bays and conservation areas, as well as sampling the cappuccino kiosks and the cafeteria. They even ventured into the massive cooling tower, where a fine but voluminous spray of water cooled the huge volumes of air that fed the museum's air conditioning system.

Leaning against a stainless-steel balustrade overlooking Los Angeles, they compared notes.

Andy Butler reacted to the opulence and scale of the back-of-house-facilities, compared with the plans for Bankside. 'I get a feeling of a sledgehammer to crack a nut. But we're looking at a building that's here in perpetuity, almost. So at present it looks to be grossly over-designed. I'm talking about the service facilities, and the conservation areas, and the crate-packing areas. They've got workshops down there where they've got four guys working in seven workshops.'

Peter Wilson had been questioning the members of the museum staff he met about their experiences of the design process. 'Most of the key people we talked to have worked for the Getty for years, from way back in this project. I think I only talked to one person who didn't have a wholly satisfactory relationship, having been involved for that long, and that was a guy who'd had all his area taken away from him, to provide display space, which is a tendency that all museum directors impose on their back-of-house staff, so I expect we shall have some of that at some point, too.'

They were all aware of the horror stories about the lack of lavatories, but had discovered from the Getty staff that there were in fact the right number per head but some of them were so hidden, or some way from the main galleries, that visitors had concentrated their attentions on a few more prominent ones. As Serota had remarked at the Guggenheim, trouble with toilets was something that had to be avoided, and Peter Wilson had been very aware of this all through the Bankside design process. He was interested to learn more from the Getty about how they handled their visitors. 'It's actually made me feel more confident that we'd been addressing those issues as we went along, and finding out the same thing. I mean, the obvious one that is terrifying is that there will be far more people than we had bargained for, and I'm sure there will be. I think if you run a successful museum you've got to expect that for a few years. If we'd designed Bankside for four or five million visitors and only four million had come, then we would have thought it was a failure, but if we've designed it for two to three and four million come, then the same number will feel like a success. And it's probably important not to constrain yourself by assuming that we've got to solve every problem in the first place. And we've probably done that over public toilets. We've got them everywhere, and we've reacted to the dismal situation that we have at Millbank, by putting in lots. And I suspect we won't have that kind of a problem. There'll be some other problem that we didn't think about, like the cloakroom, or queuing for tickets, or whatever.'

Andy Bramwell felt that the interiors of the museum were pleasingly consistent with the appearance of the outside and he put that down to the influence of the architect operating throughout the process – an issue which, of course, Harry Gugger was very concerned about at Bankside. 'With something that's as important as an art gallery, you need to keep the continuity and the quality of the design in what you actually put into the building. And that's something that I'm engaged in, at the moment, trying to find out what our needs are after the building is finished, from putting up shelves to finding out what our needs are for ticketing and information booths, and then helping us, as a client, decide how much Herzog and de Meuron should feed into that process. So, you know, a good example is gallery seating. I gather that the insides of the gallery weren't done by Richard Meier, and that there were disagreements between the interior designers and Meier over what the fittings were. We've got maybe fewer problems in terms of what we're displaying, because it's contemporary and modern, so it's very sympathetic to Herzog and de Meuron's ideas – we're very unlikely to bring in a French interior designer to make replicas of Parisian town houses. But I think it would be a great pity if we don't involve Herzog and de Meuron in helping us select the right sorts of seating that keep the quality. We're all trying to achieve excellence, and we don't have the budget that the Getty has, but I think we clearly could learn a lot from the way they've handled their fitting-out.'

The group had been on the lookout for signs around the museum, since the Tate was just beginning to try to devise some sort of design policy for Bankside. In fact they hadn't seen many.

'Signage is a specialized thing,' Peter Wilson said, 'and the content of signage and the way in which you dispose of it all is very specialized, and I'm sure that Herzog and de Meuron think they know all about that, and probably don't. But, on the other hand, it really needs to have a relationship with the architecture. And the trick will be for Andy [Bramwell] to make sure that when we get round to having someone on board to help us out with the professional know-how of signing, that we actually get someone who can work with Herzog and de Meuron and not fight with them. But I think there's the potential for a real disaster there, if we don't get that right. Because I imagine black-painted, mild steel columns and rivets and bolts and things, with nice satin finish: stainless-steel signs adjacent to it aren't going to work too well.'

One overwhelming impression the group had gained from their visit was the atmosphere among the people who worked there. Andy

Butler commented, 'I think the one thing that's struck me, here more than anywhere, is the human angle. Everybody we've met was completely engrossed in this. They've all been here nine years, ten years, and you get the feeling it's a family. I'm an outsider to the Tate project. But it doesn't seem as comfortable, if I may say that.'

'A bit functional,' Andy Bramwell chipped in.

'It's all to do with money,' said Peter Wilson, defensively. 'It's easy for them, because they've got lots of money, and everyone's been able to be involved in deciding what their own working environment's going to be like, and how it's all going to work, because there was a chance that the funds to solve their problems would be there. We operate in a much more constrained climate, and we're trying to do an immense amount with our money. And we could have built a museum half as big, with twice the cost per square foot, and behaved towards art handling and education in exactly the same way as people have been here – very closely involved – and that would all have worked fine. But we're trying to do an incredibly lean building, much leaner, with far fewer facilities than we have at our existing site. And people's preconceptions are all towards what they've been used to, and making it a bit better and having a bit more, whereas we've been trying to do a really stripped down kind of job, and that isn't so comfortable. So, we're not quite the cheerful family that we might be.'

It might be thought that any lessons learned from the Getty visit would have come too late to be applied to Bankside, but in fact there was still room for the design to be adapted in ways that would improve visitor facilities. This was because on the plans the area of the Turbine Hall floor was still much as it had been left after the first stages of proper design work back in 1995–6.

The first designs for the Turbine Hall, where most visitors were intended to enter the museum, were laid down in Herzog and de Meuron's competition entry. But a closer inspection of the computer graphic of the Turbine Hall that accompanied their winning proposal, at a time when it could be compared with the finalized design, hinted at a story that showed how the built structures in a complex building can arrive at their final shape via a tortuous route.

The Herzog and de Meuron computer graphic showed a view of

the Turbine Hall looking from the west end. Across the middle was a bridge, running from south to north. It seems little different from the bridge that was eventually built, apart from the fact that there is in the graphic a south–north oriented escalator running from it to the floor below, instead of east–west stairs. But in fact this bridge is lighter and thinner than the one that was eventually built and there are no steel columns underneath, as there are today, so that there is a clear view under the bridge from one end of the Turbine Hall to the other.

Once the design team started turning the competition entry into a real design, they took an additional factor into account, as Peter Wilson explained. 'There are two travelling cranes on the gantry above the Turbine Hall and at least one of them has a very high lifting capacity. There was a debate about how we could get an object in here that was big enough to lift with such a heavy crane. There are artists who are very happy to create very heavy objects, and our handling team would no doubt love using a crane. The working solution is that we'll bring them in through the main doors of the Turbine Hall and on to the bridge.'

Here's where Herzog and de Meuron's bridge, as originally drawn, would have to change if the Tate decided to keep the gantry cranes. To build the bridge for the new museum would have meant destroying the existing bridge, a pretty solid affair supported by steel columns and used for bringing heavy equipment into the Turbine Hall when the building was a working power station. But to make the new bridge – 'a sort of light plank', in Peter Wilson's words – strong enough to carry the sort of loads that would justify refurbishing the gantry cranes, would require deep, heavy steel beams to support it. It didn't take people very long to see that instead of making Herzog and de Meuron's light structure heavier it made more sense to keep the heavy structure they already had, a bridge that they knew could take heavy loads because it had done so throughout its working life. But they lost their clear view from one end of the Turbine Hall to the other, and acquired – or retained – a set of steel columns that in four years' time were to constrain the decisions about how to deal with the visitors who would pour down the Turbine Hall ramp.

The design that was finally becoming fact in late 1998 was a bridge that had trebled in width from the old power station bridge, and still relied on the old steel columns to support heavy loads. Then there was a staircase going down to the Turbine Hall floor from near the Boiler House end of the bridge and facing the ramp. These stairs, it was generally agreed, were for people to go down rather than up. This was because the main body of visitors was expected to come into the Turbine Hall down the ramp, leave their coats if necessary, ask questions or get a map, and then go up an escalator on the left of the Turbine Hall under the Boiler House. This escalator would take the visitors up two floors to Level 3, where the first permanent collection galleries were to be. If the visitors who had arrived at the foot of the ramp chose to go up the stairs, there would be nowhere useful for them to get to, since those stairs were intended for visitors who had entered the museum at ground level, by walking from the river walkway across the landscaped area and in through the north entrance.

So the essential fixed elements were: the bridge with a staircase to go *down*; a space under the bridge that could be used for information desk, ticket desk, cloakrooms and so on, and an escalator to one side to go *up* (or down). This was really how things were left until 1998. There was so much going on in the rest of the building that needed everybody's attention, and in any case the works that would have to be done on the Turbine Hall floor were more in the nature of fit-out work than serious construction, or so it was assumed.

When the time came for detailed design decisions to be made about the floor of the Turbine Hall, the Tate hired a company called LORD who knew about this sort of thing, and after studying the building and reading projections about visitor routes, numbers per hour, and so on, the LORD consultants brought their recommendations to the Tate and spelt them out during a meeting in early December 1998 with Dawn Austwick, which was also attended by a puzzled Harry Gugger. Gugger had turned up to the meeting late after a delayed flight from Basel. He seemed slightly shell-shocked as the meeting progressed as he heard recommendations – such as reversing the position of a staircase – made firmly about his beloved Turbine Hall by someone he'd never met or spoken to, and they were statements about the detailed design of the fit-out of the area that he would have expected to have some warning of. At one point he asked about LORD and its background, and about their qualifications for making these kinds of statements.

LORD were, of course, doing the job they had been paid to do – think through in some detail issues that the Tate, and indeed the architects, had neither the time nor the expertise to follow through. There was a considerable emphasis on making sure that the maximum number of visitors were channelled in the direction of the shop, by the way visitors were guided by signs and information desks, and perhaps by reversing the direction of one of the escalators so that it disgorged people more directly towards the shop door. Rob Lamarre, one of LORD's partners, was concerned that as currently configured, people would come off the escalator and have to walk round past the cloakroom and lockers before they would realize there was a shop. By this stage, Gugger was openly hostile to Lamarre and his colleague.

As the meeting wound up with no firm conclusions reached, and people packed their bags and left the room, Gugger spoke privately of his unhappiness at the situation. 'The timing is at least a bit strange,' Gugger said, angrily. 'I think we had discussions two years ago, and as I am not used to this kind of building, with this amount of visitors, I would not have minded to bring someone on at the time to have a more fruitful discussion. And I find it a bit odd that they are bringing up these people now and that we have not been introduced to each other. I assume if I, as an architect, would be asked to assess the design of someone else, the first thing is, I would pick up the phone and talk to the guy – "What have you done? Why have you done it?" – because I would have a sharp learning curve in this way. So I am a bit surprised that we have not been sent all this information and discussed it, and they just dropped me into this meeting, into cold water.

'I'm still convinced the design is very robust. Maybe one judges the situation on your own experience, how you behave, and for example this whole issue about the shop – I go to the shop because I want to buy a book and not because I am forced into it. I don't need to be pushed in a shop, I would not allow this to happen. I believe in reasonable human beings who know what they want. There is nothing worse than somewhere like the Guggenheim in SoHo in New York, where you have to walk through the shop to go to the museum. I really think if this is the future of museums, I'm not interested any more. I'm very aware they have a large revenue and they are important, but I think we've done everything to make it an attractive location and we'll do everything to design a beautiful design.'

It was difficult to work out how much of Gugger's anger was to do with the fact that he felt that LORD's recommendations had been sprung on him without consultation, and how much was to do with the actual substance of what they said. It might even be that, as Gugger admitted himself, Herzog and de Meuron had such little experience of visitor patterns in a large building like Bankside, that they realized there really *were* aspects of their design that had to be changed, much as they hated the idea.

Looking back at the situation three months later, Gugger gave a graphic illustration of how he still felt about the whole situation. 'I feel similar to the *Angelus Novus* [a painting by Klee]. Walter Benjamin describes this figure as being an angel being blown backwards into the future, and this angel is representing history, and the storm which blows him backwards into the future is progress. I'm far away from being an angel, but my experience is a very similar one, because you're blown backwards and you would like to try to fix things – you never reached the optimum. And I think at the time, as far as we could adjust the situation, our proposals for circulation were fine, and I'm sure there are people out there who have more experience and know more about these kinds of things and could have made a contribution. It's more, for me, a timing problem to bring these people in, and the wings are so large you can't fight this wind, you can't reach back, it's just not possible.'

One other event took place in December 1998 which caused the Tate some unhappiness. Six months after Dale Sager was appointed to bring sweetness and light to a troubled client, Sager himself was taken off the project by Schal to return to a high-profile project Tarmac were managing at GCHQ, the government's security headquarters in the west of England.

Peter Wilson was very unhappy about this. 'We took exception to the speed with which Tarmac removed him, and the lack of consultation. So we have a dispute with Tarmac about lack of good manners, or maybe it was just lack of ability to communicate, but that all happened rather rapidly and could have been better managed, and so we were pretty annoyed with them.'

Wilson was reflecting a general Tate discontent, which was shared by Nick Serota himself. 'You can't have changes at the top taking place without some sign that there's disruption below. We were in delay last summer on two particular contracts and we have had to try and catch up time. And Schal responded very positively by bringing in Dale Sager. In December they told us they were withdrawing him and taking him elsewhere, and I think they didn't do it in a way which was helpful to our project. If they'd given us plenty of warning and introduced us to the person who was taking his place, and there'd been an overlap, that would have been one thing, but to have a sudden withdrawal of the key person struck us as being not the best possible way to manage a project; and we're absolutely determined that this project should run to time and on budget. We can't afford for it not to.'

23

Places for Art

By autumn 1998, the four genres that Morris and Blazwick had presented to Nick Serota back in March – *The Nude/Body*, *Landscape/ Environment*, *History/Society*, and *Still Life/Real Life* – had been through the mill of their colleagues and some outside advisers and, on the whole, had resisted being ground down or changed very radically. There was a certain nervousness about how the new director would react, since he'd had nothing to do with the original concept, and he himself wasn't sure about them when he was first confronted with them.

'I had concerns, definitely,' Nittve said, 'because there are certain risks connected with doing it in a different way. One thing may be that you're trying too hard to be different in a certain way. And it should really feel that this is another equally natural way to approach the material, so it doesn't look like you're trying to be smart. Also, if you envisage yourself as a visitor, coming into one of these suites or galleries, you really have to think through whether this way of relating works to each other is helpful in order to answer the basic questions that most people have coming into the galleries: "Why does this look the way it does? And what does it say to me? What does it tell me?"'

'I think, at the beginning, he was very, very sceptical,' Iwona Blazwick said, remembering Nittve's initial reactions. 'Partly because a number of museums are trying to reinvent the wheel at the moment, and there have been one or two attempts which proved to be rather hokey, and had attempted to get out of the canonical way of doing things, and ended up doing stuff which was a bit gimmicky, a bit shallow, and didn't really work. So I think he was concerned that we didn't lose the scholarly or canonical in the way that we were approaching it.'

The evolving ideas that the curators had come up with had a comforting philosophical rigour about them which nevertheless didn't impose itself on the visitor, and Nick Serota seemed very happy with the new framework, particularly the way it focused on the intentions of artists rather than just their works: 'It's going to be organized in a way that allows people to test for themselves ways in which artists have responded to certain central ideas within the making of art over the last hundred years. And we're going to try and examine the way in which attitudes to making art, and indeed the kinds of solutions which artists have come up with, have changed during the period. But not in an evolutionary sense. Because what you will find quite frequently within the displays will be contemporary art alongside, or adjacent to, a historical figure. And it means, for a visitor, that they're going to encounter contemporary art, the art of their own times, at every point in their journey through the gallery, rather than simply coming across it as they are fatigued and about to leave.'

He contrasted the new scheme with the more conventional approach of some other twentieth-century museums. 'You walk in, you turn left, and you find yourself in 1900. And you walk through the galleries on an enfilade basis, and you come out in the year 2000, and you exit. And we're not going to produce that kind of a tunnel.'

As with any specialized discipline, modern and contemporary art experts can seem obscure and forbidding to the outsider. Vocabulary can seem like jargon; analysis like persiflage; and the exchange of ideas like spies communicating in code. And yet the serious outsider doesn't want to be talked down to either: he or she just wants to understand what everyone is on about. Lars Nittve's cricketing analogy explains *why* we should take the art experts seriously but not how.

Iwona Blazwick is an example of how it is possible to straddle the world of insiders and outsiders without compromising your own beliefs. Her analysis of movements and works in contemporary art is rigorous, but if you listen carefully you can grasp the origins of her excitement and interest. 'I was thinking about a work which was in the Turner Prize in 1993, by Vong Phaopanit, who is a Laotian artist who is an exile here in Britain, and he made this incredible work, which was a field of rice, but it was literally an entire gallery filled with rice, which led towards a series of neon Sanskrit letters. It was stunning. And the field was marked and lit just by light. And going to see it, I was struck at how accessible and how exciting it was. It was a very compelling experience for people who were completely uninitiated. So I was there, hanging out, looking at the way people were interacting with it, and the guards, older people, kids, et cetera – a vast spectrum of people – went through and totally responded to it, almost intuitively. They got it, and they were excited and puzzled by it. And there were a ton of newspaper cartoons about it and it became notorious, this work. But people engaged with it and they didn't feel aggressive towards it. And it struck me that if they'd seen that, they could then go and look at Carl Andre's bricks, which is also horizontal, which is also about a very banal, poor material – instead of rice, you know, the bricks, and so on. And that, maybe, that kind of experience opens doors, you know. If you've found one thing that you can relate to, maybe that leads you to looking further at things which seem more hostile or impenetrable.'

As the four genres became more defined, Frances Morris and her colleagues began to appreciate some of the difficulties they were presented with by the gaps in the Tate's own collection. 'The process is fascinating,' Morris said in September 1998, 'but extremely problematic, because we're thinking both about the twentieth century in a limitless way, and we're also trying to think about the twentieth century as constrained by the particular collection we have in London. And there are additional constraints imposed by a number of loaned works that we would like to find room for. There are constraints given by the building. And then there are constraints of interpretation – that there are maybe some areas of practice of discourse that we're finding extremely difficult to frame in ways that are popular and accessible.

'So, we begin with an ideal scenario. What would we do if we could deal with the twentieth century in the way we really want to? And we're moving slowly, but inexorably, into trying to translate that, now, into a real vision, with works of art in it. And, over the last few days, I think we've almost met a reality checkpoint, where we've realized that some of the vision cannot be expressed with works in the collection. So, not downhearted, we're just readdressing those issues and trying to maybe find more imaginative or more inventive ways of approaching the same questions. Say, for example, we have Cubism. Cubism exists in the public conception of art as a movement locked into time, but also as a series of conceptual leaps and innovations. Now, we have enough works in the collection to suggest Cubism as a movement, but once we try and break it down into the kind of moments of innovation that then span out across the century it becomes much weaker. And so, now, what we're having to do is put Cubism into a wider time-span, to try and show how those moments of innovation spread out over time. Now I think we may end up with some more interesting display ideas than if we had been unconstrained by the collection, and that would be the ideal result.'

It seemed surprising that Morris brought up the fact that the group was trying to keep Cubism as a movement together, since this seemed to go against an early suggestion that looking at modern art as 'isms' was an outmoded response. But she clarified this point: 'We are beginning to try and think about making a distinction between isms that existed, because people said, as it were, "Hey, let's have a movement, let's write a manifesto, let's sign up to some rules, let's all believe in the same things, let's have some books that are our bibles". And then, isms that really have been coined latterly, by art historians, to group together similar tendencies. And although I wouldn't want to say at the moment which isms might feature *as* isms, I feel at the moment confident that in a number of the suites of galleries, there will be displays that will feel familiar to people who are familiar with certain isms. So, rather than dispersing all our Surrealist works between each suite, it's likely, I think, that there will be a concentration of them in one suite, sufficient for a visitor to think, "Oh, here are the Surrealistic holdings".'

One of the hoped-for consequences of the new arrangement of art was that, merely by the choice of which of the four suites of galleries (one for each genre) works were placed in, an ism would acquire new significance for visitors. They might come across works of Abstract Expressionism in the *From History to Society* suite, for example. 'Most people don't associate Abstract Expressionism with social or political content,' Blazwick said at a time in 1998 when discussions about what to put where were in full flood. 'And what we're arguing is that, actually, it is part of another story which is to do with the exile of Jews from Europe, the exile of intellectuals and artists from Europe through the course of the Second World War, and actually post the First World War; the shift of power, of cultural power, to America; the emphasis on individualism, freedom, democracy and propaganda. As we know now, the CIA were very heavily involved in backing Abstract Expressionism. [The artists] themselves, as a group, formed a group the "Irascibles", and protested on the steps of the Met. Barnett Newman, apparently, stood for Mayor of New York. So there are all these kinds of interesting stories that people don't normally associate with that movement. Similarly, much earlier abstraction was tied in with ideas about social change. It was a very utopian kind of practice.'

In January 1999, Nick Serota was awarded a knighthood in the New Year's Honours. As people do on these occasions, he pointed out that he thought carefully before accepting it but decided to do so on the basis that it was really for everyone at the Tate, not just for him personally. It was an unsurprising honour. Every previous director of the Tate since the war has been awarded a knighthood, and the Tate clearly had become part of the Establishment but in a rather odd way. Like a court jester, the Tate was the part of the Establishment whose job it is to shock the Establishment.

Later in 1999, when Tracy Emin's rumpled and soiled bedclothes, seen in the Turner Prize shortlist exhibition, formed the focus of yet another media outrage, it was clear that Sir Nicholas's Tate had not lost its power to shock. But during the year, as the plans for Bankside matured and filled out in the hands of Frances Morris and her colleagues, it was clear how little of what they were doing had anything to do with what might or might not shock, surprise or appal visitors to the museum. Their discussions were driven by a determined attempt to understand, classify and display what artists were producing as a legitimate response to the society they were in. To shock the public was as far from their intentions as to bore them. And yet both reactions could be the result.

By March 1999, there had been a series of meetings about each genre with curators and advisers. The aim was first to divide each of the four genres into ten or a dozen subcategories, each of which would then be featured in one of the rooms that made up each suite. Then the subcategories would have specific works allocated to them. Finally, the hanging or placing of those works would have to be specified.

Just before 11 a.m. on 24 March 1999, a group of senior curators, along with Lars Nittve, gathered round a table in the Duffield Room at Millbank. They were there to run at a breathless pace through a hundred or so works of art that were candidates for the *Nude to Body* suite.

Frances Morris started the meeting by addressing the issue of traffic flow. Morris told the group that they had, for the time being, assumed a route that had a beginning and an end, and that they would discuss the individual galleries in that order. The first room to be discussed was called 'The Naked and the Nude'.

One of Morris's colleagues asked, 'Are you just hoping that people will go into "Naked and Nude" first, or are you going to direct them?

'Well,' said Morris drily, 'I rather thought you could say "Entrance".'

'Yes, but would you stop them going into "Traces and Imprints"?' This was the last room in the suite.

'It's something that we have to discuss quite soon,' Morris said. 'I think Nick's quite keen, at the moment, on allowing people to take that decision themselves, and therefore, allowing people to have a very loose sense of orientation, so that people can wander, at will, from suite to suite. Now, I think our thinking about that is that it's quite difficult to construct a plan without a sequence of rooms and without, therefore, jarring notices. But it's something I think we have to think about, once we've got all four on the table.'

Because the two different suites on each floor were either side of the chimney, there would be a gallery linking them, which meant that, if the rooms were arranged in a specific order within a suite, someone coming from the other suite on the same floor would enter a carefully planned sequence of rooms at the wrong end.

After loading a full carousel of slides into a projector, one of the Tate curators, Matthew Gale, sat down to take his colleagues through the selection he and another curator, Jennifer Mundy, had made of works of art for the first room. 'The premise really is to look at the treatment of "The Naked and the Nude" through the idea that there is a continuing studio tradition of depicting the nude, which can be set against a more intimate, psychologically charged set of images, and so to bring together works across the century which bring that confrontation together.'

Gale went through a series of slides of paintings – each of which represented one or other of the two categories. Clinically painted, studio-based nudes as object, by William Coldstream, against the more intimate, psychologically charged paintings of, say, Bonnard. And there were other artists whose paintings seemed to combine the two approaches – people like Sickert.

One of the group, Toby Jackson, asked why there was no sculpture in this room.

'It's not that it's been excluded out of hand,' said Gale. 'We were talking about this only yesterday, actually, how, particularly the classical figure, sculptures of Maillol . . .'

'I was thinking Maillol, Rodin, or Matisse,' Jackson said.

'Possibly even a Degas, *The Little Dancer*, which is a clothed naked figure,' said Frances Morris, cryptically.

But another member of the group, Theodora Vischer, disagreed. 'We also thought that to start with Rodin and Degas would be a very conventional way of telling the story of the body, and we thought that this already opens a kind of discourse which would be a bit controversial.'

Blazwick joined in. 'I was thinking about the painting thing. Could one make an argument that it is this very intense and close relationship in the studio which sculpture doesn't have? Sculpture's something different, because you're in a foundry, there's a much longer process, whereas here you get this very intimate sense of either a series of formal experiments being carried out, quite ruthlessly sometimes, or else a kind of psychological tension between the artist and the model, but it's definitely within the confines of the studio. And I wonder if there's an argument to even make that more intense, and that maybe sculpture would dilute that.'

The discussion continued, ranging over whether the Coldstreams should be 'edited out' – 'I think they're awful,' someone said – and whether Kossoff and Auerbach were guilty of 'visual rape'.

Then Lars Nittve voiced a fear he had. 'Just going through these images, it's too early for me to say whether this will look good, also, will make a great room. In some cases, a room kind of announces itself. The problem, of course, with this kind of theme is that, if you're not really careful it might look like some exhibitions, where you come and you see portrait paintings, and a room full of portrait paintings of all sorts. And, I mean, it usually looks pretty horrible, actually. I don't think this will look horrible, but I don't know to what extent you've tested it as an actual possible installation, or whether it's a list of possibilities. How is it to be understood?'

'I think it's between the two,' Morris said to Nittve. 'I don't think it's just a kind of pick-and-mix ragbag flipped up from a subject . . .'

'Of course not, of course not . . .'

'. . . but it has got some great paintings in it, really, really major, large-scale, things like the Freud, they're big gutsy things. I think they'd hold their own.'

The next room was called 'Savage Beauty'. Gale described it as looking at a particular moment when so-called 'primitive' art became a source for Western artists. He rattled through slides of a series of modern paintings derived from African and Far Eastern objects and then described how, to accompany these works, he and his colleague were suggesting documentary background material 'ranging from the ethnographic study of these objects, gathering them together in the Trocadero and the Museum of Mankind, across to the sense of the Harlem renaissance and the rediscovery of a sense of cultural identity amongst black people; Negritude in Paris; through to jazz and popular films, popular magazines'.

'I was reading this morning,' he went on, 'that Greta Garbo appeared on the cover of *Vanity Fair* with an African mask, which would be a nice thing to bring in, to show that this is across all layers of society. And to ask some of those questions that those postcards that opened the Picasso and photography show at the Barbican [raised], where the French colonial authorities are publishing photographs of naked women, which is allowed because they're black, and then they're being adopted by an artist like Picasso for his own work, and building towards *Les Demoiselles*, as the show suggested.'

After some more discussion, Nittve told the group what he thought. 'My gut feeling is that this is going to look really great. If I compare my reaction to the first gallery, where I wasn't immediately sure it would look great, this *is* going to look great, because of the coherence . . .'

'My feeling about this display,' said Morris, 'is that you need something like the previous display for this to ground things, to show this as a tabula rasa, an attempt to break out from an academic tradition.'

Blazwick was very enthusiastic about this room. 'I also see it as an absolute fundamental engine of modernism, this kind of idea about going back to archetypes and to primal origins. Then you can see how it's disseminated through popular culture, even to art deco, actually: it's an interesting cultural moment which this sits in the centre of.'

'Yes,' said Matthew Gale. 'And those imperial exhibitions and that sort of promotion of the other as part of our culture.'

Jeremy Lewison came up with a point that highlighted one of the problems he kept coming across with certain themes. There was a desire that the galleries should include British art wherever possible, but it wasn't always possible, either because there wasn't anything appropriate in the Tate's collection or because it just wasn't justified by the context. 'Did we consider Epstein's *Doves*?' he asked. 'Would you consider Dobson's *The Man Child*?'

'Absolutely not,' said Morris firmly.

'It is a primitivised, primitive sculpture, made of stone. I mean, one of the problems we've been having is getting British art into some of these displays, and this actually is a moment where you really can quite legitimately . . .'

'There's quite a lot here,' said Morris.

'But not that many,' said Lewison.

'I think the Dobson seems particularly relevant,' Matthew Gale said, agreeing with Lewison.

The next room was a small room containing works on paper.

'The interesting thing about this,' said Morris, 'is that it's the small gesture, it's the connection between brain and hand rather than the gesture of the body.'

As the rooms had been planned there had been some attempt to reflect the characteristics of size and location of the gallery spaces. The next room, a monographic display devoted to Giacometti, was in a gallery that looked out on to the Turbine Hall and benefited from daylight coming in. Matthew Gale raised the issue again of whether the rooms had to be followed in sequence.

'At the moment, the thinking is that that is the way we have to go. And, in a sense, Giacometti plays a role in the sequence as well, between the automatism and the primitivism spaces, and the spaces that are about to be discussed.'

Morris raised the issue of displaying something she called "Giacometti's walls".

'What are they?' said Nittve. 'I'm not sure I know.'

Frances Morris told him. 'When Giacometti's studio was pulled down, his widow, Annette, organized – literally – the walls from the studio taken away first, so that the plaster and the brickwork were cut out in big chunks and stored by the Giacometti Foundation. And what's interesting about them is that he not only continuously worked on painting and sculpture and drawing, but he scribbled and scratched at the walls all the time, so that one of them has a very recognizable portrait of Diego on it, another has a leg . . .'

'It's basically drawing on the wall,' said Nittve.

Toby Jackson felt that the Giacometti room didn't need to be seen as part of a sequence at all. 'I think the placing in there is excellent: I just like the idea of being immersed in an artist's work. We were talking about people coming into this show in different places – it wouldn't really matter. It acts like a nodal point rather than a reaction to or an introduction to anything previously or coming. I think that works extremely well.'

The fifth room was described by Matthew Gale as 'a sort of undoing of the figure'. It led to a brief discussion involving the definition of 'nude' in the pictures.

'They're not nude, of course,' said Lars Nittve, 'some even have hats.'

'Very few have arms,' said Frances Morris, as if that made them more nude.

In spite of all the best efforts of the Tate team and its architects to provide lifts and doors through which the entire collection could pass, there was a flurry of concern about the size of one particular painting, a Graham Sutherland.

'The problem is, can you get it through the door?' said David Fraser Jenkins, one of the curators.

Jeremy Lewison said, 'It used to hang in the Duveen Galleries, and it's probably about twelve feet tall or more.'

'You'd get it in the lift, couldn't you?' Sarah Tinsley, another curator, said.

'Yeah, easily,' said Frances Morris. 'Whether you'd get it through – well, what is that doorway?', she went on, pointing at a plan of the gallery. 'And that doorway, that doorway, that doorway.'

'They are all the same height, aren't they?' said Tinsley. 'So, you get it through one, you get it through three?'

'But it's not on the list of problematic works, Sutherland,' Morris said.

Nittve started to say, 'Because no one thought it would . . .'

And Morris added, 'No one thought that David would suggest it.'

As detailed plans for another seven rooms were laid out before the group, it was clear that the 'genres' way of thinking was a rich and fertile way of showing the collection. Looking at familiar works and considering them within one of the room settings immediately forced them into a less familiar framework.

The sixth room was a monographic display of Picasso's treatment of the female body, which Nittve suggested would actually be an exciting display to put at the beginning of the whole suite. Frances Morris had already tested that idea and decided that it didn't work.

The seventh room included an area called 'Acting Out', which looked at a time when artists started doing very simple, very methodi-cal, often studio-based experiments with their bodies: using their bodies as painting implements, making sounds, pulling faces, using their body as subject or object, often with a humorous or ironical edge.

The eighth room dealt with the body of the spectator, through works which had their effect by forcing the spectator to interact with them, by walking round them, through them or under them, for example. It was interesting to see how an artist like Carl Andre, whose works make no obvious reference to the *form* of the human body, was nevertheless placed firmly in this room, as Blazwick explained. 'I thought that *Venus Forge* would be a particularly appropriate work, simply because it's so directional. This really leads you, and it really does embody the sense of walking.'

'But presumably it's destroyed if people can't walk round it,' Frances Morris said.

After describing several other works in this area, Blazwick said, 'And finally, another work, which is a very small piece, but which is the key to the whole display, I think, is this Robert Morris location piece, which is this very beautiful plaque which simply has a number of letters and arrows, and it's all about locating the viewer and about ambient architecture.'

David Fraser Jenkins raised a general point about the chronology of different rooms. He had noticed that some rooms had works spanning a century and others only a decade. 'Do you think it's slightly unnerving, as you wander from one room to the other without any kind of rhyme or reason for finding an overall spread, or just ten years?'

'Well, there are reasons for moving between individual rooms,' said Frances Morris. 'It may not add up to an entirely coherent sequence, but we've tried to make relationships between displays evident, even if they're not chronological relationships.'

'But I think we mustn't lose sight of the fact that, actually, the public aren't necessarily going to walk in a particular order,' Jeremy Lewison said.

'No, of course not,' said Morris. 'But on the other hand, we can offer a guide to a suite which does suggest a route.'

'One of the things with these suites, firstly, is actually the walls are quite fat, quite thick,' Lars Nittve said, 'so when you walk from one room to another, you actually *really* move from one space to another. It's a very distinct feeling of transition. So, in that sense, the individual routes are quite defined.'

Morris defended the coherence of the plans they were coming up with by a dig at Millbank. 'At the moment, in Millbank, you can go into that cluster of new displays and there's Damien Hirst and Bacon and narrative painting. Every time, you screech to a halt. You think, "What?" And your brain has to go, "Ch, ch, ch, ch," and you have to go into a different time zone and a different philosophical background. You almost spin around like Superman in a telephone kiosk. These junctions we're talking here are nothing of that order.'

The final room, called 'Traces and Imprints', was to have a range of works where the human body was represented or hinted at in various ways, ranging from direct imprints of body parts to fragments of bodies standing in for the whole. The fact that it was last in the sequence brought the group full circle to talk again about whether the 'Naked and Nude' room was an exciting enough start to the suite.

'I feel it's a bit bland,' said Jeremy Lewison.

'You didn't listen to Matthew's amazing exposition,' said Frances Morris, referring to Lewison's late arrival at the meeting. 'I think that's really unfair. It's going to be a lot of in-your-face nudity.'

'That's still a bit of a concern I have,' said Nittve, 'at least, as an opening.'

'I think we're all slightly concerned,' Morris said, 'but I don't think it's a dull display, as I heard Jeremy say.'

'Bland,' said Lewison.

'"Dull", earlier, I quote,' said Morris.

'OK, "dull" earlier,' Lewison admitted, 'it doesn't matter. OK, I think it's bland, I think it's dull, I think it's too one-dimensional.'

'Two-dimensional,' Morris corrected him.

'It's two-dimensional.'

'It's two-dimensional,' agreed Morris, and the little spat was over, as a result of Morris's verbal dexterity.

By late spring 1999, the Tate curators no longer had to rely on architects' plans to plot the positions of works of art in the new galleries. As each theme was finalized on paper, Morris began to take groups of curators to the galleries themselves, where they could finally come to grips with all the factors that mattered when it came to hanging or placing a work of art. Light from windows or skylights; height of walls; position of floor grilles; the scale of a human being in relation to a painting or sculpture; the location of water and power for more adventurous works of contemporary art.

On 25 May 1999, Frances Morris took a group of curators and art-handling staff to the suite of galleries on the third floor at the west end of Bankside. This was the suite that included the double-height gallery, and the theme of the exhibits in this part of the building would be *Landscape and Environment*.

As if they didn't have enough to think about, the curators had had to take into account the fact that certain galleries had to be available for entertaining. The Tate had a profitable sideline in parties and dinners for corporate sponsors and special occasions, and it liked to hold these in galleries so that the eaters and drinkers could be surrounded by the best in modern art. Unfortunately even the best classes of people – and the richest – could not be relied upon not to splash their drinks and food on the walls, and the caterers the Tate allowed in might not even worry about the contribution the odd splash of tomato soup would make to a nearby Jackson Pollock. So there were strict rules about which works of art could be in galleries identified as suitable for entertainment because they were near specially designed kitchens and serveries.

As Frances Morris stood on the third floor of Bankside in hard hat and wellies along with a dozen similarly clad colleagues, she explained that, as far as possible, they planned to have glazed works of art in this particular room. 'This is, broadly speaking, a Surrealist hang,' she said.

'Will there be any spillover into the Monet and Long?' asked Derek Pullen, one of Morris's colleagues concerned specifically with sculpture. He was talking about human bodies rather than Hollandaise sauce. 'Not if you say there can't be,' Morris said.

Morris led her crocodile into an adjacent room, and when everyone was listening she said, 'So this at the moment is Cézanne, Matisse, Mondrian and possibly Nolde – work from early in the century, very much deriving from real experiences of the landscape but moving away from mimesis to interest in structure and sensation. That is a sort of an introductory space, and then we go from there into this gallery here which is Long and Monet – Monet's waterlilies.'

Another factor that the curators had to take into account was the emergency services in the building, which included a room designated as a safe zone for wheelchair users. Morris explained that this meant that no sculptures could be placed there that might impede the passage of wheelchair users.

'And this presumably has to be an escape door?' said someone. 'And you're going to have a lovely escape sign?'

'Yeah, a big green one we were thinking, really big,' Morris replied.

As the group marched from one room to another, Morris's quiet voice was often drowned by the sound of loud drilling and hammering, as the interior fit-out was carried out around them. Morris poked her head into one of the 'fat walls', where she hoped to be able to install a monitor for a video installation.

In a small room with tall windows looking west, someone asked whether Auerbach's pictures were 'light-vulnerable'. The conservators at the Tate have assessed each work of art, on the basis of the materials it is made out of, as to whether it can safely be exposed to daylight for long periods without fading or deteriorating. The plan was to open with Auerbach pictures in this gallery but the room got a lot of light and so the light-sensitivity of the art needed to be checked.

With a flourish, Morris led the group into the next room – the double-height gallery. Even though it was still unfinished, with unpainted walls and scaffold towers lying around, it was clear what a magnificent space it was going to be.

Morris described the decision that had finally been made about what to display here. After talk early in the design phase that 'because it's big it won't necessarily have big works of art in it' it had now been decided to put two big works of art in it.

'The idea for this gallery,' Morris said, 'is two Beuys pieces – *The End of the Twentieth Century* and this big loan, which is seven metres, has a girder that has to span the corner of the gallery, and on that is hung the cast of a mountain of earth. Then, across the floor are strewn different bronze elements, from tiny little turdy-like things to self-sufficient free-standing sculptures. So I think the technical question is whether we can get the big bronze element through the door and then how we actually hang it.'

It was sometimes painful to contemplate breaking into the walls of the new galleries while the surfaces were being lovingly finished. But this particular piece of sculpture had an I-beam that supported the weight of the 'mountain of earth', which had to look as if it was resting on the floor, a floor that was not load-bearing and therefore couldn't support the weight itself. To make the illusion work, the height of the I-beam had to be adjusted precisely once the mound had been hung on the beam. What still had to be decided was how to make fittings for the ends of the I-beam in the double-height gallery wall so that the precise adjustment could be made when everything was in position.

'So in effect,' said Morris, 'the I-beam needs to be hung on things behind the walls and then adjusted. It's not entirely authentic.'

The group's attention turned to *The End of the Twentieth Century*. This is a Beuys work that consists of thirty-one large basalt stones of various sizes. The artist had not specified exactly where they had to be placed, and Morris and her colleagues now considered the matter. Since the pieces would be scattered over half the floor area of the gallery, the curators had to think about how the visitors would be channelled through or round them.

'How do we create a passageway for the public, preferably without barriering? It may be the case that we have to have somebody in here all the time.' Remembering the labyrinth at Bilbao, Morris did not want to have to arrange for the full-time supervision of hordes of visitors to this room.

Derek Pullen said, 'My experience of *The End of the Twentieth Century* is that it would need half this gallery unless you cut it down.'

'We're not allowed to, are we?' said Morris. She turned to a colleague. 'Is there any question of being able to split *The End of the Twentieth Century*?'

'You can't leave sections out, but you could make it more compact,' was the reply. 'There's thirty-one stones and they've all got to be in.'

Someone pointed out that when exhibited in Edinburgh, part of *The End of the Twentieth Century* went through the floor of the gallery, along with the forklift truck carrying it.

'This floor is very robust,' said Morris optimistically.

When they moved to the next room they were joined by Andy Butler, and Morris asked him about the possibility of leaving light-recorders in position in the galleries to measure the levels of light that fell on the walls at different times of day and times of year. This would be important data to decide finally where certain works of art could be hung safely, and where they would be exposed to too much light. (Although in fact there would always be the option of drawing the blinds.)

Like most of the construction people, Andy Butler found the world of modern art a closed book. When Frances Morris started talking to Butler about the Beuys I-beam, he said in a puzzled tone, 'Do you need an I-beam?'

'The work *is* the I-beam,' Morris said.

As they worked their way back along the north side of the third floor, they came to a room where it was planned to place a sculpture by Roland Penrose called *Captain Cook*.

'It's interesting,' said Derek Pullen, 'because we've never shown it in its original form.'

'What's its original form?' Frances Morris asked.

'There's the story that Penrose remade the base because he thought it was lost, and then about ten years ago the original base turned up at the back of his garage and turned out to be quite different from the base that he'd remade.'

'Where is the original base?' Morris asked.

'It's here, it's part of the work but it's never been presented.'

'Perhaps we should "unveil" it?'

'It shouldn't just be done, it needs to be done with a bit of oompah.'

'Well, what more appropriate than the opening of the Tate Galley of Modern Art?' asked Morris.

One room had been designated for the Tate's Rothkos, currently in their own gallery at Millbank. 'So this is Rothko? asked Morris, 'This feels enormous.'

There is apparently a concept known as a 'Rothko room', defined by the artist with specifications that have to be adhered to by exhibiting galleries. The Tate were planning to put four Rothkos in this room, partly because they thought that was the minimum number permitted. But then they investigated further.

'After all this canonical view of the room,' Morris said, 'we have on paper that *three* constitutes a Rothko room. We've gone for the bigger option [of four pictures].'

As the group walked through the room on their way out, Morris looked back. 'Ooh, it looks so lovely,' she said.

24
Through the Glass, Darkly

Early on in the Bankside project, the architects described a concept for lighting the Turbine Hall that turned out to be extraordinarily difficult to achieve. They designed a series of bay windows overlooking the Hall, framed by a series of light boxes which consisted of sheets of translucent glass in front of batteries of fluorescent lamps. The glass was required to conceal the lamps yet still allow the maximum amount of light through. By 'conceal', the architects meant 'to even out the light so much that it was impossible to distinguish individual tubes behind the glass'.

The architects knew the amount of diffusion they needed; they told the glass suppliers; the glass suppliers came back with a sample where the diffusion was achieved with an interlayer; the architects said, 'Yes, that's fine', and then everyone got on with their work.

A year later, it wasn't fine at all. The technique that had been used for the small sample the architect approved seemed not to be possible with larger sheets of glass, and as months went by, people stood on the floor of the Turbine Hall looking up, squinting, turning to each other, looking again, and shaking their heads. What was the problem and why was it so difficult?

The architects had a very clear idea of the job they wanted the bay windows to do in the Turbine Hall. 'You will have this enormous steel structure,' said Harry Gugger, speaking of the Turbine Hall wall, 'which will create the boundary of the space, and we will have light interfering with the steel structure. It's like cutting through the steel structure, and that leads to the solution where these light objects [the bay windows] will almost hover. They should act as the main light sources, but they are also elements where people can walk in and can have a view into the Turbine Hall, so it's also about transparency – that from the Turbine Hall you can get orientation by these light objects [the bay windows with their surrounding light boxes]: you see people up there, they see you. So it's not just at first sight a simple transparency but also a mental transparency.'

Perhaps there was a danger sign in that phrase 'mental transparency', if anybody had been alert enough to notice it at the time Gugger was speaking, back in February 1997. Because it was adjectives like 'transparent', 'translucent', 'luminescent', 'opaque' and 'diffuse' that dominated discussions of the Turbine Hall bay-window light boxes, as technological fixes failed time and again to provide the solution.

The glass contract was won by an Austrian company, Bug (pronounced 'Boog') Alutechnic in 1997, but it was only late in 1999, three months before the building was handed over to the Tate and many months after the glass should have been up and Bug been off the site, that an agreed solution was put into action.

Jonathan Raynes was one of Schal's on-site construction managers, and it was his misfortune to have to wrestle with the glass problems on a day-to-day, almost hour-by-hour, basis when it became apparent that the architect had been told by Bug that he could have what he wanted, and then it turned out that he couldn't. Raynes is a tall, cheery, matter-of-fact engineer, who viewed the whole situation with mounting disbelief. His starting point was what the architect – and the Tate – had decided was the effect they wanted. 'There is glass which, basically, acts as a diffuser, behind which there are lights. From the architectural point of view, when standing in the Turbine Hall, the architect doesn't want to see any light at all. He purely wants to see a nice white, glowing luminescence. That is what the architect wants. Unfortunately, we're right on the cutting edge of what is achievable with glass technology, certainly in Europe.'

Initially, the success with the small glass sample lulled everyone into a false sense of confidence. 'Everybody's sat back for three months saying, "Oh, we have control samples," and we never had a viable control sample, was the reality,' said Andy Butler of Stanhope Properties. 'What's let them down here is that their glass supplier left it to the last minute to say, "By the way, I can't put an interlayer in at 4.5

metres, sorry." Bug are relatively new into the market, and I think they've had some bitter lessons.'

In November 1998, having discovered, to their own dismay as much as anyone else's, that they could not recreate the effect of the original sample in large sheets of glass, Bug prepared some alternative samples that *could* be reproduced at large scale and set them up on the Turbine Hall wall at Level 2. The Tate and the architects were told that they had to choose one of these.

Harry Gugger and Michael Casey from Herzog and de Meuron, along with Andy Butler from Stanhope and Jonathan Raynes from Schal, Peter Wilson from the Tate, and several uncomfortable people from Bug, stood around near the concrete ramp and assessed the situation. Butler, on behalf of the Tate, was not happy with the gun that was being held to the client's head. 'Bug have put the client in a position now where he's having to take a "yes or no" decision when, basically, he's not been offered an option now, because what everybody thought we were getting, a white interlay on the glazing, isn't achievable. And they only brought that to the notice of the team six weeks ago, having been appointed since last November.'

Harry Gugger did not like what he saw, and had no intention of choosing between two samples that didn't do the job he was promised a year ago could be done. 'I have a very clear opinion,' he said. 'If they can't provide what's specified then they have to come up with equal at no extra cost.'

'There are two types of glass we are now offering,' said a man from Bug. 'As we've said, it is not possible to produce the white interlayer with the height of the glass. But here we have acid-etched glass, and glass that has been sand-blasted.' He was asked which was which, and made a call from his mobile phone to find out.

'Having that up there is a waste of time,' said Michael Casey. 'They originally provided us with a sheet of glass with a white interlayer and reneged afterwards.'

Reluctantly, after further discussions, Herzog and de Meuron and the Tate accepted an alternative solution based on the sand-blasted sample, but with some extra precautions. Jonathan Raynes was relieved. 'The issue about sand-blasting is that when one touches the glass, it is very receptive to oil and grease, and difficult to clean.

So in conjunction with the sand blasting we will have a protective treatment. And we have actually agreed with Bug a combination of sand-blasting and protective coating on either one or both sides, according to the location of the glass.'

So carried away was Raynes with the fact that a decision had been made that he next made a rather rash statement. 'I think the architect's actually getting a better solution than we had originally, that's in my humble opinion. He probably will disagree. So the end result will be an enhanced solution.'

For Bug, this was an unhappy situation and one that was likely to cost them a lot of money through the effects of delays and a type of glass treatment that was different from the one they had budgeted for. Reto Barblan, the senior Bug man on-site, put some, at least, of the problem down to differences in people's perceptions – a reminder of Gugger's 'mental transparency'. 'If somebody looks at an elevation with glass and light behind, I think everybody sees that in a different way, and that is the biggest problem we have.'

For the time being, since a decision had been made, the architects and the Tate could get with other important areas of the building, while Bug set about organizing the manufacture of the large panes of glass in a Europe-wide operation, as Jonathan Raynes explained. 'The basic glass is manufactured in Spain. It's toughened, heat-soaked and laminated in Spain; it then travels to Austria, where it has the sand-blasting treatment applied; it then travels to Germany to have the protective coating applied; back to Austria, where it has the fixings applied; and then it's crated and shipped here.'

By February 1999, Nick Woolcott, the latest Schal senior construction manager, who had replaced Dale Sager, had visited the glass manufacturers in Austria. 'The factory's very impressive,' he said. 'We've seen the glass for the balconies, which are very large sheets of glass, and there's a load which left Austria on Monday. It is generally encouraging. We will put up an area of that in advance of the rest of it, with lights behind it for the designers to look at. But effectively the rest of the glass is either made or in production now, so we don't have time to be able to go back and re-alter it before it's fixed.'

There was now an increasing sense of urgency in the matter. Without the glass, which should have been in weeks ago, the wall between the

Turbine Hall and the Boiler House couldn't seal the Boiler House galleries from the elements, since the Turbine Hall was always seen more as a street than an interior space, potentially open to the elements at the west end, where the main doors were, and unheated.

'The immediate milestone is that we've got to get the Boiler House watertight and we've got to get the environment controlled, because there's no point pumping heat into a building that's spewing out into the Turbine Hall.'

Ruddy Joinery, the contractors for the wooden floor, were waiting to lay this down in the Level 3 galleries and couldn't do so for fear that it might be damaged if stable temperature conditions were not maintained.

As the panes of balcony glass processed in a Grand Tour around Europe, Bug were kept busy in several other parts of the building where they were also supplying and fixing glass. A meeting in February, called to plan how to put pressure on the company to improve the quality and speed of their work, revealed a litany of problems.

'They have problems with brackets; problems with tolerances where they are attaching glass to the substructure; there's panels missing in certain areas,' said Dave Ward, a Schal site supervisor.

'The panels are made,' said Jonathan Raynes,' but they can't find them, so they are remaking them. That'll produce a two-week delay for Tommy Clarke's [the electricians].'

Ward said, 'They were saying the panels were stuck in the snow, but now they say they're lost.'

'They can't just carry on swanning around like they are,' said Nick Woolcott. 'We must hit the dates for balcony glazing. Send them a letter, explaining all these issues, and then arrange a meeting with Peter Wilson.'

In April 1999, the first long-awaited, much-needed panes of balcony glass, with their sand-blasted, protective-coated diffusing surfaces, arrived on-site. Everyone waited on Level 1 to see the panes installed in front of a battery of fluorescent tubes. Once the glass was in place, everyone could see very clearly the outlines of the light tubes behind the glass. Now time was not on their side.

It might be asked at this point: what was so awful about seeing fluorescent tubes behind the glass? Would it *really* be so bad if the

Tate and Herzog and de Meuron accepted the fact that dozens of 4.5 metre sheets of glass were wending their way across Europe, expecting to be installed in the Turbine Hall wall, and let matters take their course?

But Peter Wilson put the argument very strongly for not giving up at this stage. He saw that there were times when an architect's vision, particularly since it was a vision shared by the Tate, *had* to be pursued until there was no alternative to accepting second best. 'I think if it does end up looking as it does at the moment,' said Wilson, 'like glass covering a lot of lamps that are very visible, then it will look not like a piece of Herzog and de Meuron architecture and, actually, rather like certain kinds of artwork that we might one day want to display, and I think it would be wrong not to resolve the problem. The question is how and when, and we've got a fair amount of time to solve it, but for technical reasons we have to get the glass in place because the glass is the edge of the air-conditioned envelope and without it we can't condition the building.'

The plan, therefore, was to keep the existing glass on-site, install it to allow the Boiler House environment to be controlled, find a solution that could be executed nearby, and then take down the panes and treat them. Herzog and de Meuron, in discussion with Bug, came up with two possible solutions to add to the treatment the glass had already undergone.

'One was a diffuser behind the glass,' Jonathan Raynes explained. 'The other was an alternative screen-printed epoxy film on the back of the glass, to help diffuse the lighting further. Both the architect and the client are happy to go down the route of the epoxy film on the back. I suspect the diffusers on the back of the glass are not really a very acceptable long-term solution, for two reasons: one's the cost, and one's the time it will take to do it. What we have done is to take the view that, "OK, it will be done". It's not going to happen now, so we've actually instructed Bug not to put any glass in the balcony areas as it stands at this moment in time.' They would have to seal the Boiler House from the Turbine Hall as effectively as possible with temporary plywood partitions.

Andy Butler's view of the story was suffused with hindsight. 'To be perfectly frank,' he said, 'I think the architect tried to make the glass do something that it isn't really capable of – in other words, to act as the only medium to diffuse the light. He also closed the centres up between the tubes, and there's a sort of rule of thumb, that the light tubes should be no closer together than their distance from the glass, and it didn't get picked up, and it should have done – the centre's closer. So the glass was never the right medium.'

One side effect of adding the new treatment to the old was that it would cut down the light levels more than the architect had specified. 'But with two thousand, six hundred tubes or whatever it is, I don't think that's going to be a particular issue,' said Andy Butler.

According to Michael Casey of Herzog and de Meuron, 'Ove Arup's assumed a worst case over lighting. That's why we have all these light fittings.' A lucky decision.

In spite of his experience of events over the previous year, Casey was incurably optimistic in his view that they were on the last lap. 'It's nothing that we can't solve,' he said. 'It's not rocket science.'

If 'solving' the problem meant producing what Herzog and de Meuron originally wanted, Peter Wilson took a different view, as the treatment of the glass began in a corner of the Turbine Hall in a small treatment plant that had been set up for the purpose.

'I don't think it will be perfectly evenly lit,' Wilson said. 'I think pragmatism comes in deciding what does "evenly lit" mean. I'm reasonably confident about it because, even though you can't get sheets of glass any longer in the size that would have done the job in one go, the fact that you *could* put a sheet of glass that near the lamps and not see the image of a lamp means that there must be a way of making the characteristics of the glass provide that kind of effect. It's not impossible, which some people have tried to say it was.'

Andy Butler was more direct. 'The balcony glazing took on a life of its own. We set the basic parameters out; the engineers [at Bug] who were involved in the design almost fell by the wayside and were taken out of the loop. It then became an issue of architectural focus, and we missed the trick.'

Thursday 29 July 1999 was a hot, hazy day at Bankside. And the emotional tone was hot, too. The Practical Completion Date – a milestone, originally set for 31 March 1999, then May and then July – had come and gone. It was meant to mark the handover of a functional building to the Tate, but there were still areas of the building where power and ventilation were not functioning. The big guns – Peter Rogers of Stanhope Properties, Peter Wilson, Nick Serota – were gathering on-site to address the issue of how to inject even more urgency into the contractors who were doing the work.

The building was now an impressive sight. Whole rooms were beginning to resemble an art gallery, with dramatic swathes of uninterrupted white walls, light-coloured wooden veneered doors, high windows letting in diffused daylight, smooth concrete floors and rough wooden ones. This was the flesh on the bones, the finishes that at last allowed the architects' vision to be tested against reality. And they were usually right. It had been an unusual decision, to give a prestigious art gallery the untreated wooden floors that Herzog and de Meuron had insisted on. Varnished or sealed floorboards or parquet are such an essential part of modern architecture that it's difficult to imagine a new building with any other sort of floor. And yet, the yards and yards of narrow, untreated floorboards looked and felt just right. And it was the *feeling* of them that was as important as the look. They were rough and therefore non-reflective, and gave a crisp, workmanlike feel to what was still a workmanlike space. And for Herzog and de Meuron, the fact that without any protective coating the floors would gather grime and dirt was in keeping with their desire to reflect the industrial feel of the original building.

But for every finished room there was another that showed signs of the work that still had to be done, that should have been completed weeks ago. And there were also signs of several of the long-running design issues which should also have been solved ages ago but had become caught in the triangular relationship between the Tate, the architects and the contractors. Would Harry be happy with the wooden finishes to the doors, doors he had always wanted to be black anyway? Would Bug be able to come up with a solution to the continuing problem of the visibility of the fluorescent tubes behind the Turbine Hall lighting arrays?

In the Induction Room, a Portakabin opposite the cafeteria, the weekly gathering of contractors assembled to be addressed by Peter Rogers on the subject of the schedule. Heaped plate-loads of bacon sandwiches and trays of tea and coffee provided fuel for the fiery arguments that Rogers expected to ensue. Earlier in the week one observer had remarked on the sense of panic that ran through the site as one problem after another reared its head to thwart the progress of work. The door ironmongery, for instance, had turned up in a total muddle. Instead of being neatly organized in sets, so that the fitters dealing with the thirty-eight different door types could find the right kit of parts to install, they were all in a bugger's muddle, with pieces for many different doors bundled up together, and in some cases pieces supplied that were meant to be flush but were designed to be inset. As the meeting got under way, the representative of the doors company explained that the entire load of ironmongery would have to be sent back – it sounded as if he said to Denmark, but fortunately it was only to the London suburb of Denmark Hill. Even so, his forecast that the pieces would be back 'after the weekend' sounded very optimistic to some. Literally it was bound to be true, but everyone expected they'd have to wait another week before they'd be back and the mammoth task could begin of fitting knobs, finger-plates and other ironmongery to 900 doors.

As each person in the room spoke in turn about his own problems or, occasionally, about the fact that he was on schedule, Rogers would turn to Nick Woolcott, Andy Butler or some member of the Schal team for confirmation. Meetings like this revealed how interwoven all the tasks were and how it was always possible for one link in the chain to blame his own delays on the previous link.

At the end of the meeting Rogers gave the kind of pep talk people always give in this kind of situation, as if everyone in the room didn't already know how at risk the revised Practical Completion Date (now rescheduled for December) was. Then, at a brisk trot, Rogers, Peter Wilson, Andy Butler and Nick Woolcott led Pat Starborough of Tommy Clarke's around the building on a troubleshooting exercise.

It was a display of Rogers at his best, a conjuror who snatches solutions to problems out of the air when everyone else has stood around scratching his head. Sometimes, there is nothing new in what he says. He is merely the piece of grit in the oyster; the person who throws in one small technical suggestion, knocks a few heads together, won't take no for an answer, and breezes off before anyone can disagree. We could all probably do the same if we were vested with his power, authority and brashness. As Andy Butler said later, 'Peter says things that I've been saying for ages, but somehow people listen to him and things get done.' At the top of the building, on the roof of the Turbine Hall, someone had installed the base of a parapet incorrectly so that now the parapet itself could not be fitted. With some toe-pushing of the offending hardware, a quick interrogation of the three different technicians and some rattled-out instructions, Rogers and his entourage headed for the door back into the Light Beam – which had closed firmly shut behind them when they came on to the roof. In a flash, Rogers' Swiss Army knife was probing the latch, and the door swung open to let them through.

As Peter Wilson looked at a couple of doors on Level 5, he was gloomy. 'See those marks?' he said. 'Harry won't like that.' He pointed to a regular pattern of small dark knotholes across the top of the door, and some areas of grain lower down that were also rather dark. To anyone else, it looked rather as you would expect wood veneer to look. But Wilson knew that Gugger wanted a very even tone right across the doors. But you only get that by using veneer from the outer edges of the tree, and the suppliers had not been told that this was required. Doors had already been installed throughout the building, and yet Wilson was contemplating the possibility that the only way to solve the problem – if it was a problem – was by staining each door black. This would be a radical step and a return to what Gugger had originally wanted, a course of action that had been rejected quite early on. Wilson was one of those who didn't like it. He felt it would look as if there was a dark tunnel leading off each gallery.

It was, of course, surprising that at this stage anyone was even contemplating such a major design change. But it was a sign of how unusual the project was. When you talked about it with the construction management team, they contrasted it with a 'commercial' building, and made clear how they felt that different standards applied because it was an art gallery, whose director listened to the architect much more than the average client would. The issue of Serota's relationship with the architects was a particularly touchy one for Peter Rogers, who saw Harry Gugger getting his way time and time again because he had Serota's support. In fact, this Thursday Rogers and Serota had arranged to meet at Bankside to thrash out this very issue.

On his whirlwind walkabout, the paths of the two men had crossed on Level 5 as Serota passed by with a group of VIPs.

As the Rogers group headed back down the building, they stopped off in the men's lavatories by the auditorium. There was a lot of dissatisfaction with the workmanship here – dark speckled tiles that seemed misaligned; slightly askew panels at the back of the cubicles; a strange design feature due to which the tiles above the sinks would have to be chipped away if access was ever needed to a stopcock behind. As usual, Rogers had a solution to this last problem at his fingertips. 'Can't you access the pipes below, where the tiles are already removable?' he asked one of the Schal people.

'There would be too much dead space,' the man replied, referring to the fact that a lower stopcock would mean that a larger volume of stagnant water would remain between the stopcock and the taps, providing a possible breeding ground for germs.

Towards the end of the walkabout one of the group received a call on his mobile to let Rogers know that Serota was now waiting for him in the visitor centre. By doubling an already rapid pace, Rogers swept his group down to the basement level, rattled off a couple of final points, and then set off by a very circuitous and occasionally erroneous route to the back of the building, where Serota was sitting calmly signing his daily correspondence.

Rogers had a central objective for this meeting – to get Serota to stop siding with the architects every time a new design issue came up that they wanted to change, even at this late stage. This had happened several times recently, and today's concerns over the doors threatened to turn into another delaying situation.

'With Harry, the seriousness of the situation we're in really needs to be got through to him,' Rogers said to Serota. 'He's got to help finish this building. The guys are nervous about hanging the doors because they think the timber veneers are going to be rejected.'

With Peter Wilson, who had joined them, Rogers ran through the various alternative treatments that could disguise the patchiness of the veneers, but he was keen that the best solution for the schedule and budget be adopted, not the one the architect wanted most. The trouble was, Schal kept listening to the architect.

'Schal are trapped, legally trapped,' Rogers said, 'in respect of having to comply with the architect's instructions. And they're in a very difficult position: they've never been particularly strong, and they're not willing to have a fight with the architect.

The trouble was, as Serota pointed out, there was only so much he could do, even if he turned up personally to discuss some crucial problem, as Rogers suggested. 'When I walk on-site,' Serota said, 'everyone comes up, they're all very sweet, and tell me how well it's all going, and they know I'm interested in quality, so they talk to me about quality and all the rest of it. And if I stay for a bit longer, we can end up with having quite an interesting discussion, but otherwise it's whitewash. So the question is, is there any point in my coming?'

Rogers then said what he'd been wanting to say for the last few minutes. 'Nick, you have to make clear to Jacques and Harry the position. They both believe, and the site believes, that if there's a real issue, they will come round the back door to you and you will side with them. It doesn't matter how true it is, that's, you know, that's what they think.'

'There are plenty of examples where we haven't,' Serota said.

'Harry's got to understand the pressures on the job to finish,' Rogers went on. 'The contingency is going to come under pressure, you are going to get claims. Contractors are here longer than they should be. We've already got two big claims, and I'm not as confident as Schal are that all the other contractors are going to play ball financially.'

'But at the moment we're talking as though the problem is the architect, and I recognize that there are some problems with the architect, but the architect isn't the only problem,' Serota protested.

'But it's the only problem you can help us with,' Rogers replied. 'It's no good getting you to walk the site and bully the contractors – that's our job – but the one problem you can help us with is with the architect. Even to the point of saying, "If you don't like the doors, leave them, do them later." They'll be better done later, anyway. It's important that Harry and Jacques realize there are going to be some compromises; there will be an opportunity at the end of this job to go back through and pick up the details.'

'Right,' said Serota to Rogers, 'so Peter will talk to Harry next week; I will call Peter on Wednesday or Thursday with a view to coming the following week, especially if Harry is here.'

Rogers scented a bit of buck-passing here by Serota. 'Can *you* also call Harry?' he asked.

'Yes, I'll call Harry, sure,' Serota agreed, and Rogers had achieved his objective.

At three-thirty, smoke rose into the sky from an area near the cafeteria. The Tate had organized a barbecue for the entire workforce, a kind of thank-you for the work done so far. The notices posted all over the building said, 'At 15.30 (half-past three in the afternoon) there will be a barbecue . . .' Clearly there was uncertainty amongst management as to how many of the operatives would understand the 24-hour clock. Soon after three o'clock a queue had started to form next to football-sized baked potatoes, long thick sausages, chicken legs and slab-like hamburgers. Men hurried back and forth with eight cans of Foster's lager cradled in their arms – it was a hot day and they had been involved in thirsty work. At four o'clock or so a small crocodile of Schal managers made their way into the crowd, fraternizing rather uneasily with a workforce they had been blaming earlier in the day for poor workmanship and inefficient work practices.

Part Five

1999–2000 Tate Accompli

25

Handover time

When Herzog and de Meuron submitted their competition entry, with its vast, uncluttered Turbine Hall, their computer illustration showed Rachel Whiteread's *House* plonked in the middle of the basement floor, dwarfed by the rest of the building. It demonstrated an idea the Tate liked, of using the Turbine Hall to display some art. When the large industrial company Unilever came to the Tate in 1997 with an offer of money to sponsor a sculpture for the new gallery, Frances Morris and her colleagues sat down with Unilever to decide how to spend their money.

'Over a period of months,' Morris said, 'we came to a mutual understanding that it would be rather exciting for the Tate and Unilever to collaborate over the commissioning of a major piece, a big, or important, or striking, or awe-inspiring, or 'wowish' piece of sculpture to act at the threshold of the Tate Gallery of Modern Art, in the Turbine Hall, so that visitors would have an experience of art as they encountered the building; to bring architecture and contemporary art together in the most lively and dynamic way. We needed to come up with an artist who was ambitious enough and fantastic enough and confident enough and established enough to cope with possibly the most major project of their career at the opening of the new Tate Gallery of Modern Art. And our shortlist quickly boiled down to one person, and that person was Louise Bourgeois because she is not only an extraordinarily accomplished artist but, being born in 1911, she is an artist whose career spans the twentieth century. And one of the ambitions of the Tate is that it should span the twentieth century and beyond. It should bring the history and the present and the future together in a dynamic and engaging way, and Louise's career seems to do that.'

Shortly after Lars Nittve became director of the new Tate he joined the discussions with the sponsors. Although Morris was sure she wanted Bourgeois, there was an initial feeling that several artists should be sounded out. But with Bourgeois' name on the list the feeling changed. Nittve explained: 'I think when we were getting closer to that process we felt that Louise Bourgeois is not really an artist that you sound out and then possibly say "no" to. Either you have to take the risk or not.'

Louise Bourgeois is eighty-eight and still producing works of art. She was born and brought up in France but now lives in New York. She has produced a large volume of work over the last sixty years, in painting, sculpture and even writing, and, in Nittve's view, her work is always changing. 'She's always been pushing at the forefront of her own work and the work of her own contemporaries. She grew up alongside surrealism; she matured alongside abstract expressionism; and yet she's still maturing and growing up and being young through the years of early feminist art, conceptual art, engaged art, and remains one of the most important influences, or role models, for contemporary artists now. And her work has consistently moved and engaged with its time but always maintained this singularity.'

Morris tried to give Bourgeois as much freedom as possible in deciding what to create. 'The guidance that I offered to her was to think about the fact that thousands of people will need to use the space, that the work needs to be accessible, that it shouldn't be barriered off. And that somehow it should engage with the architecture and experience of being in that space.

'She sent us a transparency of a maquette, of this very striking tower topped by these distorting mirrors and we were completely taken aback and delighted and thought, "This is really a goer." Two weeks later there was another transparency and another tower. And two weeks after that there was another transparency and another tower and then a week later there was a spider. And it just seemed to unleash in her mind this kind of torrent of new ideas.'

The spider was a Bourgeois motif. She had made several cast iron spiders a metre or two high for other museums, but the one she was proposing for the Tate was far larger – ten or twelve metres from its bulging body to the tips of its spindly legs.

On 24 July 1999, Frances Morris and Phil Monk, a colleague at the Tate who would be responsible for the logistics of Bourgeois' installations, walked along West 20th Street in New York towards the brownstone house where Louise Bourgeois lived. It was in the area of Manhattan known as Chelsea and her street was tree-lined, with a very English-looking Episcopalian church right opposite the house. On the steps of the church was a group of people sitting or standing around talking or smoking or just contemplating the New York heat, which was typically thick and muggy for July.

This would be the first time Morris had met Bourgeois since the Unilever award had been announced, and she had no specific agenda for the meeting other than to consolidate the relationship with the Tate now that Bourgeois' commission was confirmed and under way. It would also be a chance to see the models of the sculpture and the beginnings of construction of the very large spider that was to dominate the Turbine Hall near the three towers.

Even though Morris has obvious intelligence, sang-froid and quiet determination, she cannot have expected an easy ride with Bourgeois. At eighty-seven the sculptor had earned the right to be idiosyncratic, cranky and incomprehensible, and she was all of these during the meeting. Morris and Monk were let into the house by Jean-Louis Bourgeois, Louise's son and an architectural historian in his fifties, who was treated by his mother as if he was twelve years old. They walked down the long dark hallway, made darker in contrast to the bright sun streaming through the glass front door, and were led to Louise, perched like a small queen receiving an audience. With a healthy disregard for anybody's sense of fashion but her own, she sat on a stool wearing a very short skirt revealing her painfully thin legs, which dangled in space like one of her own suspended life-size mannequins. A model of one of the three towers stood on the wooden floor in the middle of a room lined with books, files, posters, letters, certificates and awards proclaiming Louise's fame.

Also at the meeting was Gerry Gorovoy, Bourgeois' assistant for the last twenty years, a tall Christ-like figure with a curly beard and long brown glossy hair which he twirled absently in his fingers from time to time. During the conversation, Bourgeois would wave him off on some mission to gather a drawing, book or picture from the shelves. Sometimes he succeeded, sometimes not, but you got the impression that by the time he returned the conversation had moved on anyway and Bourgeois had forgotten what she had sent him for. 'You can never lose anything in this library,' she said, 'and you can never find anything.'

As an intimate of several key members of the French and American surrealist movements in the 1930s and 1940s, Bourgeois threw this sort of remark into the conversation at regular intervals. She had clearly been interviewed many times over the years and any conversation was in danger of turning into a series of pressed buttons releasing epigrams about art and life. Morris skilfully tried to avoid pressing these buttons as she concentrated her attention on the Tate's commission, but she didn't always succeed.

Bourgeois had prepared herself for the meeting with a joke, which she had got Gorovoy to print out in large type on a piece of paper. The rationale for the joke was that it was the sort of discussion that might take place between a father and a son who had climbed to the top of one of Bourgeois' towers when it was on public display in the Tate. Laboriously and in the strong French accent that had clearly not changed for the last forty years, she read it out.

' "Father, who made the day and the night?" Smart Alec . . .' (an explanatory aside to Morris). ' "Well, my child, that is a very good question, but I simply do not know." "Thank you, Father. Father, where do we come from?" "Well, my child, that is a very, very good question, but I simply do not know." "Thank you, Father. Father, when will I know where I am going?" – that is the kind of conversation they are having at the top of the tower stairs,' Bourgeois said, 'so it relates immediately with my sculpture – "Father, when will I know where I am going?" "Well, my child, that is a very, very good question, but I simply do not know." "Thank you, Father. Father, why does the touch of my friend's skin feel so nice?" "Well, my child, that is a very good question, but I simply do not know." "Thank you, Father." And then, "Father, what are we here for?" A very, very deep, searching question. "Well, my child, that is a very, very good question, but I simply do not know." "Thank you, Father, I'll pass on your wisdom to my children." And after all of that, the father said that he didn't know!'

'And he'll never know,' said Morris politely.

'So this is the kind of conversation they are having at the top of this tower,' Bourgeois said, 'philosophical questions. "Is it worth living or isn't it worth living?" '

'Is the tower then a stage for those kinds of questions?' Morris said, searching for a possible underlying theme for the sculpture. 'Is it designed to prompt those questions?'

She was disappointed in the answer.

'No, it was not set up as a stage for that,' Bourgeois said. 'It was set up as a visual pleasure-giving monument.'

'But it seems more profound than just pleasure,' Morris said.

'Yes, because when people see that thing, they are really wondering, "What does that damn thing mean? What is it there?" Well, it is there in order to give us pleasure and in order to make us think, and to make us meet.'

'Each other?'

'Yes, yes. Sometimes you are wandering in this world, and you are anxious as to who am I going to meet? Am I going to meet somebody interesting? Or am I condemned to meet only idiots? So you make a great effort in circulating, socially, among people who amount to something.'

People like Morris, Serota, Nittve and others who have spent their lives immersed in contemporary art are very comfortable with uncertainty. What does it mean? is not a question that they very often ask an artist, at least not in such bold terms. But Morris was keen to pursue this conversation about what Bourgeois intended as the function of the towers, for example, since they were there not just to be looked at but climbed, sat in, observed from and generally used by visitors. There ensued a dialogue during which Bourgeois created a small world of secrecy at the top of the tower, where intimate conversations could take place a dozen metres up in the air.

'Your tower will be the site of encounters with strangers?' Morris asked.

'Absolutely. That's absolutely it. Are you going to be lucky or are you at your best yourself? You know, you shouldn't always put the responsibility on the other one. Do you feel all right today? Do you feel up to par . . . ? For instance,' Bourgeois went on, giving an example that must have left Morris wondering if she had missed a key step in the way the encounter was proceeding, 'I have been working on a musical scene, because up there you might meet a musician, or somebody who is interested in listening – listening is not only words. So what I was listening at, when I got there, was a call, it was a call. And I am trying to bring up the call, why does it escape me?'

At this point she embarked on a long and intriguing meditation on Switzerland, which started with a challenge. Bourgeois cupped her hands round her mouth and gave forth a series of sounds which were like a muted cow mooing rather tunefully.

'Do you know what that is?' she said to Morris.

'It sounds like a very distant call,' Morris said in an inspired guess.

'Very, very distant,' said Bourgeois. 'And it is a piece of music which is played on an Alpine – Alpine horn. Is it Alpine horn?' She turned to Gerry, as she often did, for confirmation and, as often happened, she didn't get it.

'And it is a call, in a Swiss tragedy. It is not a happy call.' She put her hands up to her mouth and sang again, to show what a happy call would sound like. 'It is not that. That would be a marriage, it would be a baptism, or it would a . . .'

'A celebration,' said Morris.

'Celebration, right. This is not at all that, it is what is called *éclat* – *éclat*.'

'*Éclat*?'

Bourgeois sang with *éclat*.

'So it's like a funereal call?'

'Absolutely, absolutely.'

The conversation was taking Morris to places she hadn't particularly needed to go to, but you don't get an hour's conversation every day with a twentieth-century icon and so she was happy to explore with Bourgeois a range of issues to do with the disturbing nature of Switzerland, spiral staircases as a metaphor for rage, and the three towers as father, mother and child. At one point Bourgeois said, 'Art is a guarantee of sanity, right? If you are an artist you are not going to go cuckoo. If you are an artist you are cuckoo already.'

Then Bourgeois asked Gorovoy to fetch a book for her. It featured artists whom Bourgeois had chosen for an exhibition she had curated.

'My gallery asked me to choose,' she said, 'I choose Bacon, Messerschmidt and myself.'

Frances Morris seized the opportunity to move the conversation back to Bankside.

'You'll be pleased to hear that when you look down on your towers from the fifth floor of the Turbine Hall, you will look down on them from a room of paintings by Francis Bacon . . .'

'Oh, that's interesting,' said Bourgeois.

'. . . which are fabulous paintings.'

'Wonderful, wonderful,' said Bourgeois. 'My association really would also be with Shakespeare, certain aspects.'

'Well, we are next door to the Globe.'

'Oh, I see. Shakespeare, because there is the question of the father and son, Shakespeare . . .'

'Would you want us to show our Rodin holdings?' Morris asked.

'Rodin? Not at all,' said Bourgeois, forcefully, 'I'm not interested in Rodin in the least. He was a naturalist.'

'This book is full of Rodin,' Morris pointed out.

'I see. Well, that's not my fault.'

'Giacometti?'

'Yes, well, you see, if you talk about people I knew personally, it becomes embarrassing, because Giacometti had become a very sour-puss in his old age.'

'Why?'

'He found out he was not appreciated.'

'I remember reading Brassaï,' Morris said, 'when he went to take some photographs of Giacometti. In his memoirs, he writes that Giacometti stopped him from taking a photograph and said, "Just wait, I look too happy; wait till I get myself looking agonized and exhausted." And there seemed to be a certain amount of staging of his personality.'

'Yes, I see,' Bourgeois snapped, 'but we are not going into name-dropping now. If you want a session of name-dropping, we have to organize something else.'

As Morris and Monk stepped out into the hazy sunlight, it was as if they had spent an hour in another world. Dark furnishings and dark ideas; a wood-lined cave inhabited by a wise and inscrutable old woman behind them, yellow cabs and skyscrapers in front of them. There were plenty of unanswered questions for Morris, though she had a real sense of the richness of the sculptures the Tate would be acquiring. For Phil Monk, there were more practical issues that faced him and his team. In spite of all the effort that had gone into providing new foundations for the Turbine Hall, there was some concern, from the initial information about the sculptures, that a floor slab might not bear the weight of the all-metal towers soaring thirteen metres into the air. At certain points the weight might be concentrated in such a way that it exceeded the loads the floor was supposed to support, and Morris didn't want there to be any sort of platform to spread the load.

Two months later, Gerry Gorovoy was standing on a patch of land in Ridgefield Park, New Jersey, outside the premises of More Specialized Transportation, an ambiguously named company that specialized in moving unconventional loads. In a far corner of the yard was a container which, according to one of the managers, the company had made to carry Yuri Gagarin's capsule when it was shipped ignominiously to the US to be auctioned when Russia faced a sudden need for ready money. Today they were to rehearse assembling and taking apart Louise Bourgeois' spider, which had now been manufactured in pieces and trucked out to More's premises. Over the course of a day, with the help of a small crane, the giant legs were assembled, each one two or three pieces bolted together, and connected at the body end to a large metal ring. The four or five men doing the work were unperturbed by the fact that what was rising before their eyes was a realistic, strangely biological object with a convincing appearance of lightness that came from the fact that each leg tapered to a delicate tip upon which the weight of the spider rested. One task for today, apart from checking that everything went together properly, was to ensure that the tips of the legs were all in the same plane. In fact, they weren't. When all eight legs had been linked to the central ring, on which the body would be placed, two or three of them hovered a few centimetres above the ground, and there was a certain amount of banging and adjusting of bolts to get them to the same level as the others.

As the sun set behind More Specialized Transportation's American flag, drivers on the nearby freeway heading home from their Manhattan offices might well have been momentarily distracted by the sight of an anatomically accurate spider ten metres high poised delicately outside a low, undistinguished building off to their right. The next time the spider would be fully assembled was likely to be nine months later when it would finally be installed on the wide bridge across the Turbine Hall, keeping a watchful eye on its three accompanying towers on the floor below, as visitors climbed the spiral staircases in the hope of meeting a musician or somebody interested in listening . . .

In November, as the race was on to finish the fit-out, a number of doors began to appear in the galleries. The surfaces were elegant, smooth, polished veneers – and the Tate and the architects hated them. 'Until I saw them on-site I'd no idea how awful they were going to look,' Peter Wilson said, '– kind of stripy and loud and over-varnished.' The lines of wood grain and the knots in the veneer stood out from the plain rather richly coloured background.

'I think it's caused by the way the veneer is peeled off the log,' Wilson said, '– getting too near to the centre of the trunk before you decide that that piece of veneer is unacceptable to you. It might be simply that somebody didn't actually check that there was a shared understanding about what we meant, because most people buy timber wanting it to have quite a patterny kind of look. Whereas we wouldn't ever buy timber like that for a gallery because it's too busy, and Herzog and de Meuron don't like it particularly either.' In fact, Herzog and de Meuron had a bigger worry. Regardless of the fussiness of the pattern, they had argued for a long time for some kind of darker coating for the doors, another instance of 'Herzog and de Meuron black' rearing its head, although Herzog and de Meuron blacks were rarely really black. The Tate had been concerned that a series of black doors would create a 'dark tunnel' effect through a suite of galleries, but when Harry Gugger spelt out what he meant to the Tate, their initial worries evaporated. What Gugger was after was a kind of dark grey stain that reproduced the quality of old, weathered oak. Even as the over-varnished veneered doors were being installed, the Tate was supportive enough of the architects' desires to consider the additional cost and inconvenience of taking them down again to be stained. But the next problem was to find someone who could reproduce consistently the stain that was in Gugger's mind over dozens of pairs of doors. When Schal thought they had found a company to do it, the first samples were unpromising. So Peter Wilson and Michael Casey travelled north to Doncaster, to the subcontractor who was doing the work.

'It's always the case,' Wilson said, 'that when you go and talk to the guy who's doing it and tell him first-hand what you want, he's got several tricks up his sleeve to help achieve it. And the two guys who do the spraying of the doors up in the wilds of Yorkshire in the factory could very easily get that kind of pared-back, just slightly stained look that we wanted. They didn't have exactly the colour we wanted, but they did have stocks of wood outside in the yard that had been aged, so we could say, "Look, exactly like that", and they said "Oh, yes, exactly like that. We know how to do that." So we mocked up several things by mixing the wrong stains, and got near to the colour that everyone wanted, and then they got in contact with their supplier of stains, who matched the sample, and the sample came back to the site the other day and we approved it straight away.'

At the beginning of December, within days of the official Bankside handover date from Schal to the Tate, the door saga was still a live issue. Having agreed the stain, Wilson now needed to discuss the implications with Schal of changing the doors that had already been hung, and re-staining – and thus delaying – the doors that were still in the factory. Nick Woolcott, Schal's project director, was the person Wilson needed to consult.

'We had the stain approved on Monday evening,' Woolcott said on Thursday 9 December, 'which doesn't give you that long before the doors are due to be here. Gut feel tells you that you should just say, "No, sorry, it's too late", but it was clearly a very painful thing for Peter, so we said, "Look, we'll see what we can do." We had quite a concise conversation with the people doing it, and they've agreed to do whatever they can, and to work all the hours available to them, and rather than be here tomorrow, the doors will be here next Wednesday, and the fixers will work extra hours to fit them in time; but the doors will be here stained, and the client will get what he wants.'

Woolcott's attitude reflected the Tate's attitude when aesthetic issues came up late in the day: 'If humanly possible, do something.'

It was one example of how much further the Tate went than some clients might have done to accommodate the architect's desires. The fact that some of the doors with the 'wrong' stain were actually installed and others being transported to the site did not deter the team from getting things right. Michael Casey, who was supervising the doors' appearance for Herzog and de Meuron, explained. 'It's important that the client understood that this is important to us. And in many ways they only understood how important it was to us when they got the industry standard door in the place.' He laughed, remembering the inspection of the first installed door. 'When that turned up, everybody thought, "Well, it's not quite in the spirit of the rest of the building, is it?" So then we went through the exercise of looking at the stain, and we have come up with a solution.'

With the stain approved, the company Wilson and Casey had visited, C. W. Fields, started work on thirty-five pairs of doors destined for display areas on Levels 3, 4 and 5. The company was located in the village of Epworth, halfway between Scunthorpe and Doncaster, and the installation of the doors was supervised at Bankside by a company called Martin Roberts. Their site representative was Mark Parry, a cheerful man who was familiar with every one of the 800 doors in the museum. When Parry came into his site office on Monday 20 December he was looking forward to the doors arriving later in the week so that installation could start. But there was some bad news.

'We came in to work Monday morning at seven-fifteen,' Parry said, 'and went into the office to see what post we'd got; any e-mails, or any faxes, and there was a fax – "Phone Stacey urgently" – from Martin Roberts. I phoned him up, and he just said, "We've had a major disaster." "What's happened?' I said. He said, "The factory burnt down at the weekend."'

When Parry told Jonathan Raynes of Schal, he was dubious. According to Parry, he said, 'Well, we've had this before from a previous contractor', although the idea that a contractor would invent a story of his factory burning down to explain delays in his contract seemed a little far-fetched. But this story must have been true – it was in the newspapers. *The Epworth Bells and Crowe Advertiser* had a front-page story under the headline 'AFTER THE INFERNO

– £2.5 million blaze horror' describing, in passing, how 'the thick black smoke pouring from the buildings killed two sheep in a nearby field'.

Although the Tate's doors were not featured in the news story, they were in fact all destroyed. Michael Casey was resigned about the news. When Andy Butler said, 'Well, you wanted black doors,' Casey replied, 'Yeah, and I've got them now. But I didn't want ash, I wanted oak.'

The further delay in the doors was just another irritation factor in the days leading up to Christmas. In spite of the Tate's desire to acquire the entire building by Christmas 1999, Schal and the architects were effectively handing over half the building. It was the latest missed deadline in a whole host of missed deadlines, though as Andy Butler described it, there were unavoidable reasons for some and a deliberate rescheduling of the rest. 'Back in July 97 when construction started we had a completion date of the end of March 99, and for a plethora of reasons, including the asbestos and the steel delays, as we've gone through the construction process that completion date has progress-ively moved from the end of May, to mid June, to the end of July, to September. Then we rolled the two distinct phases of the project [the Practical Completion Date, otherwise known as base-build, and the fit-out works, and Level 4, which was excluded from the original project] so we had a completion date of the end of December 99.'

The Tate had expected to begin moving art into the building in September 1999 and finish a couple of months before opening. With the building not being handed over till December, that meant a compressed programme that they still felt was achievable. But now, December had arrived and the galleries were just not in a fit state for art to be installed. There was a mixture of reasons. One of them was to do with Level 4, excluded from the early planning because there wasn't enough money to turn it into finished display spaces. Then the Tate applied for, and received, a grant for the work from the Arts Council, but the news came rather late, delaying final design and fit-out. Level 4 was for special exhibitions and would start with a display called *Between Cinema and a Hard Place*. These galleries would not now be available until the end of February, and so the art-handling staff had to concentrate their attention on Levels 3 and

5 until then. But even in these, the more finished areas, there was a lot to be done. For Andy Butler of Stanhope, progress was agonizingly slow. 'What is frustrating – and I've never worked on an arts project of this size before – is it just seems to take us an eternity to grind out what are the most basic issues. We've got intelligent people who sit round a table who should be able to make decisions, but everything just bounces backwards and forwards, and too often we've put the decision in the client's lap and it shouldn't be. I mean, he employs professionals to make those decisions for him. I've said to Peter [Wilson], "Have me here every day and I'll make decisions. You know I won't get them all right but I'll get eight out of ten right," but if we don't have that, somebody to say, "Yes, do it," we'll bounce around for another week.'

As Colin Berry of Schal, who had recently left the project, looked back in November 1999 at the delays that had taken place, he was critical of the Tate's pliancy in the face of design problems. 'It's very difficult to finish a building if the client defers ten per cent of it because of delays in design such as with the glass. You can't finish any of the lobbies if the glass that goes through them is not there. You can't finish the ceilings, you can't finish the services, you can't finish the floors, you can't finish the balustrade. And the specification for that glass was not decided till probably about two months ago. There are enormous chunks of the building which were deferred by the client because the architect was still designing it right the way up until spring or summer 1999, and the decision was taken then that we can't fundamentally delay the handover from base-building to fit-out, so we had to defer those works and do them within the fit-out period. So the base-build was completed on time and the only bits that weren't were the bits that the client and the designers between them couldn't make up their minds on.'

In fact as the millennium arrived, marked by an informal Bankside party on Level 7 to see the River of Fire that had been promised, it seemed as if Andy Butler was the only person left to make decisions. Whether or not the building was complete, Schal was meant to be off the job by now. But for Butler, representing the Tate's consultants, Stanhope Properties, responsible on their behalf for bringing the job in, there was no escape. Even though he moved to new offices and started work on other projects, he was back on-site nearly every day to deal with the host of problems that still arose.

At this stage, he was concerned about a general lack of activity all over the site, in the areas that had not formally been handed over to the Tate and still needed serious fitting-out work. He was particularly unhappy with Schal. 'Before Christmas,' he said, 'there was a huge effort by everybody, and we sat down and said, "Listen, let's wake up: we're not going to finish this building by the end of the year. Let's focus on Level 3, Level 5 and Level 4." Now, people worked right through to that last week, but we come back this week and it's like a morgue and I'm extremely frustrated that there doesn't seem to be the urgency in there to focus on Levels 3 and 5. Art goes in there on Monday and I bet if I go up there today I'll not be a happy bunny.'

Of all the paperwork that was generated in the course of designing, constructing and operating the new museum, the most impressive was a chart Jim Grundy drew up for his teams of art handlers and installers as the date approached – and then receded – for art installation to begin. Grundy, who is in charge of the art handling at Millbank and Bankside, is a quiet, round-faced man, thin on top, and his chart was clearly his pride and joy. It had about 150 columns and 150 rows. Each column was a day and each row was a room or individual display area, and it covered the new Tate Gallery of British Art as well as the Tate Gallery of Modern Art. By this stage, the two museums had acquired new names: after agonizing internal discussions and highly expensive external advice, the Tate at Millbank was called Tate Britain and Bankside was called Tate Modern. (A pedant would have quibbled at the fact that one Tate had a noun and the other an adjective, but at least it made the names end with the same syllable.)

The fact that there were two galleries with overlapping needs – for British art – posed a few problems for Frances Morris and her colleagues when they were breaking their four genres down into actual works. As she visited the empty galleries on Level 3 a few days before the first art was to be brought in, she described some of the issues. 'There are a number of instances where curators wanted the same works for different displays, not just within Tate Modern, but also Tate Britain. So there have been questions about "Where does Francis Bacon fit in?" "Who should premiere Spencer?" There are also key displays that we never got right at the beginning. We're sitting in a room which is a key important space, it's the opening to the *Landscape* suite, and we only resolved the content of this room about two weeks ago, and we resolved it by making the decision to go to a private collection and borrow one or two items that would lift what we have, and resolve it thematically.

'I'm probably the only person who can walk round the building now, walk into each space and tell you the title of the display, and name aspects of the content. And that makes me quite a useful person because we don't even have adequate and up-to-date layouts of those galleries. And it's a symptom of doing everything at such a pace and not being massively resourced to do it, and it being done in an ad hoc way. We're doing it once, we'll never do it again, so we don't need those systems.'

The room Morris was in, W316, was part of the suite called *Landscape: Matter: Environment* and, adventurously, would contain the works of two very different artists, linked in a way that had emerged from the curators' discussions of the four genres.

"This is the Monet/Long room, behind me: Monet's *Water Lilies*, juxtaposed with Richard Long's *Red Slate Circle*, which is a loan from a private collector. And also, Richard Long has now visited and offered to do us a mud wall drawing along this wall here, which will be very liquid. The display is about the expanded field of landscape, and trying to demonstrate that expanded field isn't just something that has evolved historically, it's something where the potentiality was there in Monet, and interestingly, Richard was very thrilled by the pairing, and is making this work almost in response to the Monet.'

On Jim Grundy's chart if you ran your finger along W316, a room on Level 3 on the west side of the central concourse, called 'Claude Monet and Richard Long', you would have found a yellow square with the letter 'T' on Thursday 27 January, which meant that for Team 6 (yellow), who were to install the art in that room, the artworks would be in transit on that day. The following day, a yellow square with 'O' meant that the boxes were to be opened. Then the following week, the five days had squares marked 'L' which meant that the team had to remove the works from their boxes and lay them out roughly in their final positions. There was then a gap of a week while the same team went off, according to the chart, to one of the other rooms to open boxes or lay the works out. Then in the week beginning 14 February Team 6 would be back to hang the works, deciding on their final positions and fixing them in place.

There were six teams, and every day from January to mid April their tasks were predetermined in one of the eighty or so art display areas at Bankside. Just to complicate things further during the autumn, every change in the fit-out schedule, which was changing all the time, meant a change in Grundy's chart. If one room, for some technical reason, was going to be finished a week later than planned, all the coloured boxes had to shift around to accommodate the change.

Frances Morris described how it would work. 'The process is that every room has a number of people attached to it, a mini team: a curator, an assistant curator, a programme curator, an art-handling team and an education team, and the curators are responsible for putting together a layout. So what they need to do is think in advance about how this room is going to work. They actually have to do a drawing that says, "Piccaso goes here, Matisse goes there". So when the art-handling teams bring in the works, and they bring them in per suite, we start with Level 5 West, starting at the west end and we do that as one, then we move to the next suite. Art-handling teams bring in the works, unpack them and lay them out according to that layout. Then a curator, or the curatorial team, will arrive and work with the art-handling team, to begin to adjust it, and to see what should be in, what should be out; and I will supervise that process, but Lars and Nick will be closely involved in that too. So we'll be a sort of mini team for three days on-site, working in the whole suite. Because one of the things that I hope to achieve is that these suites will feel more like exhibitions than just miscellaneous rooms. There needs to be a family feel. So there'll be three days working in the space with art-handling teams, and then, on the fourth day, there'll be a kind of quiet "Is this right?" session with a small number of people, after which, if major adjustments need to be made, the curators will come back and make them. And then the works go up.'

For Morris, installing the displays at Bankside presented a number of challenges. One of them was a management issue. 'I work with people from all sorts of different departments, in a very flat and transparent structure, but within their own departments they're part of a linear hierarchy. And during the first months of the autumn, I found it quite difficult to work within two systems. Trying to run a team with people, meeting deadlines, and taking responsibility and authorship for aspects of their work in my team, when they're also called upon outside that team to work in a very different way. And it was difficult to control who was part of my team, because their line managers might step in and take them off my team and put them on to another project, so the thing has evolved, not always happily, and at various times I have lost people who I thought had been, as it were, "given" to the team for the duration.'

At a meeting in the autumn to discuss the art-handling schedule, Morris had explained to the group, including Serota and Nittve, the difficulties she faced. 'I'm concerned about just keeping my team of curators on board together now, during the period when some quite tricky decisions have to be made about design issues, plinths, placing of monitors, and so on, and there seems to be a little bit of crumbling on the curatorial side, as a kind of reality checkpoint comes into view.'

'And what form is that crumbling taking?' Serota asked, intrigued.

'The two quite senior curators who were assigned to the display delivery team both want out,' Morris said. 'They both want to leave the team at this stage.'

'Why?' Serota asked.

'Both of them because they've got other work priorities, and I'm being offered as a replacement a very good curator, but one instead of two; one who can't cover the twentieth century or international British . . .'

'Have you talked to Jeremy [Lewison] about this?' Serota asked.

'Yes, I have.'

'And what was his reaction?'

'Talk to the curators.'

'Well, I'll talk to him,' Serota said.

A little later, Morris described another problem with getting curators needed at Bankside away from their Millbank work: 'I did manage to get two of them to work on Fridays for the whole day at Bankside, so that we have our meeting and then they do the actions on-site, there and then.'

'Free lunches, perhaps,' said one of the group.

'And a stretch limo,' said another.

On Thursday 6 January 2000, Joseph Beuys' *The End of the Twentieth Century* set off on its journey to Tate Modern. On Jim Grundy's chart, W301, the double-height gallery, was the top line and because the work consisted of thirty-one separate pieces, the 'T' boxes, turquoise for Team 7, occupied three days, to allow for several journeys by the Tate's lorries. At the Tate's Southwark stores, the basalt blocks were loaded into two trucks. Each piece of stone was in a wooden case, with its identifying number – '12 of 31', for example – written on the side, and a label saying 'FULL' on the top of the case. There was a twenty-minute drive through London's rush-hour traffic – light that morning, because it was the first week back to work after the millennium celebrations – and then the truck was backed into the Tate's brand-new loading bay on the east side of Bankside.

There were several reasons why this was a good work to inaugurate the whole Bankside art installation juggernaut, as Jim Grundy explained. 'We want to try and start off with some large-scale work that creates some space at the store for preparing the next shipments. We've also chosen *The End of the Twentieth Century* because of the amount of space that it takes up while you're laying it out – and it takes up two or three rooms around about it with all the empty cases as you're taking each one out. And that seems to be one that was a popular one with the delivery team to have early photographs of the double-height space. So that one basically is ready to go.'

Phil Monk was supervising the logistics of the art installation and he had a wry, resigned air even at the beginning of the day when nothing had gone wrong. Everyone accepted that there had to be a first work of art in the new museum and that, whatever it was, it would test the system; and Monk and his colleagues accepted that the system would probably fail at some point. The chances of some kind of technical hitch were all the greater because of the general state of the building – a hotchpotch of completed areas, half-completed areas and uncompleted areas. But art installation had to begin in the first week in January 2000, or all the art would not be installed by the target date, mid April.

So when the wide loading hoist failed there was no sign of panic or even frustration. Just a sense of inevitability as half a dozen men stood around and watched buttons being pressed to produce nothing but a whining sound. The hoist was needed to provide a floor surface that was level with the inside of the truck so that the boxes could be wheeled out. Then the hoist would be dropped to the floor level of the loading area so they could be wheeled away to the galleries. That task would be carried out by a team of art handlers. One of them here today to supervise the journey of *The End of the Twentieth Century* to the other end of the new Tate Gallery was Richard Forbes, a gentle, diffident man with grey hair and round spectacles, who was himself an artist and had taken up art handling as his day job. He was carrying a file, a sort of 'Bible' of the Beuys work, setting out descriptions of each stone – one was 'slightly flaky', for example – and suggestions for how to install them.

As the lift engineers fiddled with the hoist, Phil Monk looked on. 'It's a good start, isn't it?' he said cheerfully. 'Fallen at the first fence.'

An hour after the truck had arrived the hoist was fixed and the first stone, Number 18, rolled off the truck, followed by half a dozen others that were laid out on the hoist. Lars Nittve and Iwona Blazwick leant on a rail and watched the process for a few minutes, paying quiet homage to an important moment.

The next small hitch was a lift door that wouldn't close after a couple of boxes had been wheeled in. A lot of shaking failed to move the door, various keys were tried in locks, and then art handlers and security staff formed a huddle and tried to decide what to do. While they were still deliberating the door closed behind them, as someone discovered the trick.

Up on Level 3, a path of plywood had been laid from the lift door to W301. Stone Number 18 was wheeled at a fast pace through the Level 3 concourse, with its unvarnished oak floorboards, through doors into the galleries at the west end of the Boiler House, right through its final destination, the double-height gallery (looking splendidly vast and white) to a gallery beyond where the stones would all be laid out in their boxes and then brought in one by one to be positioned on the floor. Forbes turned the pages of the 'Bible' and looked at the layout that had been approved, and signed off, by a Tate curator. Also in the file were two previous layouts from an exhibition of the work in Edinburgh and another in Liverpool. There seemed to be no common ground at all between the three layouts, and indeed, as Frances Morris had suggested during her walkabout with the other curators, there wasn't even any agreement about whether all the stones were necessary to the display.

Over the next three days, the rest of the stones were brought to the gallery and by late January they were all in position. There was a pleasing symbolism in the fact that *The End of the Twentieth Century* was the very first work of art to be installed in Tate Modern at the beginning of the twenty-first century.

For the Tate, installing the art was more than just another phase – the final one – in the project. This after all was what the gallery was all about. It was a moment – or a series of moments – that Serota had awaited for six years and Lars Nittve for two. However talented and creative the team of curators and art handlers were, the two men at the top couldn't hand over entirely the process of positioning the paintings, drawings, photographs, sculptures and installations.

Serota was admired for his hanging abilities, and would often roll up his sleeves at important exhibitions at Millbank. But clearly he couldn't personally decide where everything had to go in every display space in Bankside, and he described how he would fit into the final phase: 'What I've said I will *not* do is come in when they've done it and say yes or no. I'm not prepared to come in and be the final arbiter, nor am I prepared to be a policeman. If I'm going to wave a wand it has to be much earlier in the process, because in my experience working at Millbank, it's really irritating to everyone, it's embarrassing for me and awkward to come in right at the end and start changing things.'

Serota had to temper his desire to get everything the way he wanted it with the need to pass on some of his own considerable hanging skills to his colleagues. 'I think you can help to develop their eye and their sense of space and a feeling for interval. You can, for instance, insist that no one uses a tape measure, because there's a tremendous tendency to take that wall there and have one picture on it and you make the space on either side equal, but actually that wall there has a door at this end and a corner at that end and therefore it's not an equal balance and therefore you need to adjust the work of art on that wall accordingly by eye. You can remind everyone that there are going to be large numbers of people wandering through the galleries. No one will see it in quite the privileged way that we see it when we're hanging the spaces. You can comment on juxtapositions that are being made and point out why they seem to work or seem to fail, as a way of passing on some experience.

'I always remember when I was in my mid twenties, in 1972, having the opportunity to hang or place a show of Miró sculpture at the Hayward Gallery, working with David Sylvester, and he would turn to me and say, "Well what do you think? Is that looking good?" and I would say, "Yes." And he'd say, "But I think it would be better half an inch to the right," and I'd say to him, "Well, let's try it," and he would move it half an inch to the right; and David was usually more right than I was. So I can begin to do that kind of thing, I hope, with other people. And certainly looking at the curators who've been working at Millbank, some people have an innate ability to hang galleries, others learn it and yet others never will, and they may be able to do other things. So it's not a skill which is given to everyone, and you have to try and find the curators who have a feeling for it.'

Phil Monk was a busy man in the first few weeks of 2000. In addition to overseeing the movement of the first artworks, he was in demand to deal with other issues that arose in the galleries and that might jeopardize the flow of works of art that had to come into the building at an increasing rate from now on. As Monk walked around with Frances Morris on 6 January, they were both particularly concerned about the state of the walls and floors. In Morris's view, there were still too many cracks in the walls. This was a worry not only from an aesthetic point of view, but also because of the possibility that any remedial work would have to take place once works of art were installed. She did not want valuable paintings and sculptures exposed to dust and paint splashes. She and Phil Monk identified room after room that had hairline cracks at the joins of the MDF panels and discussed – somewhat despairingly – what could be done about it.

'You know,' she said to Monk, 'it may not be something that we can deal with now.'

'What concerns me about the cracking,' Monk said, 'is that it does seem to be throughout this floor, and that would require a lot of art to be shifted in order to remedy it.'

'Although we'll probably open with some cracks, people will be so

stunned by the displays they won't see the cracks, I would hope,'
Morris said, unconvinced.

Part of the problem was that neither of them really knew whose
responsibility it was to fix this problem. In the rush to hand over the
building to the Tate and get Schal off the site, responsibility for these
final clearing-up works seemed to have slipped through the cracks,
so to speak. "I suppose we should speak to Andy Butler," Monk said.

The problem was acute. From the following Monday, artworks
would arrive in a steady stream, and be taken to their predetermined
rooms where the curatorial staff would take them out of their packing
and put them in position on walls or floors. This could not take place
in rooms which still required remedial work, and yet that seemed to
be the majority of the rooms. And it wasn't only the walls. Morris
was appalled at the state of the concrete floors on Level 5. Here there
was more room for manoeuvre. It was part of Herzog and de Meuron's
original scheme that some levels of Bankside would have plain concrete
floors in keeping with its industrial origins, and the design team had
visited Belgium to see a warehouse that had a particular type of
concrete strengthened with tiny metal needles. The appearance of this
type of concrete now that it was in situ was mottled and patchy,
something which the architects didn't worry about. In fact they
expected it. But the trouble was there were other markings as well –
a footprint in one place, some tyre marks in another which made it
look like 'a motorcross track' in Morris's words, scattered gouges
and paint marks, and so on.

'Technically,' Morris said, 'with such a short run-up to opening,
we can't really hang major paintings and then un-hang them to Polyfilla
gaps behind them. Obviously, whenever you hang a gallery you need
to go in afterwards and paint out the art handlers' finger marks and
tidy up and all that stuff, but you want to keep it a kind of clean
cleaning, not dirty cleaning. We certainly can't do building work. And
my concern is that there seem to be a number of different problems,
none of which come within the remit of one single person. Most of
the teams here are actually working on the building, not on the display,
and it's that transitional moment where suddenly our deadlines kick
in, and if we don't have the building, then we won't have a display.'

But on her walk round the galleries Morris had found something to be pleased about. Some of the 'fat walls' were designed to hold 'vitrines' – glazed boxes with art objects laid out inside. 'I like the holes that we've cut in the walls for the vitrines,' Morris said, 'and I was very nervous about their placement. We've never cut holes in walls before at the Tate, and so having been given such beautiful walls, it seemed almost sacrilegious to get in there with a jigsaw and cut these holes out. But I think they look very good, very elegant.'

It was actually Andy Butler who ended up dealing with some of the problems, and Morris and Monk were to find out that he took a different attitude from theirs. He too was touring the building that day, and saw the same problems that Monk and Morris were concerned about, but responded more robustly. For some time, Butler had felt that there was little point in doing anything about the less serious cracks because they would only open out again. 'They're going to have to live with some of them,' he said, and pointed out that some walls were never going to be free of cracks. 'Every time the gantry crane travels past, the existing structure is physically connected to the new structure, and the walls are physically connected to the floors, so you do get vibration through there. The Tate – that is, Peter Wilson – have always taken a pretty realistic view of it: that the walls will crack.' But Butler *was* concerned about the double-height gallery.

'I think that's a different scale of problem,' he said, 'It's exponentially worse because of the double height and the huge spans, and it's extremely flexible.' Just that day he had decided to suggest a pretty drastic solution. 'I'm seriously thinking about putting an additional lining on the wall, because it's one space where people will come in and the first thing they're going to do is look up. And the long-term repairs of those walls at that height are going to be exceedingly expensive, so it may be better value to bite the bullet and put a lining on the wall now. But I'm probably speaking out of hand because I've not discussed this with Peter yet.'

In the same way, he felt less worried by the concrete floors. 'Obviously, there's paint and the like on the floor, which has just got to be cleaned up, but there are elements of scarring that you can see, where the actual trowelling process has marked the concrete, and also because there was board that was put down [as protection] that was probably moist and there was moisture in the concrete – there's been some impression marks. There's very little you can do with that, I'm afraid. I think when the art's in there it won't be anywhere near as obvious as it is now.'

As the art was moved in, week after week, during the early part of 2000, concerns about the building had to be put on one side. What could be fixed would be; with the problems that remained, the Tate team had to hope that Morris was right and that the first visitors would be too stunned to notice.

As with any complex project, with Tate Modern at Bankside there was a mix of feelings in the closing weeks as people looked back at the project that, for those who had served longest, had occupied a fifth of their working lives by the time they retired. For some people, the fact that the building was on target to open on time and on budget was in itself a major achievement. But Colin Berry, a Schal manager who had probably seen more of the inner workings of the project than any other member of the construction team, was distinctly jaundiced about the way the project had been run. One evening, with a pint of beer in his hand, and Bankside topped by a glowing Light Beam behind him, he looked back at some of Harry Gugger's complaints about the quality of workmanship that Berry and his colleagues had supervised. 'In a building project of this size you know you can't get every single piece of it exactly right. But the process is that, if we don't get it right we have a construction manager there who goes round before we offer it to the architect and we try and put it right. If Harry wants to go and look at it beforehand and then throw everything out of his pram, the ice cream off the cornet, because something isn't right that we're dealing with, that's Harry's lookout. He perhaps doesn't understand the system. I don't think anybody's got any criticism of the finished quality in that building. Some of the details, nonsensical details, that architects continue to keep pushing out on to pieces of paper nowadays, such as no cover fillets, no skirtings, five-mil gap between floor and concrete, it's very difficult to achieve, but we've achieved it. So I really don't see what his gripe is. In fact, I would say, "Apologies accepted, Harry: you got it wrong, better luck next time."'

But Berry's barbs were also aimed at Stanhope: 'You can't expect designers to manage themselves, that is not what they're good at –

they are designers. Management doesn't feature in their vocabulary, let alone them being good at it. So you need someone to manage them. The project adviser, Stanhope, has got to do it. Patently that didn't happen here because the design was two years late. So one of our biggest frustrations was the fact that nobody was getting hold of designers and bringing a design out of them so that we could get on and do it. Once we got into construction, an even bigger frustration was the fact that Stanhope never seemed to bring anything positive to the party. It was always a negative. And you have to consider that we delivered the base-build on or under its budget, on time, by summer this year, to get into fit-out and finish it by the end of the year, while we had to put up with the assassinations along the way – I'm talking about a project director, two construction managers, a couple of site managers, all delivered through this stratosphere of politics.'

But by any objective standard, the design and construction of Tate Modern was a success. For all the schedule delays, unforeseen problems, aesthetic arguments and personality clashes, the Tate had done far better in organizing, designing, constructing and paying for its new gallery than most other projects of its size. And all of this while maintaining – in the face of many obstacles – a fierce and potentially unappealing vision that had originated when Nick Serota chose Bankside as his location and Herzog and de Meuron as his architects.

Harry Gugger summed up this vision late in 1999, as he stood in one of the galleries on Level 3. 'With this timber floor, which has a rough surface, or with these cast-iron grilles, where you have an almost emotional link to them through the roughness of the oak and the familiarity of the cast iron, we make the room more of a membrane for the art. And that's somehow the secret which we try to achieve here. I think we are successful because lots of people having been here don't even bother about the floor grilles because they seem to be an obvious thing: they are placed in the front of the windows, and it's something you are used to in relation to windows, with radiators, for example.' He tried to think of a way of summing it up. 'This museum,' he said, 'is an intensive care station for the art.'

Gugger and Herzog and de Meuron had changed a lot in five years. The firm was now working on seven museums, largely as a result of their high-profile work on the Tate. Harry Gugger had started out in what seemed a subordinate role to Jacques Herzog, but he had come to dominate the project, as far as being present and making decisions was concerned. It might be thought that he had now come out from under Herzog's wing, but Gugger wasn't so sure. 'I don't know whether one is able to get out from under Jacques' wing. He has very, very large wings. But certainly I'm a different person, because I had the opportunity to be involved in this project in a different culture, and this is a different challenge than working at home. And you grow with such a project, and you change.'

Some of the Tate team had seen Gugger's role as counterbalancing Herzog on those occasions where he was being unreasonable. 'I might be seen as the more reasonable person,' Gugger said, 'but it's not Jacques' role to be reasonable. He is our quality insurance for the architecture, so it's his role to be the strongest critic of our work. And in order to allow him to be the strongest critic of our work, you have to get in a certain distance to the job, you have to know the job very well but, at the same time, if you are exposed to the daily worries of everybody in such a project, you lose the big picture, and there's a big danger. So it's good that Jacques has the opportunity to step back, more than I can; and you come back and look at it again with different eyes and with a different mindset.'

On 10 February 2000, both Jacques and Harry were walking around the galleries that were filling rapidly with works of art. Herzog was there showing some journalists around and Gugger was walking through the building with Peter Wilson, 'snagging' – identifying those small tasks that had not been completed by the contractors – as well as deciding how to spend £300,000 or so of unspent contingency money that no one wanted to leave unspent. But it turned out that there was not enough contingency money to resurface the doors on Levels 3 and 5, and so only Level 4 doors would have the dark 'old oak' stain that Wilson and Gugger wanted.

The Herzog party encountered Gugger and Wilson on Level 5 West, where, for the past two weeks, three art handlers had been up ladders drawing precisely angled pencil lines of different colours on the north wall of the room, according to the specific instructions given by Sol Lewitt, the artist whose mural this wall would become. Like *The End of the Twentieth Century*, this was a work of art whose final form was only tenuously connected with the hands of the artist.

Greetings were exchanged around a prototype of a wooden bench designed by Herzog and de Meuron, for the public to sit on in the galleries. Both Gugger and Herzog were in a relaxed mood and they squatted together on the floor to inspect the bench, an elegant light wood construction with a seat pierced with square holes that curved gently upwards. Peter Wilson lowered his bulk onto the bench and said, 'Look, it doesn't even sag under me.'

There was a distinctly 'end of term' feel in the air. As room after room could be seen in its finished form, it was clear how trying hard to stick to their principles had paid off for the architects. The art could be seen at its best, somehow detached and floating away from the plain featureless backgrounds of unfussy white walls and unpolished oak floors. Only a Carl André tiled sculpture on the floor a metre or so from a floor grille could give the visitor a moment's pause, as he might wonder whether they were both works of art, although as Herzog looked at the juxtaposition that day he felt that the design compromise that resulted in heavy cast iron grilles created a distinction between the two.

But where that confusion was far more likely to occur was with the gallery bench, which was *so* beautifully designed that in a room with other solid three-dimensional works on the floor it could definitely be mistaken for art. (Not helped by an exhibit in an adjacent room that *was* art although it looked like a canvas settee on a metal frame.) In fact, a couple of days before, an art handler had mistaken one of the benches for a sculpture and had asked Frances Morris if he was allowed to move it to make way for a work that had to be brought in to the room. Morris was very worried about the benches, precisely because they were so 'artistic', and she told Serota that she didn't want them in several of her galleries.

For Serota, the May 2000 opening was an important milestone rather than an ending. He and his team had more targets to achieve: transforming the oil tanks, the space under the Switch House, and eventually the Switch House itself. There were inevitably things he felt anxious about, although some of them were to do with anticipating the public reception of the building rather than any specific dislike of his own. Who knew whether his often-expressed concerns about the colour scheme would strike visitors in the same way? After a walk round the nearly finished building he did allow himself to admit a small regret: 'Harry and I were talking today about the dilemma over the staircase and the realization that there had been an error in the way in which it was being set out and developed, when Harry proposed a modification that he was told would cost a huge sum of money. We were walking up and down the stair today and I was commenting on the sadness that we had not been able to make that adjustment. But I guess that only a very small proportion of our visitors will notice that.'

But a bigger issue that hadn't yet turned out as he had hoped was the transformation of the area around the gallery. The design of the south end of the pedestrian bridge across the river had eventually become truncated as the Tate had wanted, although it didn't land on a mound. Unfortunately all the signs were that construction work would still be continuing on the Tate's landscape when the gallery opened, although the landscape design itself had softened, to the residents' quiet satisfaction. But on the other side of the gallery the paper merchant's building was still standing, which Serota and the Herzog and de Meuron team had identified as an eyesore during their first walk round the area in 1995. 'I would like to find a more animated use for that corner of the site than a paper merchant's,' said Serota. 'We're going to have a million and a half people walking past that corner of the site every year. It fronts on to our terrace coming from the café/restaurant and I think that we could add a facility there that would complement what the Tate is and make it a nicer place to sit, to converse, to meet people on a summer evening, and all the other things that we want to do. I wanted us to make a move to try and acquire it five years ago and I'm afraid other forces prevailed and people said, "Well, we don't have the money to do that and we can't add to our overall target for raising funds." My view was that it was going to cost £1 or £2 million and that we should do it and try and put the money down on the table. I'm afraid my view didn't prevail.

'It's the kind of thing that happens when you have a project which is being run by an institution rather than being sponsored by government. One of the great missed opportunities here at Bankside arises from the fact that this is a single institution trying to create a big public entity. We should have been working more closely with others to ensure that some of the benefit that will arise through the economic regeneration of this area came either to the project or to the public good. What I see around me at the moment is a series of buildings being planned where huge sums of money are going to be made by the private developers who happened to own them when we arrived here and it seems to me quite absurd that that should be the case while I am still struggling to raise the final £8 million or £10 million to create the building in the first place.

'The other thing I'd say is London has a lot of catching up to do. We are creating a great museum of modern art twenty-five years behind Paris, seventy years behind New York, years behind Bilbao. It is absurd that we don't already have this facility. Since we started planning this project the Pompidou has renovated itself, added another whole floor of accommodation; the Museum of Modern Art in New York has embarked on a scheme that will add fifty per cent to its exhibition space. Both of those projects have been stimulated partly by what we're doing here, but the real internal driver I think is what artists need and what we feel we need to show.'

One notable achievement was the non-acrimonious quality of much of the interaction on the project, between the Tate and its partner organizations. Towards the end, the Tate had even given everyone blue hard hats with 'Tate' on them, to try to break down the 'them and us' feel. It would have been surprising if there hadn't been *some* rows and 'assassinations' and mistakes and incompetence on a project so complex and involving so many people. But as Andy Butler of Stanhope, Michael Casey of Herzog and de Meuron and Jonathan Raynes of Schal looked back one December evening towards the end of the project, their discussion of what they had learnt and the advice they'd like to have given to the others was surprisingly good-natured with so much shared history between them.

'I've probably learnt a hell of a lot,' Casey said, 'because from an architectural point of view anything this scale only comes to you in your life once. People say your experience is the sum of your mistakes, and sometimes you make the odd one, but I don't think we made many. It's been like a whole life, really, because you sort of start off a teenager, and you end up somebody completely different at the end of it. You have to learn lots of skills, dealing with characters like these two; and they in turn have had to learn to deal with people like us, who are not necessarily the easiest of architects to be around.'

Butler joined in the post-mortem: 'Three or four key issues that I look back and think we should have done differently – we should have been more forceful in our advice to the client – as a team, that's not just Stanhope but Schal as well – about the implications of taking on Level 4 and the fit-out at the stage we did. Because when we took those things on, we were looking at them, to be honest, with rose-tinted glasses; we were still struggling along from the problems we'd had with the steel frame, et cetera, and then we took on another £10 or £15 million pounds' worth of work, and no project could take that, not with a team that's already struggling.'

Michael Casey had some advice for the construction managers on how to deal with the architect: 'Don't be afraid of him. Many times we have had situations where we've been perceived to be meddling in things that are obviously important to us that have a habit of coming round again. I think now people understand the reasons why we make decisions early on and have to revisit things, and I understand all of the issues why construction management is the way it is, but I think they need to absorb us more into the equation sometimes, because we're not that bad, you know. We do make compromises.'

'The Herzog concept and the design intent is fantastic,' said Jonathan Raynes of Schal. 'It is really good and I thoroughly enjoy it. Where we fall over as a team is in the design detail, and it's the design detail that makes it work. It's generally there in the architects' heads, but they need to be able to understand the full integration of not just the architectural design, but all the services content that goes with it. And that needs to be sorted out a little earlier, because a lot of the problems, and the challenges, that we've had is being able to overcome those as we've gone through the project, and sometimes that's too late. When you're out in the field, that's too late – you need to have done it before then.'

For all three of them, the Tate had probably been the most unusual client they had ever worked with. 'From a personal point of view,' said Jonathan Raynes, 'I think they have been an absolute joy to work with, they really have. They understand about people. Our business is about delivering what they require, what they want, and trying to make their dreams into realities. They understand not just the views of the architect; they understand the construction elements; and they understand some of the detail as well. The main conduit for that has been Peter Wilson, who's been fantastic, and he deserves a lot of credit.'

Michael Casey agreed. 'We've had an incredible working relationship with the Tate; I think they've been willing to back us lots of times when they were not quite convinced, and that's been fantastic, of course. Peter's role as a sort of a judicial father to us all is very strong, and I think he plays his role incredibly well.'

Butler analysed the client's role in a little more detail. 'Sometimes you give them advice, and they're aware of the implication but they choose to ignore it – that's the client's prerogative. But generally the client, as Jonathan said, goes into these decisions with his eyes open, and will live with it, you know. And the great thing about them, generally, is they're not looking for scapegoats; I go to their board meetings, and there's problems to talk about but they approach them in a positive manner. I work very closely with Peter Wilson and this job is a testament to that guy. He's one of the most positive, knowledgeable clients I've ever worked with.'

As Butler, Raynes and Casey walked out of Bankside at the end of the day the empty building was handed over to the Tate, the winter darkness outside and the hushed quietness inside reinforced the cathedral qualities people had remarked on right at the beginning of the project. Just like a cathedral nave, the Turbine Hall soaked up sound so that even when the crowds eventually began to pour into the building their chatter would be a background murmur rather than the roar of the football crowd. The auditorium glowed out on Level 2, its red semi-transparent glass transmitting the bright red of the interior coverings. Below the bridge, the Visitor Services desks were ready, and the staircase that no one was meant to go up was swept. The shop – not designed by Herzog and de Meuron but still a capacious and elegant money-maker – nestled in the corner by the ramp, displaying its wares to those who walked, ran or slid down the smooth concrete, although as they came in, for the first few metres they were bound to be looking up rather than to the left, at the ugly rooflights, screened but not entirely obscured by the grid that Herzog and de Meuron insisted should have function as well as form.

The Turbine Hall was lit by all the balcony lights, covered with the troublesome glass that now – more or less – smoothed out the outlines of the fluorescent tubes. The fittings – brackets that held each piece of glass in position – seemed rather prominent, and some of the team had been surprised how obtrusive they looked. It was as if they'd spent so much time on the 'mote' of the glass diffusion that they missed the 'beam' of the fittings.

At Level 3, the Grand Stair, now equipped with concealed lighting above the black handrails, looked inviting rather than forbidding as it beckoned the visitor up or down its wood-covered treads, which merged with the oak strips of the concourse floor. The wooden floor looked and felt *soft*, almost carpet-like, because of Herzog and de Meuron's insistence that it should have a rough surface and no stain or lacquer. Higher up, on Level 5, the concrete floor had an impossible-looking smoothness, the result of 'floating' a top surface of fine concrete on a coarser under-layer. Smooth walls – with hairline cracks – came down to within a few millimetres of the floor – leaving a gap that no one was very keen on, but that would be filled somehow, Peter Wilson was sure.

The plant rooms, one of Andy Butler's favourite features, hummed with life as they operated on green principles to keep the Boiler House spaces *reasonably* evenly conditioned, but not obsessively so. And the Light Beam shone out towards St Paul's, making a horizontal bar to the vertical line of the chimney.

And pervading everything, not yet entirely suppressed, was the hum of the transformers in the Switch House, a reminder of where Serota wanted to go next.

Peter Wilson, avuncular and soft spoken, but also described by one of his close colleagues as Machiavellian, probably knew more about the new museum than anyone else on the project, and, in his own quiet way, he was responsible for its success. As he looked at the completed building, he considered how it embodied the unique charac-teristics of the architects the Tate had chosen six years beforehand. 'One of the things that was very hard to appreciate about their work from photographs is that whatever they're designing, whatever kind of thing it is, it has a style and a language which is quite reticent but quite particular to them. And they've carried that through this building which is, after all, not their building to start off with, and they've actually managed to do that very effectively. And what is there now feels quite natural. It's not in any way fighting what was there originally, even though the interventions are quite considerable. And I think it's that, really, that shows it's theirs and nobody else's, rather than having a beautiful red auditorium or a particularly brilliantly lit element of balcony or anything like that. It's the whole thing.'

Index